781 L761m
LINTON
MUSIC FUNDAMENTALS AND FUNC-
TIONAL SKILLS

FV

27.20

WITHDRAWN

Music Fundamentals and Functional Skills

STANLEY LINTON
University of Wisconsin, Oshkosh

PRENTICE-HALL, INC., Englewood Cliffs, New Jersey 07632

Library of Congress Cataloging in Publication Data

LINTON, STANLEY.
    Music fundamentals and functional skills.

    Includes index.
    1. Music—Theory.   2. Music—Manuals, textbooks, etc.
I. Title.
MT6.L45M9   1984   781   83-21196
ISBN   0-13-606939-8

Editorial/production supervision and interior design: Fred Bernardi
Cover design: Lundgren Graphics, Ltd.
Page layouts: Gail Collis
Manufacturing buyer: Raymond Keating

Printed in the United States of America

10   9   8   7   6   5   4   3   2   1

ISBN 0-13-606939-8

PRENTICE-HALL INTERNATIONAL, INC., *London*
PRENTICE-HALL OF AUSTRALIA PTY. LIMITED, *Sydney*
EDITORA PRENTICE-HALL DO BRASIL, LTDA., *Rio de Janeiro*
PRENTICE-HALL CANADA INC., *Toronto*
PRENTICE-HALL OF INDIA PRIVATE LIMITED, *New Delhi*
PRENTICE-HALL OF JAPAN, INC., *Tokyo*
PRENTICE-HALL OF SOUTHEAST ASIA PTE. LTD., *Singapore*
WHITEHALL BOOKS LIMITED, *Wellington, New Zealand*

Contents

Chapter 4   Harmonic Intervals, Chords, and Chording   79

Chapter 5   Subdivision, Triplet Division, and Off-Beat Syncopation   106

Chapter 6   Other Beat Units   125

Chapter 7   The Subdominant Chord in Harmony and Melody   143

Chapter 8   Compound Meters   163

Chapter 9   Minor Scales, Melodies, and Chords   181

Chapter 10   Form, Expression, Analysis and Synthesis   203

Preface

Authors of textbooks are confronted initially and continuously with three main questions: Who are the learners? What will they learn? How will they learn? These questions place instructional focus where it belongs, on the learner, and answers to them provide good material for an extended preface.

Who are the learners? This book is intended primarily as a text for college students who are nonmajors enrolled in a one-semester course for purposes of learning basic music theory and functional skills in reading and performing music. As a group, these students have two kinds of programmatic needs and various individual interests. They come mostly from elementary education and special education programs where such a course may be a curricular requirement and from liberal arts and preprofessional programs where a course in music fundamentals probably fulfills a general education elective. Individuals usually have interests of three types: (1) They want to know more about elements of organized musical sound (such as rhythm, intervals, scales, chords, keys). (2) They want to develop at least an elementary ability to read music notation. (3) They have a desire—often of long standing—to somehow individually perform music. These students also are apt to have widely different musical backgrounds ranging from those who have no formal musical training beyond elementary school and are nonreaders of music to those who have several years of instruction on a keyboard, band, or orchestral instrument and read music with varying degrees of skill.

Subject matter in this book has been selected and structured on four premises: (1) A rather large common body of knowledge is appropriate for all students in a heterogeneous group. (2) Certain functional skills in reading and performing music should be developed. (3) Different levels of achievement in skills should and can be provided for students with different (musical, nonmusical) backgrounds. (4) Selected subject matter that satisfies needs and challenges abilities beyond those in the common content should and can be included as optional additional experiences.

What will they learn? This book has a parallel thrust in applied musical knowledge and functional musical skills. Components of musical knowledge that run throughout the text focus on how sound is organized and notated from standpoints such as: (1) melodic intervals, scales, tonalities, and melodies; (2) harmonic intervals, chords, and chordal accompaniments; (3) durations, metric groupings, and patterns of sound and silence; (4) elements of musical form and expression.

Knowledge of elementary music theory is of relatively little worth unless accompanied by at least a minimal level and scope of musical action—skills in reading and performing music. Acquisition of musical skills can lead to greater personal satisfaction with musical experiences and provide a concrete basis for applying and understanding music theory. Development of minimal skills is an integral part of this course of study from its beginning to its end. Kinds of skills include hearing and reading patterns of pitch and rhythm, singing melodic patterns and song melodies, playing scales, chords, and melodies on a piano, and improvising keyboard (and guitar) chordal accompaniments to song melodies.

How will they learn? Music Fundamentals and Functional Skills should be viewed as an instructional program that can function as a basic text in a traditional class format and that also can be used by students who might benefit from a more individual and independent method of learning. The entire book contains ten major basic chapters and five optional minichapters. Each basic chapter is designed as a learning unit in which experiences are competency-based. *Objectives* are stated at the outset as competencies to be attained by the end of the unit of study. *Study Activities* present all new subject matter liberally illustrated and demonstrated with graphic and music materials. *Practice Activities* provide further opportunities to apply and confirm what has been learned; they focus on responses such as *naming, notating, identifying, discriminating, reading, creating, analyzing,* and *performing.* Competencies that were identified in the objectives and acquired through study and practice are evaluated at the end of each chapter with an *Assessment of Progress* that consists of a self-administered and self-scored paper-and-pencil test of applied knowledge, plus skill tests administered by a teacher or student assistant.

Sequences of activities within each chapter, and from chapter to chapter, are developmental in nature. No previous (formal) musical experience is assumed at the beginning. Students are confronted with knowledge and skill with which they can immediately deal successfully. Application of learned competencies continues alongside the introduction and acquisition of new ideas and abilities. Topical subjects, therefore, are not exhausted in one extended treatment. Interval study, for instance, is not confined to one chapter; it is inserted at various points where knowledge of specific intervals is requisite to understanding, reading, and performing scales, melodies, and primary chords. In addition, one of the optional minichapters gives a concise, more complete summary of intervals for students who have further interest in, or need for, such information.

Individualized learning is characterized by learner options that derive from flexibility in instructional elements such as time, space, subject content, and evaluation. This book has been conceived and written so that students might be given choices in how they will complete course requirements. Flexible time, the *self-paced* ingredient, comes from the certainty that some students will be able to achieve their competencies in less time than others, and flexible space infers that study and practice activities can be accomplished either inside or outside a traditional classroom environment. High, independent achievers might opt to complete their work when and where they choose, so long as they are responsible for demonstrating their competencies at specified assessment or testing points.

Students also can be given a degree of choice in subject matter. This can be done most easily by setting a basic content (our ten basic chapters) common for all and providing supplementary content that can be elected or assigned on the basis of individual interest, need, and capability. Optional minichapters A through E expand into areas such as styles of keyboard accompaniment, guitar accompaniment, other intervals and chords, pentatonic and modal scales and melodies, and other metric organizations.

Evaluation of learner achievement can be flexible. Cognitive competencies can be set reasonably at the same level for most (or all) students, but achievable skills are too dependent on previous musical performance and physiological differences to apply the same level of expectancy for everyone. Each *Assessment of Progress* is comprised of two parts: Part A—applied knowledge—is a test for which each student can be expected to achieve correct, or corrected, responses to all items before continuing to the next chapter. Part B—skills—sets a minimum criterion level that allows students more choice in what they prepare to perform, and requires performance of fewer and easier materials, compared with what is required for higher criterion levels.

Finally, this book focuses entirely on music fundamentals, without attempts to cross over into other areas such as elementary music education theory and methods or "music appreciation." The subject matter is relatively complete, and it is appropriate for a one-semester course for nonmajors if we keep in mind these conditions: (1) This text establishes expectations that will both challenge higher achievers and facilitate success on the part of those with less potential. (2) Achievement of different acceptable levels of competencies is provided through optional areas of study and assessments for different levels of skills. Practice activities and assessment tools make learner success in one chapter requisite to advancement to the next chapter. (3) Teachers always have a right and responsibility selectively to delete from or add to textbook content in the process of adapting it to their course of study.

Acknowledgment and appreciation are given to the following: To the publishers and manufacturers whose credit lines appear with the material used, to Dr. Janice Klemish for proofreading and critiquing the manuscript, to John Iwata for photography, to Dr. Michael Thiele for keyboard poses, and to Jacquelyn Sandene for guitar poses.

Stanley Linton

Chapter 1

Introduction to Basic Elements and Skills

INSTRUCTIONS

1. Read the *Objectives* to gain an initial awareness of competencies you should have acquired by the time you complete this chapter. Keep these objectives in mind as you continue through the study and practice activities.

2. Complete all *Study Activities,* striving for understanding of the subject matter that is presented and illustrated.

3. Complete all *Practice Activities* for the purposes of applying your knowledge and improving your skills.

4. As soon as you are ready, or when directed by the instructor, complete the *Assessment of Progress.* You should achieve the criterion levels indicated before continuing to Chapter Two.

5. Refer to the optional Minichapter A if you want more knowledge of, or experience with, bass-clef notation.

OBJECTIVES

1. Recall and define the following terms and correctly use and interpret them in written or oral communication:

key and keynote	melodic movement	octave
ledger line	ascending	phrase
linear pitch	descending	scale, diatonic
melodic cadence	repeated	staff
complete	steps	tonality and tonic
incomplete	skips	treble clef
		vertical pitch

2. Recognize, name, and notate any of the following signs, or parts thereof, used in notating pitch:

    a. staff: lines, spaces, ledger lines, and spaces
    b. note: head (open or closed), stem, flag, beam
    c. treble-clef (or G-clef) sign

3. Quickly name any pitch written in treble clef over a two-octave range from A below to A above the staff and, given the pitch name of any of these notes, write a note head on the correct line or space to represent that pitch.

4. Immediately identify the pitch name of any white piano key and, given a pitch notated in treble clef, identify the piano key that would produce that pitch.

5. Look at a notated treble-clef melody and identify where pitches move by steps, by skips, or by repeated pitches.

6. Write, play, and sing the C major scale and identify each of its tones by scale number and *so-fa* syllable.

7. Given a melody in C major written in treble clef, identify and name its keynote (tonic) and key as well as the scale number and *so-fa* syllable for any tone. Also, name the type of cadence (complete or incomplete) in each melodic phrase.

8. Play on a piano, for an instructor or student assistant, at least three song melodies learned in this chapter, and sing (to the best of your ability) at least two of these melodies using pitch names, scale numbers, and *so-fa* syllables.

STUDY ACTIVITIES

The primary purpose of this course in music fundamentals is to provide learning experiences that will enable you to gradually develop your knowledge of how musical sound is organized in a piece of music and to acquire minimal skills that will make it possible to perform simple pieces. Knowing something about music is more meaningful if you also can do something with music. From the outset, therefore, you will be dealing with basic music theory while you are learning to read, play, and sing music. The kind of music you will encounter consists of a variety of traditional songs. These relatively short and simple pieces are comprised of the same basic elements found in more complex compositions; they also are complete pieces whose melodies can be sung and played either with or without harmonic accompaniment. We will begin with a general introduction to basic musical elements, music notation, the keyboard, and tonal organization of pitch.

BASIC ELEMENTS OF MUSIC

Creative artists in any field have certain basic elements, or materials, out of which they form their works. Painters and sculptors work with components such as color, texture, and line to create a visual form occupying space. Music is frequently defined as *organized sound and silence,* and musicians have only two primary elements out of which to create an aural art form (a piece of music) that exists, or takes place, over an interval of time. These musical elements are *pitch* and *duration:* Each sound is of a certain pitch, and each sound and silence has a duration.

Let us assume you are unable at this time to read music notation (although some of you probably do have various degrees of reading skill). Try to recall how the well-known melody of *Row, Row, Row Your Boat* sounds. While you are silently thinking or singing aloud this melody, follow the graphic representation on page 3 in line notation of its pitches and their durations as a general background for studying the definitions and descriptions that follow.

Pitch

Musical pitch has both a physical and a psychological aspect. The physical, or acoustical, attribute is sound-wave frequency measured in cycles (vibrations) per second and called Hertz (Hz) after Heinrich Hertz, who was an early researcher with electromagnetism. Pitch is the psychological correlate of frequency. A lower frequency (200 Hz) and a higher frequency (1,000 Hz) will produce sensations of lower and higher pitches respectively. We are more interested in the psychological component of pitch, for that is the attribute to which human beings respond. Pitch is a subjective sensation, arising from the physical stimulus of vibra-

ROW, ROW, ROW YOUR BOAT (in line notation)

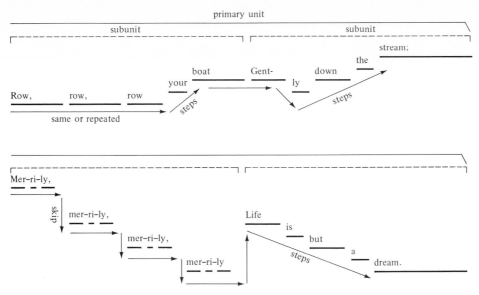

tion, and is measured according to its relative placement along a continuum from low to high. In other words, we perceive one pitch as being higher than, lower than, or the same as another.

We respond to melodic patterns comprised of two or more pitches rather than to single pitches one at a time, and the most compelling general aspect of our perception is *melodic direction.* Movement from one pitch to the next can occur in only three ways: 1) pitches can stay the same, or *repeat;* 2) pitches can move higher, or *ascend;* 3) pitches can move lower, or *descend.* Furthermore, pitch movement that ascends or descends can do so by *steps* or by *skips.* Progression by steps is to the next pitch in whatever organizational system the melody is based, normally some kind of scale. Movement by skips occurs when one or more pitches are jumped over in going from one note to another.

Return to the line notation of *Row, Row, Row Your Boat* and concentrate on how various pitch patterns sound; identify patterns comprised of repeated pitches and those that contain ascending or descending steps or skips. Pitch is sometimes called the *spatial* element in music. As a psychological feature of sound it neither occupies space nor changes location, but we have learned from early childhood to label it with references to space—high, low, up, down, above, below—for pitch movement does seem to convey a perceived spatial rise and fall.

Pitch organization in music can occur in two dimensions. *Linear pitch* refers to patterns or successions of pitches that follow one another in a single voice line such as a *melody. Vertical pitch* organization is the result of combining two or more pitches to sound simultaneously. Vertical structures of three or more pitches are called *chords,* and patterns (progressions) of chords produce *harmony.* (Chords and chord progressions are introduced in Chapter Four.)

Duration

A general meaning of *duration* is the time during which something exists or lasts. *Duration* in music refers to relative time values of sounds and silences along a continuum from short to long. Patterns of short sounds give a feeling of quick or fast pace to music, while sounds of longer duration seem to set a slower pace. Look again at the line notation of *Row, Row, Row Your Boat,* in which longer line segments represent sounds of relatively longer duration. Try clapping each sound (each word syllable) as you sing in order to become more conscious of durations that, along with pitch movement, comprise the melodic organization.

Organization of relative durations in a piece of music ultimately involves several other components (such as beat, tempo, and meter) that, along with duration, add up to a broad musical attribute called *rhythm.* (Rhythmic organization and its notation are introduced in Chapter Two and are further expanded in other chapters.) Rhythm is sometimes called music's *temporal* element—a reference to sounds and silences moving across time.

Form

Organization of pitch and duration is not a random, uninterrupted arrangement of tones from beginning to end in a piece of music. First of all, we probably have an inborn tendency to subjectively group sound stimuli into patterns, or units, during the process of perceiving and giving meaning to those sounds. Also, we have learned through experience in our cultural environment to expect certain sequences of tones in certain prevailing conditions, and these are the kinds of patterns that are most meaningful to us. Pieces of music usually have clear architectural designs into which their patterns of sounds have been structured. This architectonic property is called *form,* and all art works—painting, sculpture, poetry, dance, architecture, and music—have form.

At its largest level, an entire piece of music has form and is a form. Within this overall outer form exists an inner structure comprised of smaller *units* and *subunits* that serve as building blocks with identifiable designs of their own. These units, or configurations, have a starting point from which sounds move toward and terminate in a *point of arrival* that provides us with a sense of momentary pause, relaxation, or punctuation in the ongoing flow. Once again look at *Row, Row, Row Your Boat* and recall the sound of each of its two primary units marked with solid overlines. From the onset of sound on "Row" you expect an uninterrupted continuance to the first point of arrival on "stream," and at this point you expect another unit to begin and extend to the final point of arrival on "dream." A closer look within each main unit reveals smaller subunits (broken-line brackets) that are comprehensible patterns. If you try other groupings of tones by starting or stopping on another tone within a subunit, you probably will discover an unsatisfactory organizational pattern. (Musical form is expanded in greater detail in Chapter Ten.)

Melody

We can generalize to say that a *melody* is a succession of linear (horizontal) pitches and durations perceived as a unified configuration. (A configuration, or Gestalt, is a structure of parts so integrated as to constitute a functional unit or whole.) This definition implies that a melody has both structural and psychological attributes. Researchers who have analyzed melodies from traditional Western music have concluded that series of tones tend to be perceived and remembered more readily as melodies if their pitches are close together (steps and small skips), involve a certain amount of repetition, and proceed toward finality (points of arrival) in a somewhat direct manner.

An individual's psychological organization of sounds is based on previous experience with music of his or her own culture. Successions of tones in an unfamiliar style (such as tribal music or avant-garde music) may not be accepted as melodies by some. We can say with reasonable certainty that you will perceive as melodies all pieces used in this book, for they are traditional folk songs, carols, hymns, and patriotic songs of Western cultures; they also are part of our American musical heritage.

MUSIC NOTATION

Music itself—the aural experience with organized sound—is not a language, for it has no agreed upon, predetermined message encoded in such a way that it can be decoded by the listener. Music notation, however, is a language comprised of a system of signs and characters used to represent musical sounds and silences. Such a written language enables us to preserve music created by a composer and to communicate it between people and across generations. Now, look at *Row, Row, Row Your Boat* in conventional music notation as a preview of a more detailed study of our notational system. How, in general, does the music notation represent pitch movement and duration previously shown in nontraditional notation?

ROW, ROW, ROW YOUR BOAT (traditional notation)

1. Row, row, row your boat, Gen - tly down the stream;

Mer - ri - ly, mer - ri - ly, mer - ri - ly, mer - ri - ly, Life is but a dream.

Notes

Signs used to represent both pitch and duration are called *notes*. One note stands for one sound of a specific pitch and a relative durational value. You should learn correct names for all parts of a note and identify which parts represent pitch and which relate to duration.

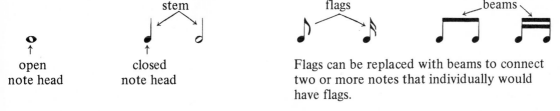

open note head

closed note head

Flags can be replaced with beams to connect two or more notes that individually would have flags.

Pitch is represented solely by location of a note head on a staff line or space. Stems, flags or beams, and open or closed note heads are related to durational values of sound. Look again at the notation of *Row, Row, Row Your Boat*, and observe that note heads for higher pitches are located higher on the staff, open note heads with stems are used for sounds of longest duration, beamed notes have the shortest sounds, and closed note heads with stems stand for durations between the longest and shortest sounds.

Staff

Our present-day single staff consists of five parallel lines and four intervening spaces. Lines and spaces are separately numbered upward—we speak of the first line, third line, second space, and so forth. In addition to four spaces within a staff, spaces for placement of note heads exist immediately above the fifth line and below the first line.

lines of the staff   spaces of the staff

Correctly written forms of notes on a staff follow standard rules:

1. Note heads on a line must be bisected by that line; note heads on a space must occupy that complete space without overlapping lines.

correct: incorrect:

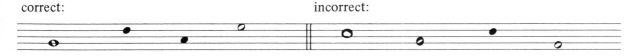

2. Stems point either up from the right side of a note head or down from the left side: Stems point down from note heads located on or above the middle (third) staff line and up from note heads below the middle line. Length of a stem is equivalent to three staff spaces.

correct: incorrect:

3. Flags are always attached to the right side of a stem regardless of whether that stem points up or down.

correct: incorrect:

Naming Pitches

Pitches are named in ascending order with the first seven alphabet letters. Only seven letters are needed, for notes eight tones apart have the same name and represent a pitch relationship called an octave. *Octave* is an important concept throughout music and is physically based on a simple 2 to 1 ratio between sound-wave frequencies of its two pitches (for instance, A 440 Hz and A 880 Hz). Octave pitches sound similar, the first overtone of any fundamental pitch is its octave, and octaves are divided into various organizations to produce scales of different kinds.

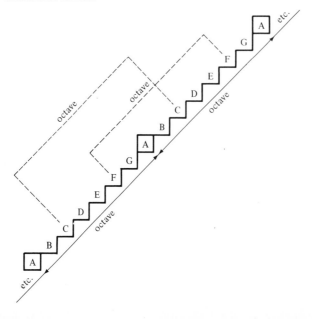

Treble Clef

Each named note is located (written, notated) on a specific line or space of a staff. But staff lines and spaces have no names until a *clef sign* is placed at the beginning. A *treble clef sign* (also called *G clef*) is placed on a five-line staff so that its large loop circles the second line, which is identified as the pitch of G above Middle C. (Middle C is an important point of pitch orientation on both the staff and keyboard. Its significance will become clear as you continue.) The space immediately above G is A, and each ascending staff line and space through an octave is named with the next alphabet letter. This same system is extended upward and downward into other octaves. Music notated on a treble-clef staff is said to be written in *treble clef.* You should be able to name quickly lines and spaces in ascending, descending, or random orders.

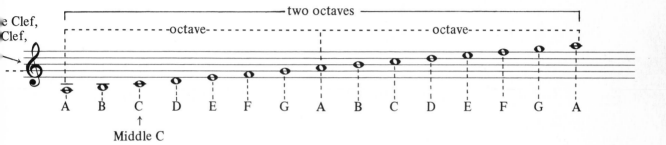

Ledger Lines

A five-line staff is inadequate for locating all treble-clef pitches. Its range can be extended by using short line segments (pieces of staff lines), called *ledger lines,* drawn above or below the staff. Ledger lines should create spaces of the same width as those between staff lines, and each should be of only sufficient length to accommodate placement of a note head on, below, or above it. You will need to be able to name ledger lines and spaces ascending at least two lines above the staff and descending two lines below it.

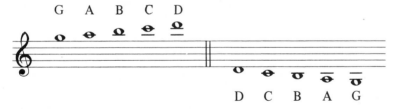

Great Staff

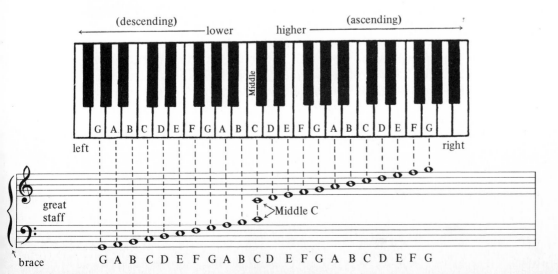

Another dimension of staff notation is represented by the *great staff* (or *grand staff*), which offers a view of a larger range of pitches. It consists of two five-line staffs connected at their beginning by a brace. The top and bottom staffs carry treble- and bass-clef signs respectively. Middle C serves as a bridge between the two clefs and can be notated on either the first ledger line below the treble staff or the first ledger line above the bass staff. You will continue to develop your skills in reading treble-clef notation, but reading bass-clef notation is unessential to achieving your objectives in the basic units of study. (Those persons who have special interests and needs for more knowledge of bass-clef notation should work through optional Minichapter A.)

Positive Identification of Pitch in Treble Clef

Positive identification of pitch is an accurate and convenient system for both naming a pitch and specifying the octave in which it occurs. Lower-case letters represent pitches in the octave below Middle C, an offset number 1 indicates pitches in the octave extending upward from Middle C, and an offset 2 identifies pitches in the second octave above Middle C.

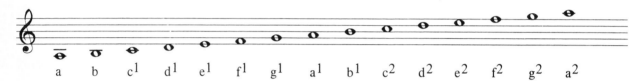

$$a \quad b \quad c^1 \quad d^1 \quad e^1 \quad f^1 \quad g^1 \quad a^1 \quad b^1 \quad c^2 \quad d^2 \quad e^2 \quad f^2 \quad g^2 \quad a^2$$

THE KEYBOARD

Another necessary skill involves the ability to name and quickly locate on the piano keyboard any pitch notated in treble clef. Your first orientation to the keyboard should be visual. Every octave contains a group of two and a group of three equidistant black keys separated by a larger space between the groups. Any white key immediately below (to the left of) a group of two black keys is a C. Middle C is the C nearest the middle of the keyboard.

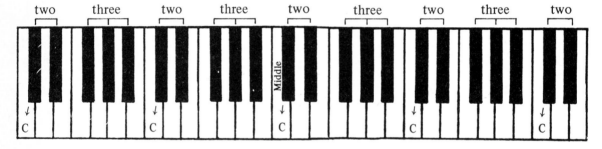

Performance

All of you have performed music to some degree, at least to the point of singing in a shower stall or informally in a group. The human voice, one's personal instrument, and the piano are two of the best instruments with which to make music audible for our purposes. You will be using both instruments in this course of study to achieve two broad goals: 1) to hear music you are studying and receive satisfaction from producing it, and 2) to make concrete applications of theoretical knowledge you are acquiring, thus increasing its meaning.

You may or may not have had previous experience in playing piano; it doesn't matter; you can start right now. First, do two things. Learn the name and location of each note in the octave ascending from Middle C on both the staff and keyboard. Practice identifying these notes in random ascending and descending orders until you have immediate recall of names and locations. Also, learn the number assigned to each right-hand finger, for a certain finger is usually designated by number to play a certain note in a melody.

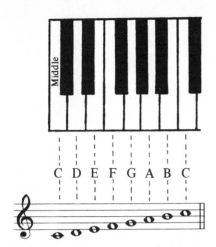

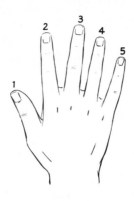

You are now ready to play with relative ease a simple melody that uses only four of the five notes from Middle C up to G. If you can go directly to a piano and accurately play *Merrily We Roll Along,* you should do so; if you are a beginner, follow these steps:

1. Sing the song to remind yourself of its familiar sound. An accurate mental grasp of the melody forms an essential model for you to follow as you play it.
2. Sing or think the melody with letter names of its pitches to increase your facility for recognizing pitch locations.
3. Sing aloud each note with its finger number (3—2-1–2–3–3–3, etc.) and simultaneously finger the melody with your right hand on a flat surface, such as a desk or table top, to establish pattern and coordination to your finger movement.
4. Study the right-hand keyboard position for playing pitches from C to G inclusive:

5. Go to a piano, assume the C-G right-hand position, and play *Merrily We Roll Along.*

6. Repeat playing the melody until it holds together as a complete unit—until it sounds the same as when it is sung accurately.

MERRILY WE ROLL ALONG

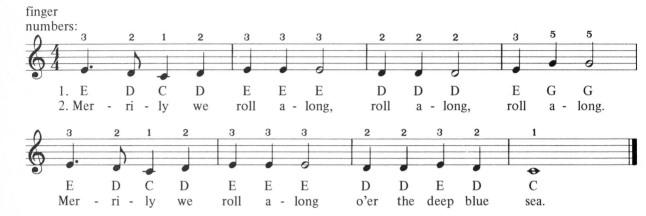

Learn to play *I Know Where I'm Going,* applying the same C-G five-note hand position and procedures you used to perform *Merrily We Roll Along.*

I KNOW WHERE I'M GOING

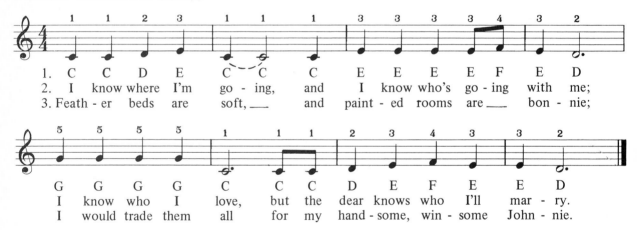

TONAL ORGANIZATION OF PITCH

Tonality

Earlier in this chapter we described three general kinds of melodic pitch movement: repeating the same pitch, ascending by steps or skips, and descending by steps or skips. But pitch organization is more definitive than that. Traditional music of Western cultures, including music in this book, is tonal music, and *tonal music* is based on an organizational principle called *tonality,* which is broadly defined in *Harvard Dictionary of Music* as "loyalty to a tonic." Among various pitches used in a melody, for instance, one pitch called the *tonic* is given preference as the most important, making it a central pitch to which all others are related. The tonic usually provides an ending tone for a melody and also is heard at other important places; it serves as a *home tone* from which the pitch moves away to other tones and to which it from time to time returns home. Tonality, then, is an overall effect produced by a selected set or series of pitches related in sound to a single tonic pitch and, therefore, to each other.

Both the aural and cognitive concepts of tonality and tonic can be illustrated by thinking, singing, or playing the familiar song *On Top of Old Smoky*. Pause on, or stop following, the next to final note, and you will discover that you mentally anticipate where the melodic pitch movement is headed—to its final point of arrival on its tonic pitch, which in this case is Middle C. We sense, consciously or subconsciously, that this pitch has occurred at points throughout the piece, that an interrelatedness and coherence exists among all pitches, and that all other pitches have an affinity for, or pull toward, their tonic. We could say the melody has a C tonality (later called the key of C major).

ON TOP OF OLD SMOKY   U. S. Folk Song

Scale

Scales are ordered series of pitches within an octave and result from dividing an octave into five, six, seven, or more tones. Scale tones are written, sung, or played in an exact ascending and descending sequence from a starting pitch that functions as the scale's tonic and gives the scale its name: A scale starting with, or built from, C is a C scale; a scale built from F is an F scale.

Diatonic Scale

Scales are very important systems of pitch organization because every piece of tonal music is based on some kind of scale. We will introduce one particular scale at this point, so that you can begin to understand the basic nature of a scale and its relation to melody (other scales are studied in Chapters Three and Nine). Our scale of the moment is the diatonic scale of C major.

A *diatonic scale* is a seven-tone scale that contains both whole and half steps (detailed interval structure of major scales is deferred until Chapter Three). Starting with its tonic, a diatonic scale contains each consecutive ascending note of the next pitch name, located on the next staff line or space, until the progression has reached a note an octave above the tonic upon which it began. This octave tonic is an eighth tone, but it is not considered as a new tone because of the octave pitch relationship explained earlier.

C Major Scale

The C major scale is a diatonic scale starting on C and ascending through every note on the staff for one octave. Its scale order of pitches corresponds with, and can be produced by, white piano keys—**C** D E F G A B **C.**

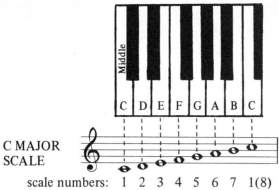

<table>
<tr><td>scale numbers:</td><td>1</td><td>2</td><td>3</td><td>4</td><td>5</td><td>6</td><td>7</td><td>1(8)</td></tr>
<tr><td>scale syllables:</td><td>do</td><td>re</td><td>mi</td><td>fa</td><td>so</td><td>la</td><td>ti</td><td>do</td></tr>
</table>

You should realize that we have included three systems, or ways, of identifying and labeling notes of a scale: 1) pitch names (alphabet letters), 2) scale numbers, and 3) scale syllables. Pitch names are absolute identifications. A pitch of a given name in a given octave will always have the same staff and keyboard locations as well as the same absolute pitch when it is sounded. On the other hand, scale numbers and *so-fa* syllables are relational tonal systems used widely for facilitation of sight-singing. Each relative tonal system serves the same dual purpose: 1) to develop an awareness of where a certain pitch lies within a scale, and 2) to acquire abilities to think (hear internally) the sound of one pitch in relation to another and to think, as well as sing or play, patterns of pitch movement in a melody. You will learn to use both systems interchangeably.

Singing the C major scale and scale patterns. Syllable systems of identifying scale tones are very old (the Chinese and ancient Greeks used tone syllables). Guido of Arezzo (980–1050) is called the inventor of our modern tone system, variously called *solmization* (from *sol-mi*), *solfege* (Fr.), and *solfeggio* (It.). The variation most often used as an educational method in English-speaking countries is the English *tonic sol-fa,* or "movable *do*," system, in which the tonic pitch (note) in any major scale or key is named *do*. Usage in the United States also has shortened *sol* to *so*. You should learn to name, spell, and pronounce all *so-fa* syllables and correlate syllable and number identifications of each tone (*do* is 1, *mi* is 3, *la* is 6, etc.).

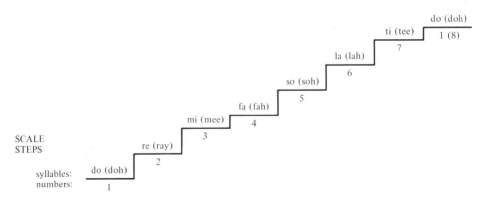

Earlier in this chapter we said that linear (melodic) pitch could move up or down by steps or skips. Now we can be more specific and refer to step movement as *scalar,* or by *scale steps*. You can train your mind to anticipate the correct sound of each pitch in a pattern of melodic tones that move through various segments of the scale and, eventually, sight-read these kinds of familiar-sounding patterns in melodies. Reproduction with your singing voice provides the best evidence that you are actually thinking specific pitch patterns. Practice singing each of the next exercises with both *so-fa* syllables and scale numbers, giving all notes the same durational value. First, play the pattern on a piano in order to match correct pitches with your voice, then try immediately to repeat singing the pattern without a piano.

Melodic scalar exercises in C Major:

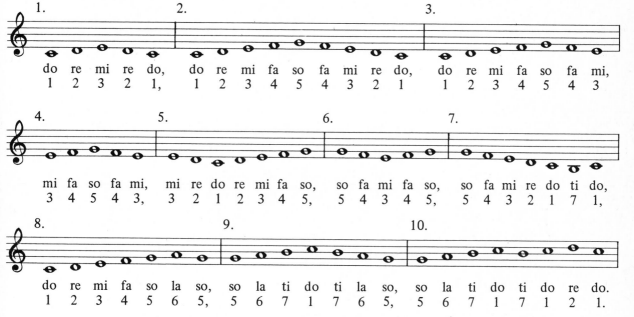

1.					2.									3.						
do	re	mi	re	do,	do	re	mi	fa	so	fa	mi	re	do,	do	re	mi	fa	so	fa	mi,
1	2	3	2	1,	1	2	3	4	5	4	3	2	1	1	2	3	4	5	4	3

4.					5.							6.					7.						
mi	fa	so	fa	mi,	mi	re	do	re	mi	fa	so,	so	fa	mi	fa	so,	so	fa	mi	re	do	ti	do,
3	4	5	4	3,	3	2	1	2	3	4	5,	5	4	3	4	5,	5	4	3	2	1	7	1,

8.							9.							10.							
do	re	mi	fa	so	la	so,	so	la	ti	do	ti	la	so,	so	la	ti	do	ti	do	re	do.
1	2	3	4	5	6	5,	5	6	7	1	7	6	5,	5	6	7	1	7	1	2	1.

Playing the C major scale.   A C major scale can be played easily if you use your five fingers in a pattern of movement that will enable you to play all eight scale tones ascending or descending. Follow the illustration, in which you will observe that the thumb passes under the third finger going from E to F ascending, and the third finger crosses over the thumb going from F to E descending.

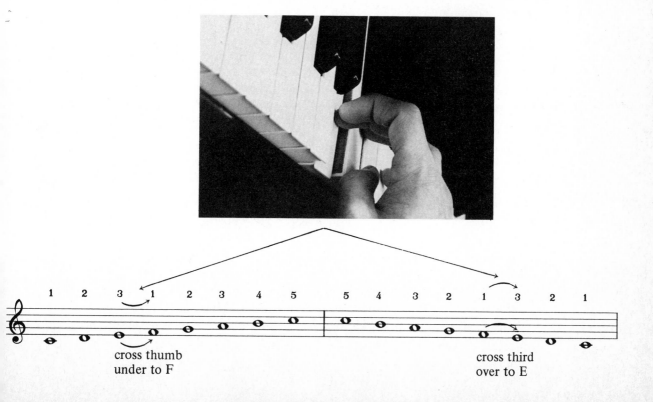

1	2	3	1	2	3	4	5	5	4	3	2	1	3	2	1

cross thumb
under to F

cross third
over to E

MELODIES IN THE KEY OF C MAJOR

Keynote and Key

All melodies arising from European and American musical traditions are based on a scale, and many of them are related to major scales. This means that pitches employed in a melody are from a specific scale (although all seven scale tones need not be used) and that the tonic of that scale functions as the tonic, or keynote, of the melody. *Keynote* means essentially the same as *tonic* and is preferred by some persons when they refer to the home tone in a piece of music. A melody that uses C as its keynote (tonic) and notes from the C major scale in its melodic patterns is said to be in the key of C major. *Key,* therefore, is related to scale and tonality; key and tonality are essentially the same. Whereas *scale* means a step-ordered arrangement of tones from a tonic, *key* refers to the tonality of a piece of music. These ideas will be extended to other major scales and keys in Chapter Three.

Phrase and Cadence

We referred earlier to building blocks of musical form as primary units of sound ending in points of arrival. These units are phrases and their points of arrival are cadences. A *melodic phrase* is a complete unit of linear pitch and duration that ends with a cadence. It is a natural division of the melody, comparable to a sentence in language, that expresses a unity and musical idea of its own, and it becomes an identifiable and extractable part of the complete melody. Melodies usually include from two to eight phrases.

A *melodic cadence* consists of the final note of a phrase. It functions as a point of arrival, closure, arrest, and punctuation for the phrase. Similarly to language, musical punctuations are of relative weight and length—lighter or heavier, shorter or longer. Melodic cadences are usually classified into two kinds: 1) a phrase ends in a *complete cadence* (c.c.) when its final note is the tonic or keynote (1; *do*); 2) a phrase that concludes on any scale tone other than the tonic (frequently 2, 3, or 5; *re, mi,* or *so*) has an *incomplete cadence* (i.c.).

Performance in C Major

Your understanding of key, phrase, and cadence—as well as your reading, playing, and singing skills—will develop best at this point through further performance and analysis of song melodies in C major.

Perform each of the next song melodies in these ways:

1. Sing the song with its text; the melody may already be familiar to you.
2. Play the melody on a piano, applying illustrated hand positions and using fingerings given above the staff.
3. Sing or think the melody with pitch names (letters), then with *so-fa* syllables, and finally with scale numbers. (In this book right-hand finger numbers always appear above the staff, and scale numbers are below. Do not confuse these two numbering systems.)

Analyze the pitch organization in each song melody from these standpoints:

1. Identify and name the keynote and key of the melody. (All of these songs have C as their tonic and are in C major.)
2. Identify by scale number and syllable the first and last notes of the melody. A very high percentage of all melodies end on their keynote (*do;* 1), but

melodies may begin on either their keynote or some other scale tone (probably *do, mi,* or *so;* 1, 3, or 5).

3. Identify each phrase and its type of cadence. Complete and incomplete cadences are respectively marked *c.c.* and *i.c.*.

4. Describe kinds of pitch movement found within phrases. Which patterns are based on scale steps, and which ones contain skips?

MERRILY WE ROLL ALONG
Traditional

names:	1. E	D	C	D	E	E	E,	D	D	D,	E	G	G,
syllables:	2. Mi	re	do	re	mi	mi	mi,	re	re	re	mi	so	so,
numbers:	3. 3	2	1	2	3	3	3	2	2	2,	3	5	5,
words:	4. Mer	- ri - ly	we	roll	a - long,		roll	a - long,		roll	a - long,		

	E	D	C	D	E	E	E,	D	D	E	D	C.
	Mi	re	do	re	mi	mi	mi,	re	re	mi	re	do.
	3	2	1	2	3	3	3,	2	2	3	2	1.
	Mer	- ri - ly	we	roll	a - long,		o'er	the	deep	blue	sea.	

You can learn to play *Jingle Bells* by applying the same procedures and five-note (C-G) hand position used to play *Merrily We Roll Along.* Short line segments in the continuity of syllable and number systems represent a repetition of the previous syllable or number.

JINGLE BELLS
James Pierpont

	1. E	—	—,	—	—	—,	E	G	C	D	E,
	2. mi	—	—,	—	—	—,	mi	so	do	re	mi,
	3. 3	—	—,	—	—	—,	3	5	1	2	3,
	4. Jin	- gle	bells,	Jin	- gle	bells,	Jin	- gle	all	the	way,

	F	—	—	—	F	E	E	—	—	E	D	D	E	D	G!
	fa	—	—	—	fa	mi	mi	—	—	mi	re	re	mi	re	so!
	4	—	—	—	4	3	3	—	—	3	2	2	3	2	5!
	Oh,	what	fun	it	is	to	ride	in	a	one	horse	o	- pen	sleigh!	

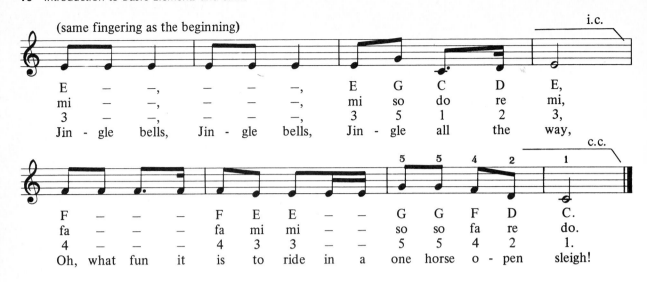

(same fingering as the beginning)   i.c.

E	—	—,	—	—	—,	E	G	C	D	E,
mi	—	—,	—	—	—,	mi	so	do	re	mi,
3	—	—,	—	—	—,	3	5	1	2	3,
Jin	-	gle	bells,	Jin	- gle	bells,	Jin - gle	all	the	way,

c.c.

F	—	—	—	F	E	E	—	—	G	G	F	D	C.
fa	—	—	—	fa	mi	mi	—	—	so	so	fa	re	do.
4	—	—	—	4	3	3	—	—	5	5	4	2	1.
Oh,	what	fun	it	is	to	ride	in	a	one	horse	o - pen		sleigh!

Kum Ba Yah encompasses the first six notes (C–A) of C major and can be played by applying the illustrated hand position and fingerings.

C-A six-note position:

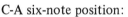

KUM BA YAH   African Folk Song

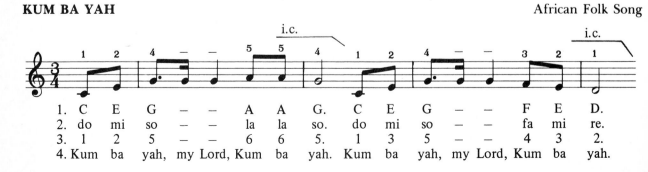

1. C	E	G	—	—	A	A	G.	C	E	G	—	—	F	E	D.
2. do	mi	so	—	—	la	la	so.	do	mi	so	—	—	fa	mi	re.
3. 1	2	5	—	—	6	6	5.	1	3	5	—	—	4	3	2.
4. Kum	ba	yah,	my	Lord,	Kum	ba	yah.	Kum	ba	yah,	my	Lord,	Kum	ba	yah.

etc.
etc.
etc.
Kum   ba   yah,   my Lord,   Kum   ba   yah.   Oh   Lord,___ Kum   ba   yah.

The opening phrases of *Joy to the World* and *The First Noel* contain all notes of the C major scale, sometimes in actual descending or ascending scale order. Apply the complete scale fingering that passes the thumb under three ascending and crosses three over the thumb descending. Also, sing these melodic phrases with syllables, scale numbers, and pitch names. Can you supply note names, numbers, and syllables for *The First Noel?*

JOY TO THE WORLD

Issac Watts, 1719
George F. Handel, 1742

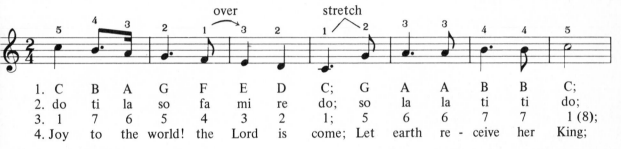

1.	C	B	A	G	F	E	D	C;	G	A	A	B	B	C;
2.	do	ti	la	so	fa	mi	re	do;	so	la	la	ti	ti	do;
3.	1	7	6	5	4	3	2	1;	5	6	6	7	7	1 (8);
4.	Joy	to	the	world!	the	Lord	is	come;	Let	earth	re	-	ceive	her	King;

THE FIRST NOEL

Traditional French Carol

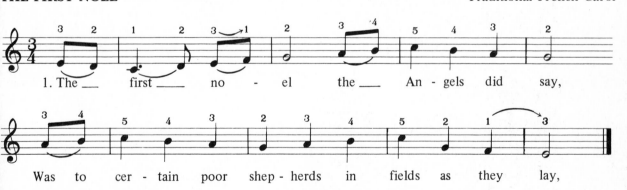

1. The ___   first ___   no - el   the ___   An - gels   did   say,

Was   to   cer - tain   poor   shep - herds   in   fields   as   they   lay,

PRACTICE ACTIVITIES

Page references to relevant *Study Activities* are given in parentheses.

Notating and Naming

1. A treble clef sign can be drawn with two strokes: a) a straight downward line, and b) a curving line that finishes with an encirclement of the second staff line (G). Follow the model and draw several treble clef signs. (5)

Model:

2. **a.** From each given open note head draw a stem in the correct direction and from the correct side.
   b. From each given closed note head correctly draw a stem and attach one flag. (6)

3. Refer to the model and notate on the blank staff each note identified by a model number.

model:

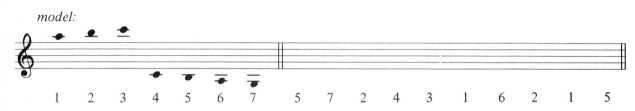

1   2   3   4   5   6   7   5   7   2   4   3   1   6   2   1   5

4. Practice naming the following notes written on a five-line treble staff. Repeat the exercise until you can name consecutive notes at a rate of one per second (do not write note names). Naming the notes in reverse order will provide additional practice. (7)

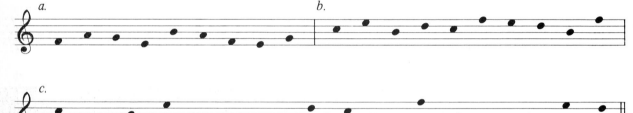

5. Practice naming the following notes above and below the staff until you can do so at the rate of one per second. (7)

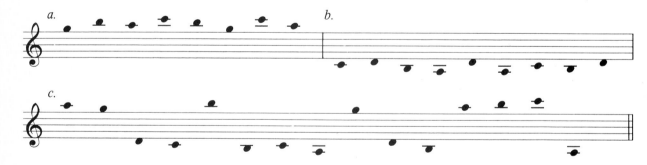

6. Place an open note head on the staff to represent the pitch given below with its *positive identification* of name and octave. (8)

example:

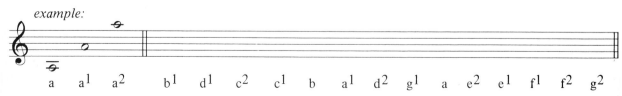

a   a^1 a^2 b^1 d^1 c^2 c^1 b   a^1 d^2 g^1 a   e^2 e^1 f^1 f^2 g^2

7. **a.** Place a closed note head one octave above the given note.
   b. Place a closed note head one octave below the given note. (7)

Identifying

8. Write an open note head on the blank staff to represent the name of, and pitch produced by, each piano white key marked with an x. (7)

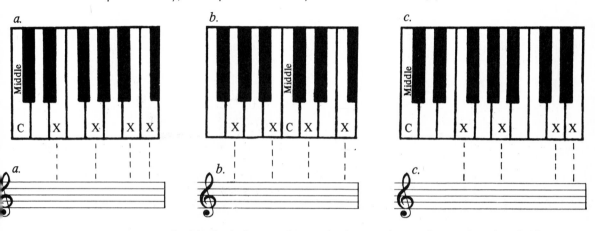

9. Write in the blanks below each note both its scale number and *so-fa* syllable. Follow the example in which tones on and below the low tonic (Middle C) are underlined, and tones on and above the high tonic are overlined. (9)

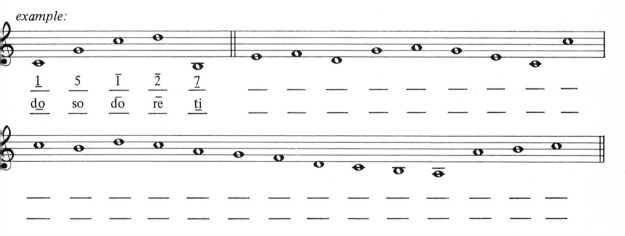

10. Write an open note head on the staff to represent the *so-fa* syllable or scale number given below.

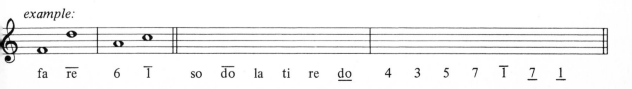

Reading

11. Sing the following pitch patterns with *so-fa* syllables and/or scale numbers. You may also play the patterns on a piano.

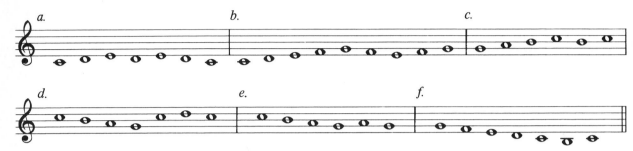

12. Sing the following melody with *so-fa* syllables, play it on a piano, and mark each of the three cadences as complete (c.c.) or incomplete (i.c.). (14)

TWINKLE, TWINKLE, LITTLE STAR   Traditional

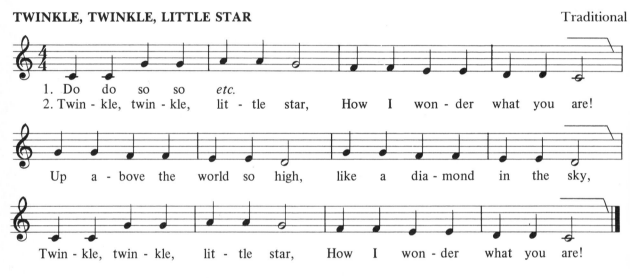

1. Do   do   so   so   *etc.*
2. Twin - kle, twin - kle,   lit - tle   star,   How   I   won - der   what   you   are!

Up   a - bove   the   world   so   high,   like   a   dia - mond   in   the   sky,

Twin - kle, twin - kle,   lit - tle   star,   How   I   won - der   what   you   are!

Discriminating (Aural-Visual)

Item 13 should be administered by an instructor or student assistant.

13. In each item (*a, b, c, d, e*) you see three (1, 2, 3) notated pitch patterns in C major. You will hear one of the three patterns played on a piano. Draw a circle around the number of the pattern you hear.

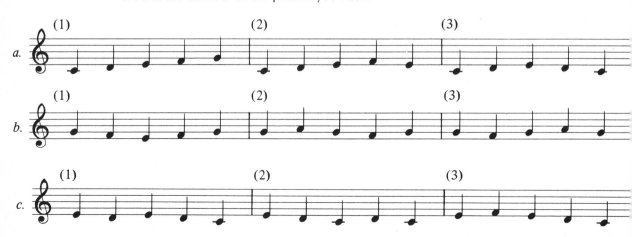

Performing

14. Continue to practice each of the following songs from Chapter One until you can perform it in the specified way for an instructor or student assistant.

    a. Play on a piano:

        Merrily We Roll Along

        I Know Where I'm Going

        Jingle Bells

        Kum Ba Yah

    b. Sing with words, pitch names, *so-fa* syllables, and scale numbers:

        Merrily We Roll Along

        Jingle Bells

        Kum Ba Yah

AFTER YOU HAVE COMPLETED ALL **PRACTICE ACTIVITIES** AND **RE-VIEWED THE OBJECTIVES,** CONTINUE WITH THE **ASSESSMENT OF PROGRESS**.

ASSESSMENT OF PROGRESS

A. *Applied knowledge.* Part A can be completed as a self-administered test without reference to any other material. Write your responses in the blanks beside each item number and, when you have finished all of Part A, check your answers with those in *Keys to Chapter Assessments,* page 249. Correct all of your errors and restudy relevant material in the *Study Activities* and *Practice Activities* before continuing to Chapter Two.

Answer questions 1 through 8 with reference to the following note and staff parts:

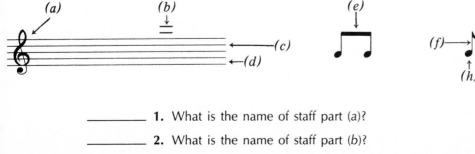

_____ **1.** What is the name of staff part (a)?

_____ **2.** What is the name of staff part (b)?

_____ **3.** What is the name of staff part (c)?

_____ **4.** What is the name of staff part (d)?

_____ **5.** What is the name of note part (e)?

_____ **6.** What is the name of note part (f)?

_____ **7.** What is the name of note part (g)?

_____ **8.** What is the name of note part (h)?

_____ **9.** Which notes (by item letter) are written incorrectly on the staff below?

Answer questions 10 through 18 with reference to the following notated pitches and numbered keys of a keyboard:

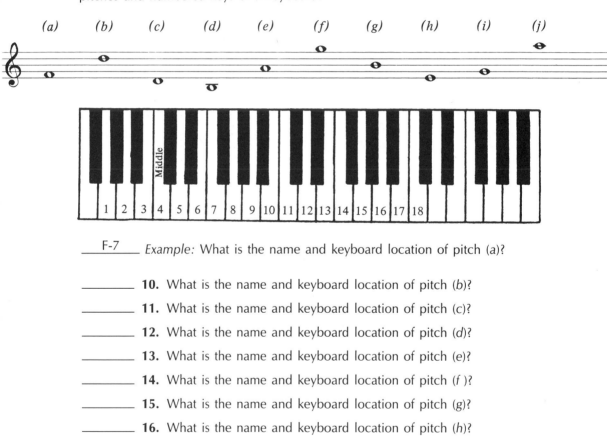

___F-7___ _Example:_ What is the name and keyboard location of pitch (a)?

_____ **10.** What is the name and keyboard location of pitch (b)?

_____ **11.** What is the name and keyboard location of pitch (c)?

_____ **12.** What is the name and keyboard location of pitch (d)?

_____ **13.** What is the name and keyboard location of pitch (e)?

_____ **14.** What is the name and keyboard location of pitch (f)?

_____ **15.** What is the name and keyboard location of pitch (g)?

_____ **16.** What is the name and keyboard location of pitch (h)?

_____ **17.** What is the name and keyboard location of pitch (i)?

_____ **18.** What is the name and keyboard location of pitch (j)?

Answer questions 19 through 25 with reference to the following notated melody:

Lon - don Bridge is fall - ing down, fall - ing down, fall - ing down;

(2)

Lon - don Bridge   is   fall - ing   down,   my   fair   la - dy - o.

_____ **19.** What is the name of the keynote (tonic) in *London Bridge?*

_____ **20.** In what key is the melody written?

_____ **21.** What is the *so-fa* syllable for the first note?

_____ **22.** What is the scale number of the second note?

_____ **23.** What musical term would be used to name each of the main units of form that are overlined and numbered?

_____ **24.** What kind of cadence occurs at the end of unit (1)?

_____ **25.** What are the (pitch) names of the final five notes?

B. *Skills.* Part B is an assessment of the level of performing (playing and singing) skills you developed during the study of this chapter. It should be administered to you by an instructor or student assistant. You should achieve the minimum level or higher before continuing to Chapter Two.

1. Minimum acceptable level of performance:
   a. Play on a piano the following song melodies at an appropriate tempo and with no more than one error or hesitation.
     1) *Merrily We Roll Along*
     2) *I Know Where I'm Going*
   b. Sing, with or without the assistance of an instructor or a piano, the following song melody and pitch patterns with *so-fa* syllables and/or scale numbers.
     1) *Merrily We Roll Along*
     2) three pitch patterns (exercises), page 13.

2. Higher level of performance
   a. Play any or all of the following song melodies at an appropriate tempo and with no more than one error or hesitation in each.
     1) *Merrily We Roll Along*
     2) *I Know Where I'm Going*
     3) *Jingle Bells*
     4) *Kum Ba Yah*
     5) *Twinkle, Twinkle Little Star*
   b. Sing, without the assistance of an instructor or a piano, the following song melodies and pitch patterns with *so-fa* syllables and/or scale numbers.
     1) *Jingle Bells*
     2) *Kum Ba Yah*
     3) *Twinke, Twinkle Little Star*
     4) any pitch patterns selected by the instructor from page 13.

Chapter 2

Introduction to the Organization of Rhythm

INSTRUCTIONS

1. Read the *Objectives* to gain an initial awareness of competencies you should have acquired by the time you complete this chapter. Keep these objectives in mind as you continue through the study and practice activities.

2. Complete all *Study Activities*. Make special efforts to understand all factors of rhythmic organization and notation that are presented and to develop skills of reading rhythm patterns contained in illustrations, exercises, and melodies.

3. Complete all *Practice Activities* for the purposes of applying your knowledge and improving your skills.

4. As soon as you are ready, or when directed by an instructor, complete the *Assessment of Progress*. You should achieve criterion levels indicated before continuing to Chapter Three.

OBJECTIVES

1. Recall and define the following terms and correctly use and interpret them in written or oral communication:

anacrusis	meter	off-beat
bar line	duple	on-beat
beat	quadruple	patterns of duration
beat unit	simple	beat patterns
elongation dot	triple	combined patterns
measure	meter signature	divided patterns
melodic rhythm	absolute meaning	rhythm
	applied meaning	slur and tie
	metric accent	tempo beat
	metric group	

2. Recognize, name, and write in the context of staff notation any of the following notes, rests, or characters:
  a. whole note, half note, quarter note
  b. eighth notes with flags or beams
  c. whole rest, half rest, quarter rest, eighth rest
  d. tied notes and dotted notes
  e. slurred notes

    f. bar line and double bar

    g. meter signatures: 2   3   4 or C
                       4   4   4

3. Given a notated song melody, provide the following information about its rhythmic organization:

    a. meter signature

    b. beat unit (kind of note receiving a duration of one beat)

    c. number of beats per measure

    d. point in measure at which melodic rhythm starts (for example: on beat one, on beat three, at the off-beat of beat three)

4. a. Given a melodic rhythm or rhythm patterns notated with a meter signature, but without bar lines, draw bar lines at places that correspond to the meter signature.

    b. Given a melodic rhythm or rhythm patterns notated with bar lines, but without a meter signature, identify and write an appropriate signature.

5. Recognize equivalent note values, rhythm patterns, and measures. This might include identifying either incomplete or incorrect measures of notation.

6. Given notated exercises or melodies comprised of patterns introduced in this chapter, accurately read (perform) for an instructor or student assistant these patterns with rhythm syllables and/or counts.

7. Identify from several notated choices the pattern of duration you hear performed by an instructor or student assistant (aural-visual discrimination).

STUDY ACTIVITIES

Chapter One introduced you to linear organization of pitch. Chapter Two will present an introduction to rhythm so that you will have an early foundation in pitch and rhythm from which we can expand and build parallel concepts and skills in both elements throughout the remaining chapters of study. *Rhythm* is a broad term that refers to everything pertaining to temporal (taking place across time) qualities of cyclical events in nature, human experience, and music. Years, seasons, tides, and sunrises and sunsets take place in a regular, recurring, orderly sequence—a cosmic rhythm. Heartbeats, breathing, walking, and other physical movements possess qualities of rhythm. Rhythm in music is an umbrella under which durations of sounds and silences occur; it also serves as the principal organizer and energizer in all music. In this chapter we will explore its components (beat, tempo, meter, and pattern) and notation and learn to read some of its basic patterns. Later chapters will introduce additional patterns and notation.

COMPONENTS OF RHYTHM

Tempo Beat

Tempo beat is a compound term containing two nouns, each with its own meaning, yet the combination has a more functional application than either word has separately. *Beat* is the regular, recurring pulsation that we feel underlying all traditional music. Beat sensations are actually part of a kinesthetic response that arises when sensory cells in the joints are excited by movements of the body (muscles) and is most noticeable during overt movements such as marching or "keeping time" by clapping hands or tapping a foot. However, our perception of beat is really a psychological phenomenon that requires no accompanying overt movement, except (probably) in early stages of learning.

    Tempo relates to speed, or rate of recurrence, of the felt beat. *Tempo beat,* then, can be used in reference to the felt beat at a certain rate, which for now we will merely divide into three broad categories—quick (or fast), moderate, and slow. Tempo and tempo markings will be considered further in Chapter Ten.

Felt beats have no signs or markings with which they are represented in music notation; we do not see beats on the written page. But we can use special markings to show onsets of beats—points in time at which we would clap or tap—in order to provide visual guidelines to their occurrence. You might think of each beat as having an onset and duration as illustrated:

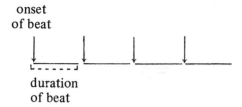

onset
of beat

duration
of beat

Tempo beats can be further illustrated with texts of songs you performed in Chapter One. Chant or sing the words in their natural melodic rhythm as you simultaneously clap felt beats represented by short vertical lines. Notice that each melody has its own appropriate tempo—a speed at which the music sounds just right. The correct tempo for *Jingle Bells* would be too fast for *Kum Ba Yah*, and vice versa.

quick, or fast, tempo beat:

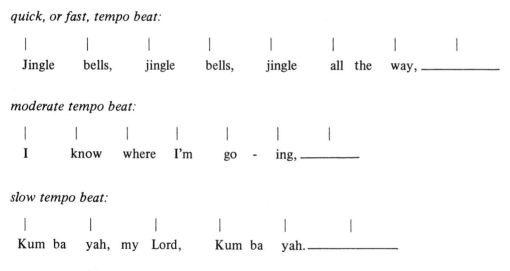

| | | | | | | | |
Jingle   bells,   jingle   bells,   jingle   all   the   way, _____

moderate tempo beat:

| | | | | | |
I   know   where   I'm   go - ing, _____

slow tempo beat:

| | | | | |
Kum ba   yah, my   Lord,   Kum ba   yah. _____

Meter

Research in music psychology has shown consistent evidence that individuals tend subjectively to group sound stimuli into patterns, and that this phenomenon includes grouping beats. We find it difficult, for example, to feel twenty-four consecutive beats as all being the same. We are inclined to place greater stress or weight on some, dividing the ongoing series into smaller units with each unit comprised of a strong beat followed by one or more weak beats.

Ordinarily, composers objectively organize beats into patterns of strong and weak pulses that create *meter*. One pattern of beats is a *metric group,* and the strong beat that begins each group is the *metric accent.* Three classifications of metric groupings used in music are shown in the next illustrations. Our two basic meters are *duple* and *triple. Quadruple* meter is really a combination of two duple groups, but identifying it as a separate meter is practical for our purposes. Also, observe that each beat in a metric group can be represented with a number, and the entire group can be "counted" (1-2, 1-2-3, 1-2-3-4). Beat 1 is the metric accent.

Meters	*Metric Groups*			
	1	2		
duple				
	1	2	3	
triple				
	1	2	3	4
quadruple				

Sing or chant the melodic rhythm of the following three familiar songs while you clap the beat. But this time try responding to metric groupings in each melody by employing a stronger clap on the metric accent (beat one). You will discover that *Kum Ba Yah* starts on the last (weak) beat of a group. This is a common occurrence in music, and one that does not change the continuing meter. Melodic tones that start at some point within a metric group preceding the first metric accent are called an *anacrusis* (see later section in this chapter).

duple meter:

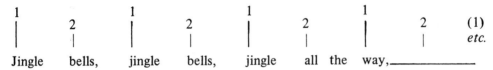

Jingle   bells,   jingle   bells,   jingle   all   the   way,_____   (1) etc.

quadruple meter:

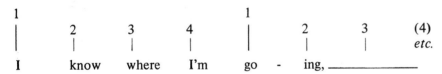

I   know   where   I'm   go - ing, _____   (4) etc.

triple meter:

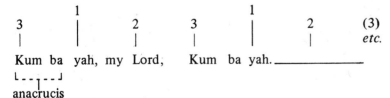

Kum ba   yah, my   Lord,   Kum   ba yah._____   (3) etc.

anacrusis

Patterns

Durations of sounds and silences in a piece of music are directly related to the tempo beat. As a matter of fact, accurate response to durations can happen only when they are correctly superimposed upon the felt beat. Patterns of duration fall into three categories: those that correspond to a beat, those that combine beat values, and those that divide a beat value. Relative durations (short to long) can be viewed initially as they are depicted in the following chart:

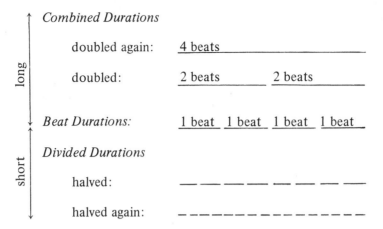

Melodic rhythm is made up of patterns of duration associated with pitch movement in a melody. Sing through the familiar *Are You Sleeping* while maintaining a clapped beat and observing durations that correspond to each word or word syllable. You will find that the melodic rhythm contains one-beat durations, two-beat (combined) durations, and divided-beat durations.

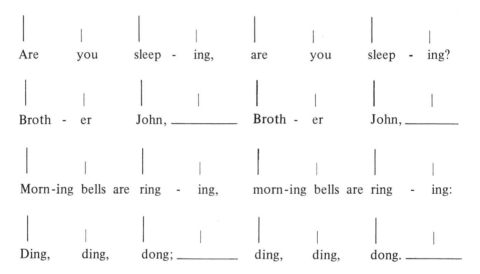

NOTATION OF DURATION

Notes and Rests

You learned in Chapter One that notes designate both pitch and duration of sound, and that only note-head locations on a staff relate to pitch. All other parts of notes represent durational values. Each note is given a durational, or rhythmic, name that comes from its mathematical value, starting with a whole and decreasing by fractions (divisions) of the whole. Rests are characters that represent silence. Each rest shares the name and durational value of its corresponding note (a half rest represents a duration of silence equal to the duration of sound denoted by a half note). Study and memorize the chart of basic notes and rests.

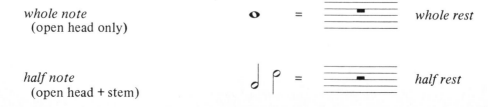

quarter note
(closed head + stem) ♩ ♩ = ₹ *quarter rest*

eighth note
(closed head + stem + flag) ♪ ♪ = ⁷ *eighth rest*

sixteenth note
(closed head + stem + 2 flags) ♬ ♬ = ⁊ *sixteenth rest*

Notes of smaller value than a quarter—eighths and sixteenths—can be connected and grouped together with heavy lines called *beams* that replace individual flags. Beamed notes, compared with separately flagged notes, facilitate visual recognition of notated patterns.

beaming eighths: ♪ ♪ = ♫   ♪ ♪ ♪ ♪ = ♫♫

beaming sixteenths: ♬ ♬ = ♬   ♬ ♬ ♬ ♬ = ♬♬

*beaming eighths
with sixteenths:* ♪ ♬ = ♪♬   ♬♪ = ♬♪

Value Equivalencies

Notes and rests represent no absolute duration. They indicate only durational values relative to values of other notes and rests in the same piece of music, and this interrelatedness arises from mathematical ratios and equivalencies between and among notes. You will encounter situations in dealing with music and music notation in which you must exercise knowledge of note equivalencies, so learn them now from the chart. (Rest equivalencies follow the same pattern.)

note equivalencies from halving or doubling values:

←———————————— doubling ————————————

1 whole = 2 half = 4 quarter = 8 eighth = 16 sixteenth
note   notes   notes   notes   notes

———————————————halving ————————————→

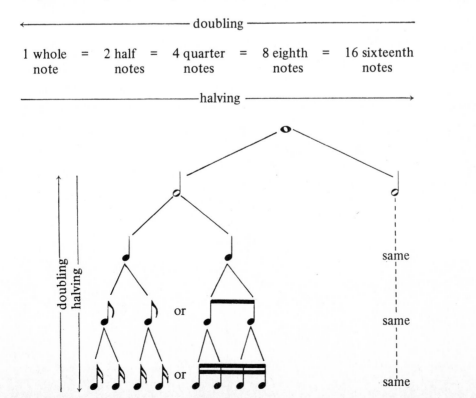

Staff Notation of Rhythm

Music written on a staff includes several features of notation that relate directly to its rhythmic organization. These basic notational elements are illustrated in the context of a notated phrase of rhythm, and each is subsequently defined and described.

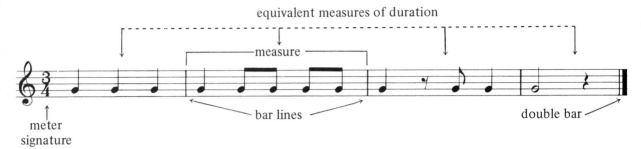

Bar lines.   A vertical line drawn across the staff from its top to bottom lines is called a *bar line*. Bar lines provide a visual framing of metric groups, due to the fact that a line immediately precedes each metric accent (beat one). But no bar line appears before the very first note in a piece of music. A *double bar* is used to close the staff at the end of a piece.

Measure.   Total duration (and all notes and rests involved) between bar lines constitutes a *measure* (also called a *bar*). Measures are numbered from the first complete measure; thus, our notated example has four measures, measure three contains an eighth rest, and so forth. Each complete measure must contain exactly the same total duration; although patterns will differ, they must be equivalent. Study the example and determine that each measure has note and rest values equivalent to three quarter notes.

Meter signature.   A traditional *meter signature* is comprised of two numbers written one above the other so that each occupies half of the staff at the beginning of a piece immediately preceding its first note (or rest). Music uses many different meter signatures, and one good way to build a fundamental understanding that can be applied in all cases is to determine two related meanings for any given signature. One meaning is *absolute* (true at all times and in all cases), and the other is *applied* (true in a specific musical situation in which it is being used). We can take the three-four meter signature from our previous notated phrase as an example:

The bottom number of a signature represents a corresponding kind of note (4 = a quarter note, 2 = a half note, 8 = an eighth note), and a meter signature can actually be written with that note replacing its bottom number. This second (applied) form is useful in separating a signature's two meanings. A three-four signature will always (absolutely) mean only that three quarter notes or equivalent note and/or rest values occupy every complete measure. Its applied meaning shows an interpretation that has a quarter note in this piece representing a one-beat duration and functioning as the *beat unit,* therefore each measure has three beats (or counts) resulting in triple meter. You should realize that three-four, or any other meter signature, has only one absolute meaning, but it, like some others, can have more than one applied meaning. Additional applied meanings will be encountered in later chapters; until then you will be involved only with music in which the absolute and applied meanings are interchangeable.

   Simple meters.   Meters can be classified into three broad types—simple, compound, and irregular or asymmetric. Compound meters are presented in Chapter Eight; asymmetric meters are treated in optional Minichapter E. *Simple meters* introduced in this chapter and expanded in Chapters Five and Six can be defined as meters in which a basic note—usually a quarter, half, or eighth note—functions as the beat unit (receives a one-beat duration), and division of the beat is a duple division into two equal parts. In this chapter you will be reading patterns notated in the three most common simple meter signatures: $\frac{2}{4}$ $\frac{3}{4}$ and $\frac{4}{4}$ (or C). Study the following summary of these signatures and their meanings:

Simple meter signatures with a quarter-note beat unit:

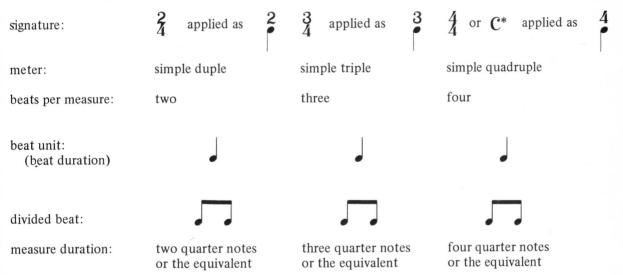

signature:	$\frac{2}{4}$ applied as	$\frac{3}{4}$ applied as	$\frac{4}{4}$ or **C*** applied as
meter:	simple duple	simple triple	simple quadruple
beats per measure:	two	three	four
beat unit: (beat duration)			
divided beat:			
measure duration:	two quarter notes or the equivalent	three quarter notes or the equivalent	four quarter notes or the equivalent

*A four-four meter signature can be written in either of two traditional ways—with the two numbers or with a **C** occupying the middle two spaces of the staff. The signatures are interchangeable and have exactly the same interpretation.

READING PATTERNS

Knowledge of names and values of notes and rests, equivalencies, meters, and meter signatures is basic to understanding how rhythm is organized and notated, but this knowledge by itself does not provide competencies to respond to, read, and perform patterns of duration found in music. Accurately reading and performing patterns requires an ability to establish and maintain a steady tempo beat and, at the same time, superimpose various patterns of duration upon that felt beat. Unless you can do these two things simultaneously, you will be unable to develop accurate, disciplined rhythmic response.

   Learning to read and perform rhythm can be facilitated by ways of practice that enable you to physically keep the beat and speak (vocalize) patterns. We use throughout this book a system in which you clap tempo beats and speak patterns with either rhythm syllables or counts.

Vocalization of patterns:

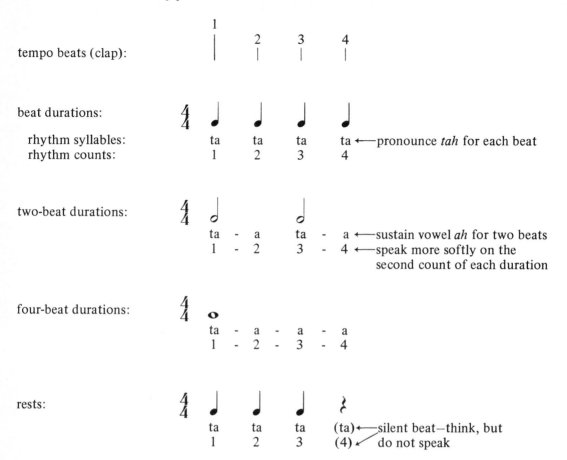

tempo beats (clap):	1	2 3 4	

beat durations:

rhythm syllables: ta ta ta ta ←—pronounce *tah* for each beat
rhythm counts: 1 2 3 4

two-beat durations:

ta - a ta - a ←—sustain vowel *ah* for two beats
1 - 2 3 - 4 ←—speak more softly on the
second count of each duration

four-beat durations:

ta - a - a - a
1 - 2 - 3 - 4

rests:

ta ta ta (ta)←—silent beat—think, but
1 2 3 (4) ⟋ do not speak

Duration must be separated from pitch in initial stages of practice; rhythm and pitch can then be read together in the process of learning to play or sing a melody. Reading rhythm patterns alone can be done by speaking their sounds with either a syllable system or the traditional counting system. You should practice both ways, for while syllables provide an easy, accurate approach to building correct responses to basic discrete patterns, counts establish an awareness of where patterns fall within a measure. Of the two systems, syllables possess a more vocal and musical quality. Learn the syllables and counts illustrated for *beat durations* and *combined* (two-beat, four-beat) *durations.*

Beat Patterns and Combined Patterns

Apply the following procedures for reading notated rhythm exercises that include beat durations and combined durations in two-four, three-four, and four-four. You should realize that observance of the exact duration of a notated silence (rest) is as important as speaking sounds correctly, and that you must keep your beat going steadily through rests.

1. Start your beat clapping at the indicated tempo—fast, moderate, or slow—during the introductory measure.
2. Continue clapping the tempo beat while you read the patterns of duration with rhythm syllables.
3. Repeat the entire exercise with rhythm counts.
4. Extract and practice any measures that present a problem.

5. Continue practicing until the beats and patterns are accurate, physically coordinated, and comfortable.

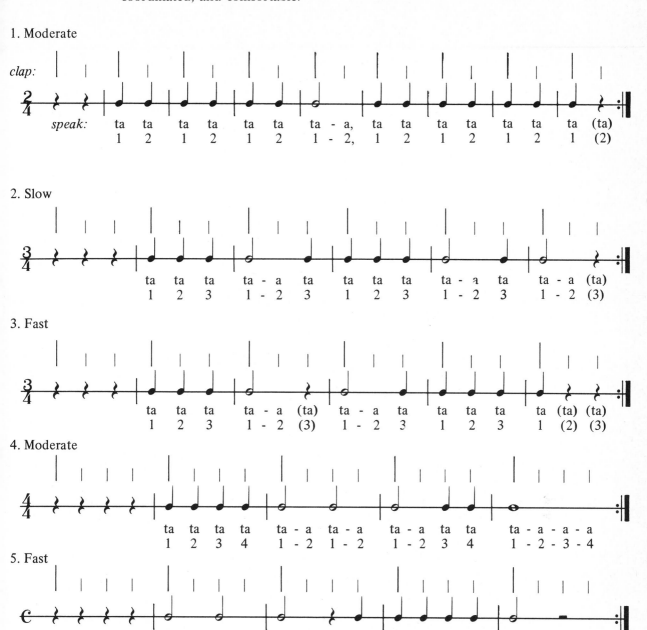

Tie and elongation dot. In the preceding exercises you read combined-beat durations based on values of single notes in simple meters. Half notes received two beats, and whole notes four beats. Duration of a note can be extended by tieing it to another note or through use of an elongation dot. A *tie* is a curved line connecting two or more notes of the same pitch and of either the same or different values. Its effect is to combine separate values into one sustained sound on the same pitch.

An *elongation dot* placed immediately to the right of a note head increases by one-half the duration, or value, of that note. Such notes are named dotted half notes, dotted quarter notes, and so forth. Use of an elongation dot also can be considered a shorthand way of notating tied notes—one dotted note replaces two tied notes. However, tied notes, instead of a dotted note, must be used in certain circumstances, such as tieing the final note of one measure across a bar line to the first note of the next measure. The elongated value that you will use immediately is achieved either by tieing a half note to a quarter or by dotting a half note, resulting in a combined duration of three beats as shown here:

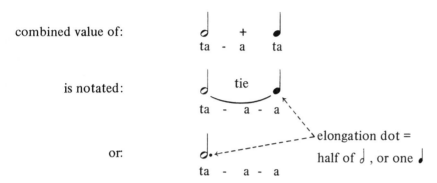

notated examples:

Read the next exercises, in which you will find various combined durations. Employ practice procedures outlined in the previous section.

1. Slow

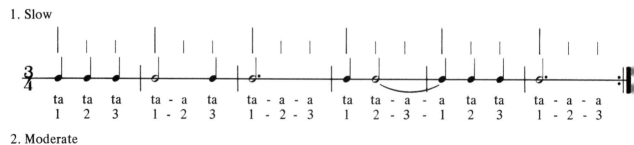

2. Moderate

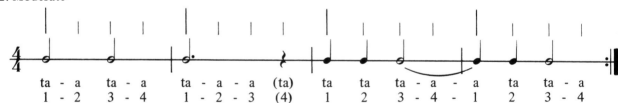

3. Fast

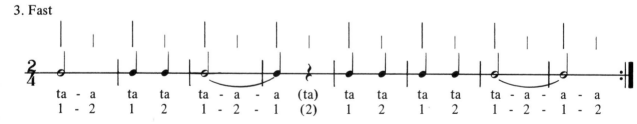

Divided Patterns

A *divided pattern* in simple meter is a *duple division* that splits the beat duration into two equal parts. When a quarter note is the beat unit, each half of a divided pattern is one-eighth, which can be represented by either an eighth note or an eighth rest. Study the pattern that is illustrated as two beamed eighth notes (two separately flagged eighth notes would be the same pattern), and observe that the first note falls at a point called *on-beat* and occurs at the onset of a beat when hands come together in a beat-clapping motion. *Off-beat,* occupied by the second eighth note, starts at the midpoint of a beat's duration and can be felt coinciding with the position at which your hands are farthest apart. You also should learn rhythm syllables (ti-ti, spoken *tee-tee*) and counts (1 &, spoken *one and* or *an*) applied to a divided pattern of two sounds. Continue to the exercises that contain divided (eighth-note) patterns and read each exercise by speaking its patterns with rhythm syllables or counts while clapping tempo beats.

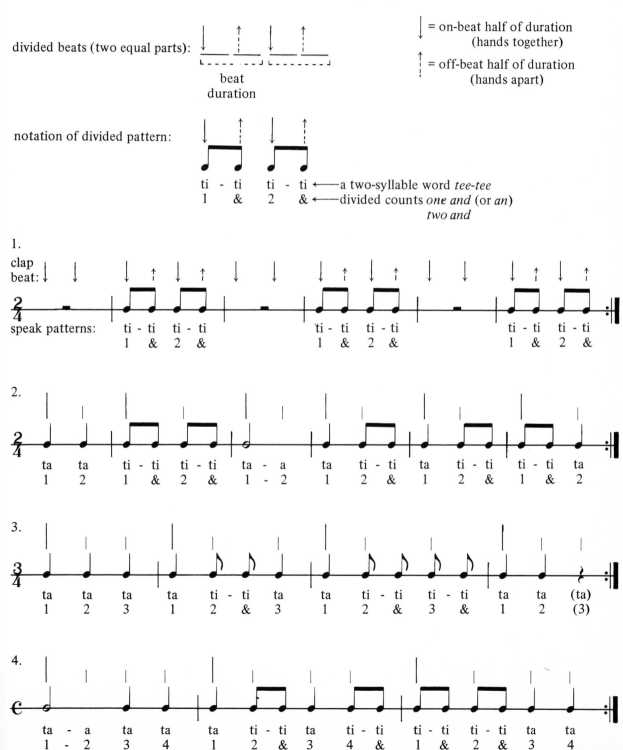

The next illustration shows a divided pattern as a combination of sound (eighth note) and silence (eighth rest). This pattern occurs in music in two forms: 1) on-beat sound and off-beat silence, or 2) on-beat silence and off-beat sound. Practice these two patterns against clapped beats until you feel exact values of sound and silence within a beat duration, then continue reading the exercises that follow. Try to see the eighth note and rest together as a one-beat pattern.

divided-beat patterns of sound and silence:

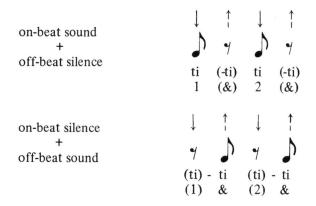

on-beat sound
+
off-beat silence

on-beat silence
+
off-beat sound

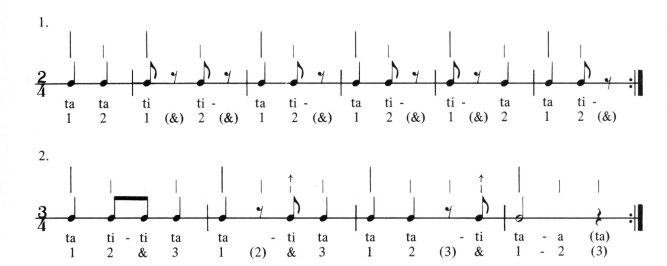

The divided pattern with a tie or elongation dot. You learned in the previous section on combined patterns that durational values can be increased by either tieing together the values of two notes or dotting a note to extend its value by one-half. At that time you experienced a dotted-half-note value of three beats. Either a tie or elongation dot also can be used to extend the sound of a quarter note into the first eighth-note value of a divided pattern.

The result is a two-beat pattern in which the first tied or dotted value extends through one entire beat plus the first (on-beat) half of the next beat and is followed by an off-beat eighth-note. As you read the next exercises, try to see and respond to this pattern as a unit (not separate notes) superimposed on two steady tempo beats.

derivation of the dotted-quarter-eighth pattern:

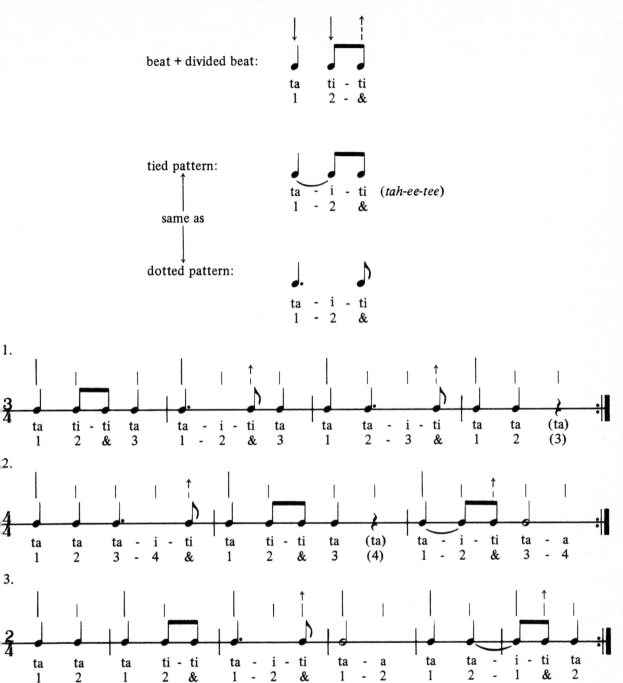

beat + divided beat:

ta   ti - ti
1   2 - &

tied pattern:

ta - i - ti   (*tah-ee-tee*)
1 - 2   &

same as

dotted pattern:

ta - i - ti
1 - 2   &

1.

ta   ti - ti   ta   ta - i - ti   ta   ta   ta - i - ti   ta   ta   (ta)
1   2   &   3   1 - 2   &   3   1   2 - 3   &   1   2   (3)

2.

ta   ta   ta - i - ti   ta   ti - ti   ta   (ta)   ta - i - ti   ta - a
1   2   3 - 4   &   1   2   &   3   (4)   1 - 2   &   3 - 4

3.

ta   ta   ta   ti - ti   ta - i - ti   ta - a   ta   ta - i - ti   ta
1   2   1   2   &   1 - 2   &   1 - 2   1   2 - 1   &   2

Anacrusis and Slur

Some melodies start on a metric accent—on the first beat of a metric group or measure. In these cases both the first and last measures, as well as all others, are complete. Other melodies start at some point within a metric group; they begin with an *incomplete measure* of duration and also end with an incomplete measure, which added together equal one complete measure.

Anacrusis is a term applied to one or more notes that precede the first bar line, or metric accent, in music that begins with an incomplete measure. An anacrusis that occurs on the last beat or divided beat of a measure can also be called an *upbeat* or *pick-up* to the following metric accent. Performing an anacrusis with accurate duration is an important factor in reading, singing, or playing a melody.

A *tie*, you will recall, connects notes of the same pitch and combines their durations. A *slur* is a curved line, similar in appearance to a tie, that groups two or more notes of different pitch, and in song melodies it is a visual indicator that those pitches are sung to the same word (vowel sound). Slurs have nothing to do with rhythm; each note must be given its individual duration. The next three excerpts from song melodies illustrate various types of anacrusis as well as slurs and ties. Try your skill in reading and singing them.

Reading Melodic Rhythm

Melodic rhythm is the overall durational component of a melody and is comprised of its various patterns of duration. Many melodies contain only patterns you have learned to recognize and read in this chapter. Therefore, sight-reading rhythm in the next melodic phrases can be done rather easily by following these procedures:

1. Identify the meter signature, meter, and beat unit (a quarter note).
2. Determine the appropriate tempo—fast, moderate, or slow.
3. Make a visual overview of the notated melody and identify familiar patterns.
4. Establish and maintain your tempo beat by clapping it, and read the melodic rhythm with rhythm syllables or counts.
5. Sing or play the melodic phrases in accurate rhythm.

WHISTLE, DAUGHTER, WHISTLE   U.S. Folk Song

Quickly

clap beats:

syllables: ta ta ta ta ta ta - a, ta ta ta ta ta - a - a (ta)
counts: 1   2   3   4   1   2 - 3, 4   1   2   3   4   1 - 2 - 3 (4)
words: Whis-tle, daugh-ter, whis-tle,   and   you   shall have a cow.

etc.
etc.
I   can't whis-tle, moth-er,   you nev-er taught me how.

SIMPLE GIFTS   U.S. Shaker Song

Moderately

ti - ti ta ti - ti ti - ti ti - ti ta, *etc.*
4 & 1   2   &   3   &   4   &   1, *etc.*
'Tis the gift to be sim-ple 'tis the gift to be free,

'tis the gift to come down where we ought to be,

And when we find our-selves___ in the place just___ right,

it will be in the val - ley of love and de - light.

PRAY GOD BLESS   English Round

Quickly

ta   ta   ta   (ta)   ta   ta   ta   (ti-) ti
1   2   3   (4)   1   2   3   (4)   &
Pray God bless   all friends here,   a

etc.
etc.
mer-ry mer-ry Christ-mas and a hap-py New Year.

MY LORD, WHAT A MORNING

Spiritual

Slowly

My Lord, what a morn - ing, My Lord, what a morn - ing,

(ta - i - ti ta ta)

My Lord, what a morn - ing, When the stars be - gin to fall.

READING AND PERFORMING SONGS

Through your combined experiences in Chapters One and Two, you now should possess the ability to read and perform some simple songs. This involves reading both pitch and duration and reproducing the melody by playing and/or singing it.

You can learn *Hanukah,* a Jewish festival song, if you follow these suggestions:

1. Identify the meter signature, set a tempo beat, and read the melodic rhythm with syllables or counts (ti-ti ta or 1 & 2, etc.).
2. Read through the melodic pitches by name (G-E-G, etc.) and realize that these pitches are from the C major scale and the piece is in C major. Only the final phrase has a complete cadence.
3. Study the illustrated hand positions and apply them in fingering and playing the four phrases.
4. Can you sing *Hanukah* with its words and also with *so-fa* syllables or scale numbers (*so-mi-so* or 5-3-5, etc.)?

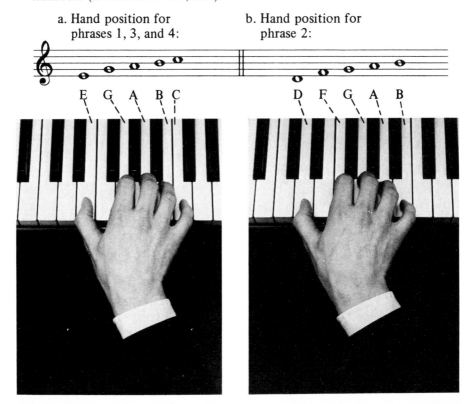

a. Hand position for phrases 1, 3, and 4:

E G A B C

b. Hand position for phrase 2:

D F G A B

HANUKAH   Jewish Folk Song

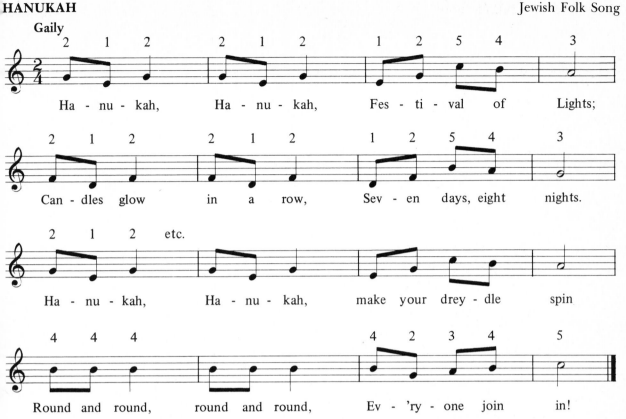

Five Hundred Miles begins with an anacrusis on count three of an incomplete measure. Read the entire melodic rhythm, then play the melody using the keyboard hand position and fingerings shown here. This melody uses five different notes with F as its tonic and actually is based on a five-tone *pentatonic* scale, not the C major scale (see optional Minichapter D).

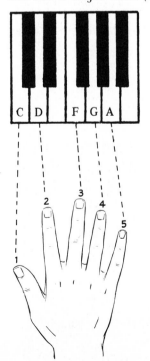

FIVE HUNDRED MILES

U.S. Folk Song

Moderately

If   you   miss   the   train   I'm   on,   you   will   know   that   I   am   gone.

You   can   hear   the   whis - tle   blow   five   hun - dred   miles, _____   five

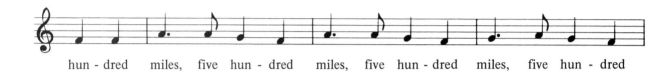

hun - dred   miles,   five   hun - dred   miles,   five   hun - dred   miles,   five   hun - dred

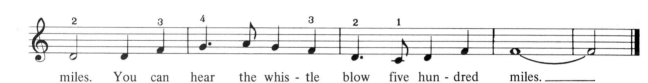

miles.   You   can   hear   the   whis - tle   blow   five   hun - dred   miles. _____

PRACTICE ACTIVITIES

Page references to relevant *Study Activities* are given in parentheses.

Notating and Naming

1. Write in the blanks provided the correct name of each lettered item as it pertains to staff notation of rhythm. (28–30)

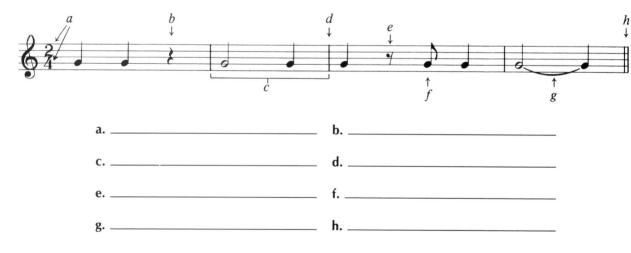

a. _____   b. _____

c. _____   d. _____

e. _____   f. _____

g. _____   h. _____

2. Follow illustrations in the model, and practice writing on the blank staff each item designated above.

Model:

meter signatures:			whole rest:	half rest:	bar line:	eighth rest in two strokes:	quarter rest in three strokes:

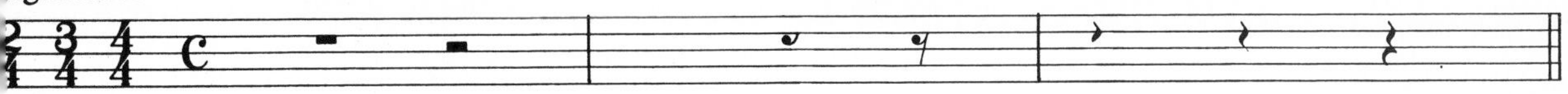

Write:

four-four signature two ways:	four quarter rests:	four eighth rests:	two half rests:	one whole rest:

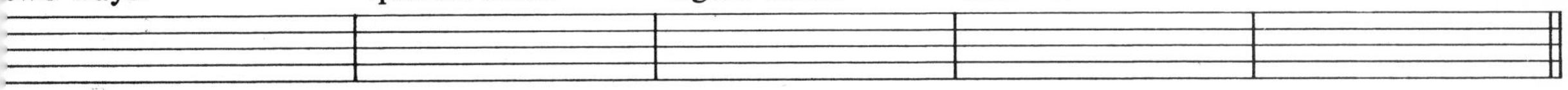

3. Follow illustrations in the model, and add stems and either one beam or one flag, as designated, to the given note heads. In a case of beaming one note above to one below the middle staff line, stems from both notes are pointed in the direction of the note head farthest from the middle line.

Model:

a. beams: *b.* stem & flag in two steps:

a. add stems and one beam: *b.* add stem and one flag:

Identifying

4. Notate on the blank segment of staff the designated equivalent of each given note or rest. (28–29)

a. equivalent note: *b.* equivalent note: *c.* equivalent rest: *d.* equivalent rest: *e.* equivalent rest:

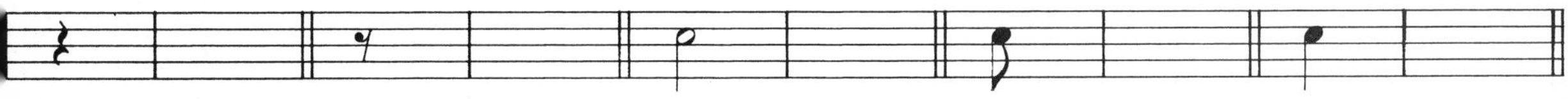

5. Notate on the blank segment of staff the designated equivalent note or notes for each given note or notes. (29, 34, 37)

a. equivalency in beamed eighths: *b.* equivalency in one dotted note: *c.* equivalency in one note:

a. equivalency in two tied notes: *e.* equivalency in two notes: *f.* equivalency in one note:

6. Write on the blank segment of staff the given meter signature in another form that represents its *applied meaning.* (31)

Example:

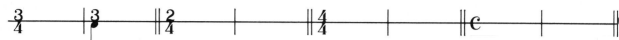

7. Cross out the corresponding letter of each measure that *does not* contain a total notated duration, or value, equivalent to the first measure. (30)

(a)　　*(b)*　　*(c)*　　*(d)*　　*(e)*　　*(f)*　　*(g)*

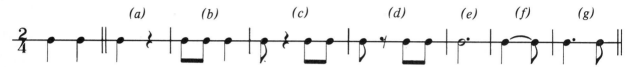

8. Each line of rhythm notation has a given meter signature. Draw bar lines at appropriate places to divide the line into complete measures. (30–31)

a.

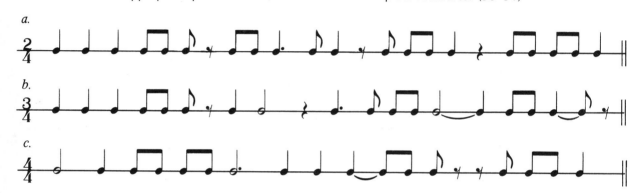

b.

c.

9. Each two-measure rhythm pattern is written without the top number of its signature. Write the correct top number in the box provided. (30–31)

a.　　　　　　　　　*b.*

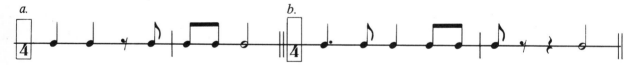

10. Each measure of rhythm is incomplete as written. Complete each measure by adding one or two notes or rests as designated. (30–31)

one note　　　　two notes　　　　　　one rest　　　　one note
↓　　　　　　↓　　　　　　　↓　　　　　　↓

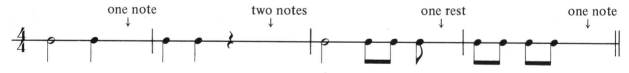

11. Write below each notated rhythm pattern both the rhythm syllables and counts used to vocalize the pattern. (32–37)

Example:

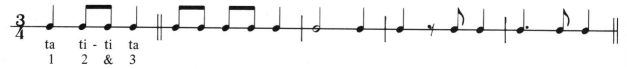

ta　　ti - ti　ta
1　　2　&　3

Creating

12.   Create and notate your own rhythm patterns, using the meter signatures given and the kinds of notes and number of measures specified.

a. four measures: with quarter notes, eighth notes, and one half note.

b. four measures: with quarter notes, eighth notes, and one dotted-quarter note.

c. four measures: with quarter notes, eighth notes, half notes, one quarter rest, and one dotted-half note.

Reading

13.   Practice reading melodic rhythm in the following song phrases by clapping a tempo beat and speaking the patterns with rhythm syllables and/or counts. All patterns are ones you have worked with in this chapter, therefore you should be able to recall them without writing syllables or counts below the notes.

AU CLAIR DE LA LUNE   French Folk Song

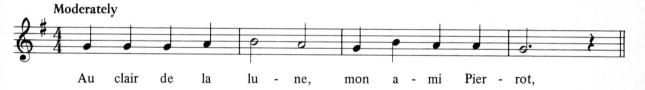

IF YOU'RE HAPPY   Traditional

FUM, FUM, FUM   Spanish Carol

AMERICA   Henry Carey
Samuel Francis Smith

THE DONKEY   Traditional Round

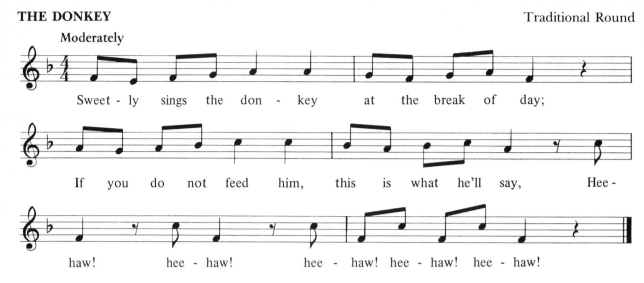

Discriminating (Aural-Visual)

Activity 14 should be administered by an instructor or student assistant.

14. In each notated item (*a, b, c, d, e*) you see three different rhythm patterns, each occupying a full measure in the same meter. You will hear one of the patterns chanted on a neutral syllable (*lah*) with an accompanying tempo beat. Circle the number of the pattern you hear.

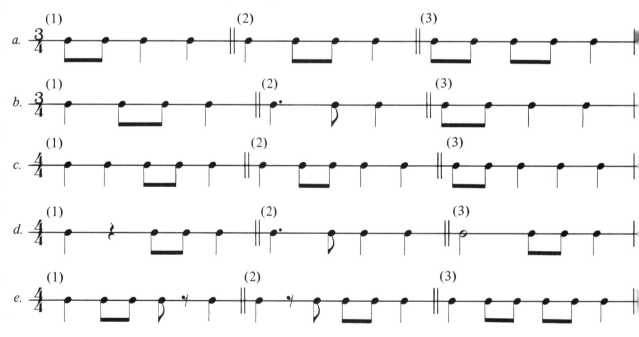

Performing

15. Continue to practice reading all rhythm patterns and melodic rhythms presented in the *Study Activities* until you can independently clap a tempo beat and simultaneously speak the patterns with rhythm syllables and/or counts.

16. Read the melodic rhythm of each song and play the melody on a piano.
   a. *Hanukah*
   b. *Five Hundred Miles*

AFTER YOU HAVE COMPLETED ALL **PRACTICE ACTIVITIES** AND RE-VIEWED THE **OBJECTIVES**, CONTINUE WITH THE **ASSESSMENT OF PROGRESS**.

ASSESSMENT OF PROGRESS

A. *Applied knowledge.* Part A can be completed as a self-administered test without reference to any other resources. Write your responses in the blanks beside each item number and, when you have finished all of Part A, check your answers with those in *Keys to Chapter Assessments,* page 249. Correct all of your errors and restudy relevant material in the *Study Activities* or *Practice Activities* before continuing to Chapter Three.

_____ **1.** Which measures (*a* through *h*) are equivalent in total duration to the model measure?

Answer questions 2 through 9 with reference to the following incomplete measures and choices of notation for completing them:

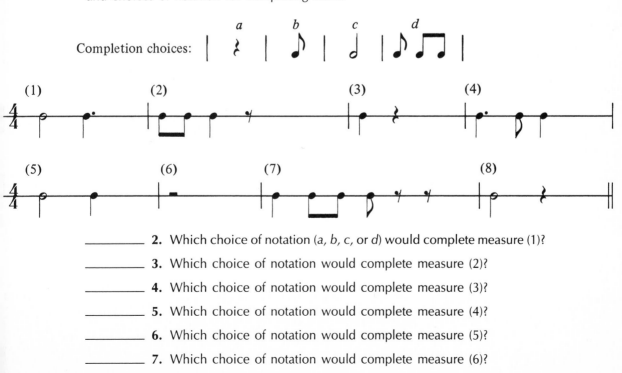

_____ **2.** Which choice of notation (*a, b, c,* or *d*) would complete measure (1)?

_____ **3.** Which choice of notation would complete measure (2)?

_____ **4.** Which choice of notation would complete measure (3)?

_____ **5.** Which choice of notation would complete measure (4)?

_____ **6.** Which choice of notation would complete measure (5)?

_____ **7.** Which choice of notation would complete measure (6)?

_____ **8.** Which choice of notation would complete measure (7)?

_____ **9.** Which choice of notation would complete measure (8)?

Answer questions 10 through 16 with reference to the following melodic rhythm:

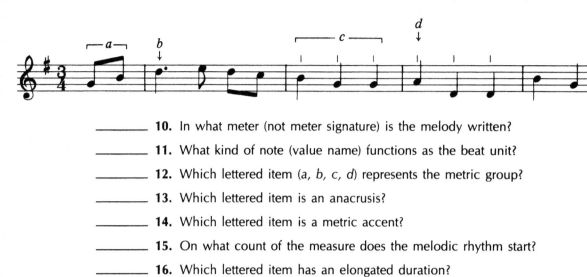

_____ **10.** In what meter (not meter signature) is the melody written?

_____ **11.** What kind of note (value name) functions as the beat unit?

_____ **12.** Which lettered item (a, b, c, d) represents the metric group?

_____ **13.** Which lettered item is an anacrusis?

_____ **14.** Which lettered item is a metric accent?

_____ **15.** On what count of the measure does the melodic rhythm start?

_____ **16.** Which lettered item has an elongated duration?

Answer questions 17 through 24 with reference to the following melodic rhythm:

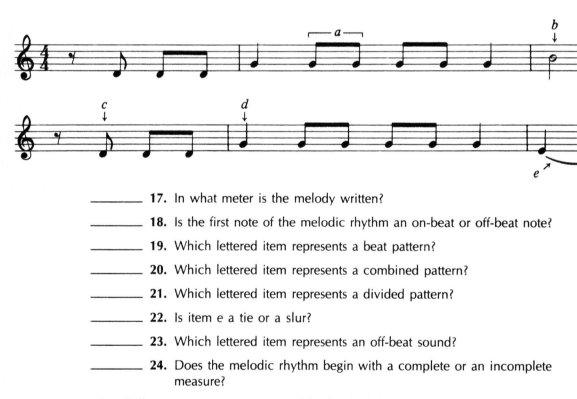

_____ **17.** In what meter is the melody written?

_____ **18.** Is the first note of the melodic rhythm an on-beat or off-beat note?

_____ **19.** Which lettered item represents a beat pattern?

_____ **20.** Which lettered item represents a combined pattern?

_____ **21.** Which lettered item represents a divided pattern?

_____ **22.** Is item e a tie or a slur?

_____ **23.** Which lettered item represents an off-beat sound?

_____ **24.** Does the melodic rhythm begin with a complete or an incomplete measure?

B. *Skills.* Part B is an assessment of the level of skills in reading and performing rhythm patterns that you developed during the study of this chapter. It should be administered to you by an instructor or student assistant, and you should achieve the minimum acceptable level or higher before continuing to Chapter Three.

1. Minimum acceptable level of performance:
    a. Read with syllables or counts the rhythm patterns in at least two exercises of your choice from each of these pages: 33, 34, 35, 36, 37.
    b. Read with syllables or counts the melodic rhythm of either *Simple Gifts* or *Pray God Bless*.
    c. Play in correct rhythm either *Hanukah* or *Five Hundred Miles*.

2. Higher level of performance:
    a. Read with syllables or counts the rhythm patterns in any exercises selected by the instructor from those in the *Study Activities*.
    b. Read with syllables or counts the melodic rhythm in *Simple Gifts* and *Pray God Bless*.
    c. Play in correct rhythm *Hanukah* and *Five Hundred Miles*.

Chapter 3

Melodic Intervals; Major Scales, Keys, and Melodies

INSTRUCTIONS

1. Read *the Objectives* to gain an initial awareness of the competencies you should have acquired by the end of this chapter. Keep these objectives in mind as you continue through the study and practice activities.

2. Complete all *Study Activities*. Make special efforts to understand major and minor seconds, major scale construction, and key signatures; try also to develop initial skills in reading and performing melodies in various major keys.

3. Complete all *Practice Activities* for the purposes of applying your knowledge and improving your skills.

4. As soon as your are ready, or when directed by your instructor, complete the *Assessment of Progress*. You should achieve the criterion levels indicated before continuing to Chapter Four.

OBJECTIVES

1. Recall and define the following terms and correctly use and interpret them in written or oral communication:

accidental	interval	key signature	steps
flat	harmonic	major key	half
natural	melodic	major scale	whole
sharp	quality	seconds	transposition
chromatic	size	major (M2)	
scale	tonal	minor (m2)	
tone	keynote (tonic)		

2. Identify and name whole steps and half steps in treble-clef notation and on the keyboard.

3. Given the name or staff notation of any natural, sharped, or flatted pitch, identify the piano key that would produce that pitch.

4. Identify and name from treble-clef notation any interval size (second, sixth, etc.) within an octave.

5. From a given note in treble clef, write a second note that would create either an ascending or a descending melodic major or minor second.

6. From a given tonic pitch, notate in treble clef a major scale showing each exact pitch—including flatted or sharped tones—in ascending order, and identify the piano keys that would produce that scale. Also, play selected major scales on a piano.

7. a. Given any sharp or flat key signature written in treble clef, name the keynote (tonic) and the major key and scale that use that signature.

   b. Write in correct left-to-right order in treble clef any key signature through four sharps and four flats.

8. Given a treble-clef melody, provide the following information derived from its key signature: a) name of its keynote, b) name of the key, and c) the scale number and *so-fa* syllable of any melodic note.

9. Play on a piano, and sing with scale numbers or *so-fa* syllables, at least two complete song melodies presented in this unit.

STUDY ACTIVITIES

We must now return to pitch organization and expand upon ideas introduced in Chapter One (you may want to review those concepts before continuing). Relationships among linear (melodic) pitches are the main focus of this chapter. We will begin with the simplest relationships—half and whole steps—then move logically through chromatic alteration of pitches via sharps and flats, interval sizes, major and minor seconds, major-scale construction, and key signatures. Finally, you will be able to read and perform song melodies written in selected major keys and built on the kinds of rhythm patterns you learned in Chapter Two.

HALF STEPS AND WHOLE STEPS

Knowledge of half steps and whole steps is often required in working with music. Applications of such knowledge are usually encountered as a need for quick recognition on the keyboard or staff of whether one tone is a half or whole step higher or lower than another and determination of the number of steps between one tone and the next. (Whole and half steps are also referred to as *whole tones* and *semitones*.)

Half Steps on the Keyboard

Half steps are the smallest pitch relationships (intervals) used in traditional Western music, and all of our keyboard and wind instruments are constructed and tuned so they can produce twelve half steps of equal size within each octave. A piano keyboard provides the most concrete representation of half steps and supplies a basis for a definition: A *half step* is the pitch relationship represented from any piano key (black or white) to the nearest key (black or white) above or below it. Our first illustration shows an octave divided into its twelve half steps, utilizing all seven white and five black keys. Other illustrations are extracted keyboard sections that show various possible ascending and descending half steps between two white keys and between a white and a black key. You should recall, in reference to the keyboard, that *ascending* and *descending* mean respectively moving right to a higher pitch or left to a lower pitch.

The twelve half steps within an octave:

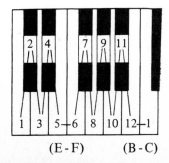

(E - F)   (B - C)

The three kinds of white-black key combinations that represent ascending and descending half steps:

a	*b*	*c*

ascending or descending from white to white, with no black between:

ascending from white to black, or descending from black to white:

ascending from black to white, or descending from white to black:

Whole Steps on the Keyboard

A *whole step* contains two half steps, which on the keyboard is from any black or white key to the next black or white key with one black or white key between.

The four kinds of black-white key combinations that represent ascending and descending whole steps on the keyboard:

a	*b*	*c*	*d*

ascending or descending from white to white, with one black between:

ascending or descending from black to black, with one white between:

ascending from white to black, or from black to white, with one white between:

descending from whit to black, or black t white, with one whit between:

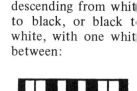

Next you will see a summary of steps between consecutive white keys and consecutive black keys within an octave. Observe that half steps occur at two locations between white keys that have no black key between them; these two points also represent a larger interval (one and one-half steps) separating groups of two and three black keys.

Step intervals between consecutive black and consecutive white keys within an octave:

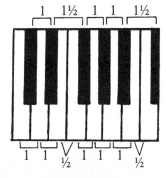

Chromatic Alteration of Pitch

You will recall that in Chapter One we used only seven different notes named with the first seven alphabet letters and represented by white piano keys. These seven tones (A B C D E F G) are *natural* pitches; naming or notating them ordinarily requires no special designation that they are natural, for their "natural" state is an automatic connotation. Music also uses pitches represented and produced by the five black keys, and these tones are derived from alterations to natural pitches.

Any pitch can be changed by either raising or lowering it one half step. Such changes are *chromatic alterations,* and notational signs (sharp, flat, natural) used to indicate them are *accidentals.*

1. A *sharp* raises by one half step the pitch of a natural tone and is notated with a sharp sign (♯) placed immediately before—to the left of—the note head.

2. A *flat* lowers by one half step the pitch of a natural tone and is notated with a flat sign (♭) placed immediately before the note head.

3. A *natural* sign (♮) preceding a note head sometimes must be used to cancel a previous sharp or flat and return the note to its natural state. A natural sign raises a flatted pitch or lowers a sharped pitch.

The following illustration shows how chromatically altered pitches are notated and named:

Notating and naming notes with accidentals:

notation: on a line   in a space

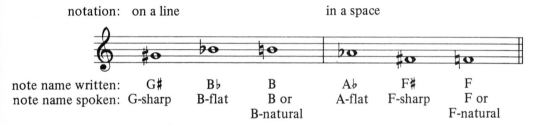

note name written:	G♯	B♭	B	A♭	F♯	F
note name spoken:	G-sharp	B-flat	B or	A-flat	F-sharp	F or
			B-natural			F-natural

Sharped pitches.   The five black keys within an octave are used to represent both sharped and flatted pitches. Each black key produces the sharped pitch of the natural tone immediately below it, or on its left. Both tones share the same letter name and staff location (for example, F and F♯ on the first space), but the sharped pitch sounds one half step higher. Notating, playing, or singing the seven natural pitches and five sharped pitches in consecutive order results in an *ascending chromatic scale* comprised of all twelve half steps. (You should always remember that each octave contains two natural half steps, E–F and B–C, where no black key exists between white keys.)

Ascending chromatic scale with sharps:

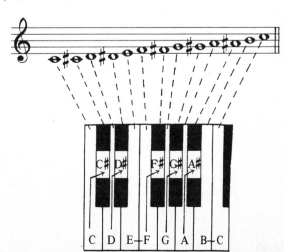

Flatted pitches.   Each of the five black keys can also represent and produce the flatted pitch of a natural tone immediately above it (on its right). Notating or performing the twelve half steps as consecutive natural and flatted pitches results in a *descending chromatic scale,* as illustrated:

Descending chromatic scale with flats:

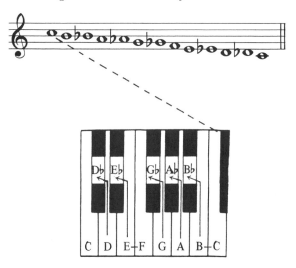

Each tone contained in the two natural half steps (E–F, B–C) also can be sharped or flatted. Since no black key is located between these white keys, sharped and flatted pitches are produced respectively by the white key above or below. Hence, E-sharp is the same pitch and piano key as F-natural, F-flat is the same as E-natural, B-sharp is the same as C-natural, and C-flat is the same as B-natural. You will eventually understand that whether a certain pitch is named and notated as a natural, sharp, or flat depends on the scale or key in which it functions. The next illustration shows all possible sharped and flatted pitches in notation and on the keyboard.

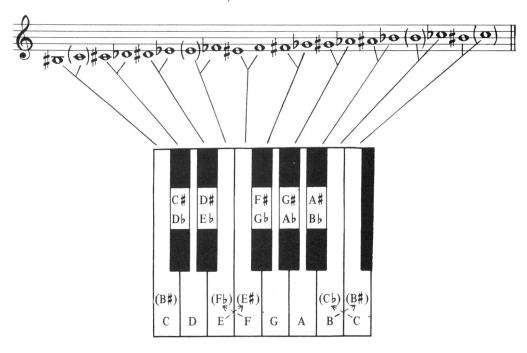

Identification of Notated Steps

Thus far your orientation to whole and half steps has been primarily in relation to the keyboard. Eventually, your greater concern will be to recognize quickly specific steps from notes on the staff. Transition from keyboard to staff can be made gradually by first checking notated pitches with their keyboard locations and then thinking directly from staff notation.

Accurate identification of notated half steps (or semitones) also requires recognition of two kinds: 1) a *chromatic half step* occurs between two pitches that have the same letter name and are notated on the same staff line or space (such as F–F-sharp or B–B-flat); 2) a *diatonic half step* involves two pitches of consecutive letter names notated on an adjacent line and space (B–C or F-sharp–G). The next illustrations include a reference keyboard and a variety of notated half steps (H) and whole steps (W).

Reference keyboard:

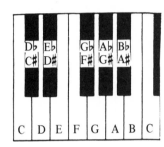

1. Chromatic half steps:

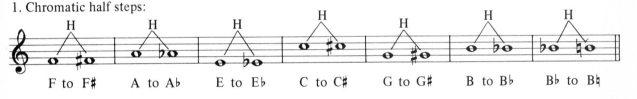

F to F♯   A to A♭   E to E♭   C to C♯   G to G♯   B to B♭   B♭ to B♮

2. Diatonic half steps:

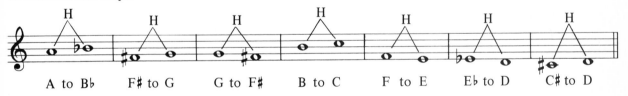

A to B♭   F♯ to G   G to F♯   B to C   F to E   E♭ to D   C♯ to D

3. Whole steps:

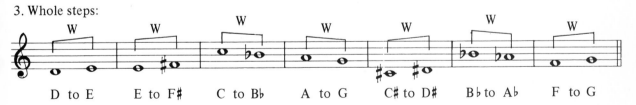

D to E   E to F♯   C to B♭   A to G   C♯ to D♯   B♭ to A♭   F to G

INTERVAL SIZE

An *interval* is the pitch relationship between two tones and is identified and named according to both its *size* and its *quality*. *Interval size* is always expressed in terms of a number, such as third (3) or fifth (5), and interval quality is designated by words such as *major* (M), *minor* (m), or *perfect* (P). Thus, complete identification and naming includes both factors: major third (M3), perfect fifth (P5), and so forth. Whole steps and half steps are pitch relationships that are useful units of measurement in defining intervals, but the terms themselves are not part of more definitive interval nomenclature for exact size and quality.

Representative calculations of interval sizes:

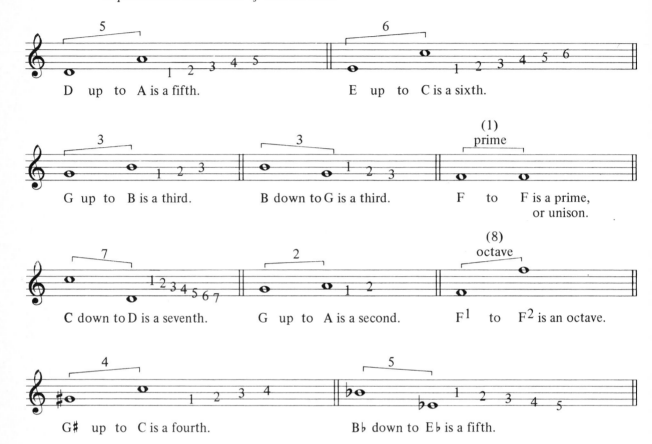

D up to A is a fifth.

E up to C is a sixth.

G up to B is a third.

B down to G is a third.

F to F is a prime, or unison.

C down to D is a seventh.

G up to A is a second.

F^1 to F^2 is an octave.

G# up to C is a fourth.

B♭ down to E♭ is a fifth.

Intervals of eight sizes are contained within an octave. These range from a *prime* or *unison*—the interval from one note to another of the same pitch—to an *octave* (eighth). Intervals between prime and octave include *seconds, thirds, fourths, fifths, sixths,* and *sevenths.* To determine and name the size of a notated interval:

1. Assign number 1 to the staff line or space upon which the first note is located.
2. Count all consecutive staff degrees (lines and spaces) up or down to, and including, the second note of the interval.
3. Interval size, then, is the number that results from counting every line and space separating, and inclusive of, the two interval tones.
4. Whether interval tones are natural, sharp, or flat has no bearing on the numerical size of an interval.
5. Interval size also can be determined by inclusively counting pitch names separating the two tones; for example, A ascending to D is a fourth (A-B-C-D).

INTERVAL QUALITY

Intervals of the same numerical size can have different qualities of sound due to differences in exact pitch between tones. For instance, some thirds contain a larger pitch interval than other thirds, creating a difference in their qualities of sound. You can imagine on the keyboard and staff that a third from C to E has a greater difference in pitch than a third from C to E-flat, and that the two thirds would sound different. A complete presentation of intervals would reveal five qualities named *major, minor, perfect, augmented,* and *diminished.* Instead of making a comprehensive study of all intervals at one time, you will be introduced to intervals of specific size and quality as you need them to develop your other musical concepts and skills. We start in this chapter with minor and major seconds, for they are intervals of which scales are made. Chapter Four includes major thirds, minor thirds, perfect fifths and octaves, and minor sevenths as they become involved in working with basic chords. Those persons who desire still more knowledge of intervals can find additional study material in optional Minichapter C.

Minor Seconds

A *minor second* (m2) is a second that contains a difference in pitch of only one half step (or semitone). Its size requirement is that the two tones must encompass a second—notes of consecutive letter names located on adjacent lines and spaces. Minor quality results from the two pitches being only a half step apart—one tone is either a half step higher or lower than the other. Study the illustrations of notated minor seconds and visualize them on a keyboard. Make sure that you understand why each interval is a minor second, and observe whether pitch ascends or descends from one note to the next.

Identification of representative minor seconds:

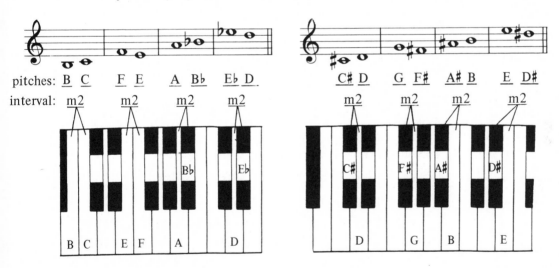

Major Seconds

A *major second* (M2) is a second that contains one whole step, or two half steps, between its two tones. Its size must be a second, and its quality must be the sound of a whole step. Major seconds are larger intervals of pitch than minor seconds. Obviously, major and minor seconds sound different. Go to a piano and play some examples from those illustrated in notation.

Identification of representative major seconds:

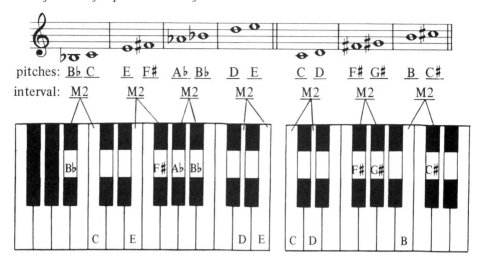

A word of caution regarding accuracy in identifying major and min or seconds is in order at this point: (1) all major seconds are whole steps, but not all whole steps are major seconds; (2) all minor seconds are half steps, but not all half steps are minor seconds; (3) some seconds are neither major nor minor.

Intervals that are neither major nor minor seconds:

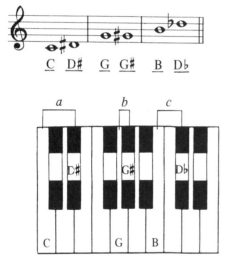

You can draw these conclusions from a study of the illustrated intervals:

1. Interval *a* (C–D-sharp) is a second, all right, but it contains one and one-half steps and is larger than a major second (its actual quality, which will be given no further consideration here, is *augmented*).
2. Interval *b* (G–G-sharp) is a half step, but it is not a second. This interval is a chromatic half step (or *augmented prime*) instead of a minor second.
3. Interval *c* (B–D-flat) is a whole step, but it is some kind of third instead of a major second.

MAJOR SCALE CONSTRUCTION

Before continuing, you should recall from Chapter One the following ideas about scales:

1. A *scale* is an ordered series of pitches starting with, or built from, a given pitch called the *tonic* and extending through an octave. The pitch name (C, F, G, etc.) of the tonic is the name of the scale.

2. A *diatonic scale* is a seven-note scale comprised of both whole steps and half steps.

3. The *C major scale* is a diatonic scale comprised of seven natural tones within an octave from C to C. These pitches are represented by white piano keys, occupy every consecutive line and space, and are named in ascending order: C D E F G A B C.

4. Tones of the C major scale can be numbered 1 through 8 and assigned the *so-fa* syllables *do-re-mi-fa-so-la-ti-do*.

5. Melodies in the *key* of C major have the pitch of C as their tonic, or keynote, and use notes from the C major scale to form their melodic patterns.

The C Major Scale As a Model

We now are ready to consider what makes a major scale and what gives it its distinctive sound. Our somewhat familiar C major scale can serve as a model from which we can generalize a structure for all major scales and transpose this organization to build other major scales from other tonics.

Scale of C Major:

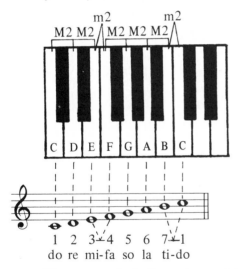

We can conclude from the model that a major scale is constructed from a tonic pitch (*do* or 1) as a step order of *seconds* in which intervals between scale tones 3 and 4 (*mi* and *fa*) and 7 and 1, or 8, (*ti* and *do*) are *minor seconds*, and intervals between all other consecutive scale tones are *major seconds*. No other set of intervals will produce both the sound and correct notation of a major scale. (Half steps and whole steps are sometimes used in place of minor and major seconds to explain major-scale structure, but, as you learned in the preceding section, half steps are not synonymous with minor seconds, and whole steps are not always the same as major seconds.)

Constructing Other Major Scales

Transposition is a term that means to write or perform music at another pitch level (higher or lower) so that it will sound like the original. An entire melody, for instance, can be sung or played at higher or lower pitch levels and still be recognizable as the same melody, due to the fact that from note to note it follows the same intervals, even though different pitches are required to form them.

The sequence of intervals that produces a major scale also can be transposed to a higher or lower pitch level by building scales from other tonic pitches. We can construct a major scale from any natural, sharped, or flatted pitch—from any white or black key on the keyboard—if we keep the same order of major and minor seconds found in the C major scale. This interval order consists of minor seconds between 3–4 and 7–1 (8) and major seconds between 1–2, 2–3, 4–5, 5–6, and 6–7. Constructing and notating major scales might be approached as a problem-solving exercise. Study the model for general procedures along with three examples that are worked out.

Procedural model for building major scales:

Problem: Given a tonic pitch (name of the scale), build and notate an ascending major scale.

Solution:

PHASE ONE

1. Notate the tonic note according to its exact pitch (G, F, B♭, etc.).
2. Place a note on every consecutive line and space ascending from the tonic to, and including, its octave. In this phase, notate all tones between the low and high tonics as natural pitches.
3. Number each scale pitch and indicate where minor seconds must be created:
   1 2 3-4 5 6 7-1.

PHASE TWO

1. Visualize on the keyboard all pitches notated in phase one.
2. Consider in ascending order each interval that exists between consecutive tones: 1 to 2, 2 to 3, 3 to 4, 4 to 5, 5 to 6, 6 to 7, 7 to 1.
3. Accept each natural pitch from phase one into the scale only if it forms the correct interval. Otherwise, determine whether the pitch needs to be raised (sharped) or lowered (flatted) to create the required M2 or m2. Correctly notate each chromatically altered (sharped or flatted) pitch.
4. Play and/or sing the scale to determine whether notes selected produce a major-scale sound.

Scale of G Major:

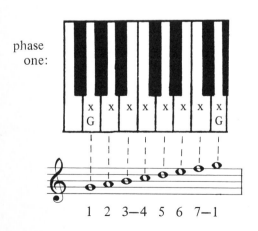

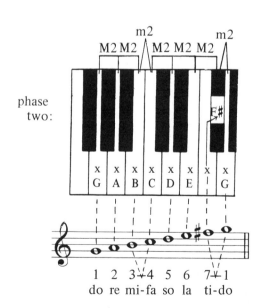

Scale of F Major:

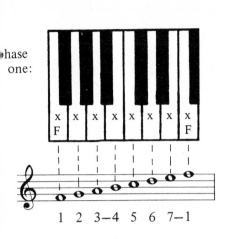

Scale of B-flat Major:

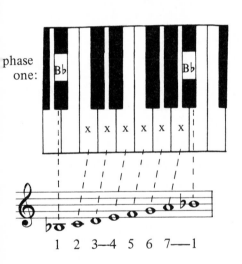

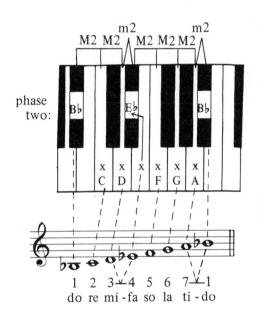

Playing the Scales of G, D, and F

You learned to play the ascending and descending C major scale in Chapter One. Although you need not perform all major scales, playing a few might broaden your understanding of scale-key structure and your skill in performing melodies. The scales of G, D, and F are notated here with appropriate right-hand fingerings. G major and D major scales are fingered like C major, but F major has a different fingering.

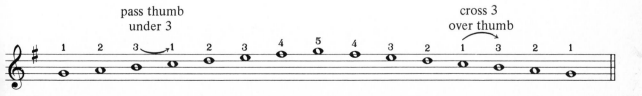

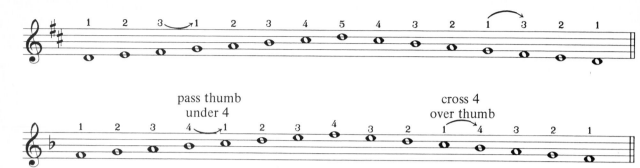

KEY SIGNATURES AND KEYS

All major scales, except C major, have some pitches that are either sharps or flats, but no major scale uses both sharps and flats. A maximum of fifteen major scales can be constructed from different tonics. This total includes C major plus seven sharp and seven flat keys in which one through all seven scale tones are either sharped or flatted. We will explore more completely scales through four sharps and four flats, for a large majority of songs are written in keys based on one of these scales.

A *key signature* is comprised of sharp or flat signs that appear immediately following the clef sign at the beginning of a piece of music. These signs are located on staff lines and spaces that identify sharped or flatted pitches in the scale upon which the piece is based and, therefore, in the music itself. Scales, too, can be written with signatures instead of with accidental signs placed before notes. Our next examples of scales have key signatures, but flat or sharp signs are also placed in parentheses before note heads to provide clear indications that signs in the signatures came from them.

Key signatures provide us with two essential kinds of information. First, we can determine which and how many pitches are sharped or flatted; all other scale tones are natural. Thus, if three tones are flatted, we know these are B-flat, E-flat, and A-flat, and we know the other four tones are natural. Second, we can identify the tonic note, or keynote, and name of the key (these are synonymous) from the signature. Classification into sharp keys and flat keys is necessary for further discussion of key signatures.

Sharp Keys

You should learn three kinds of operations with sharp key signatures: 1) names of the sharped pitches, 2) placement of sharp signs in the signature, and 3) location and identification of the tonic note from the signature. Study each of these four sharp scales notated with key signatures and apply the operational ideas that follow.

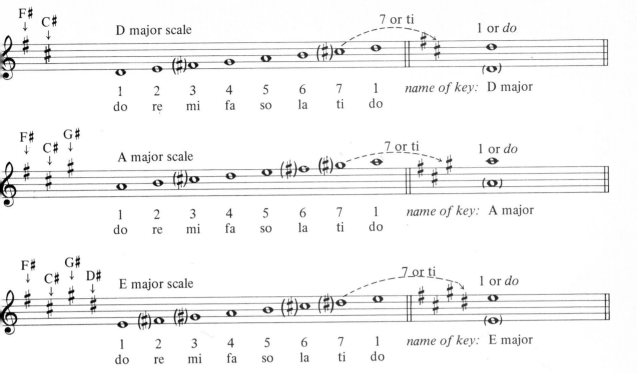

Names of the sharped pitches.   Each sharp sign in a key signature is placed on a staff line or space to indicate that the note of that name *in any octave* is sharped. For example, a sharp sign on the fifth (top) treble-clef line signifies that in this scale or piece of music any note on the top line or bottom (first) space is F-sharp; F-natural is not involved. You must remember to play or sing F-sharp, instead of F, whenever this note is encountered in the music, for the sharp sign is not ordinarily written again before the note in a melody or chord.

Placement of sharps in key signatures.   Sharp signs in a key signature are always written in the same left-to-right order and on the same lines and spaces, and this order is unrelated to the ascending sequence in which sharped pitches occur in scales. Beginning with a signature that has one sharp on the top line, each successive sharp key uses the same sharps as the previous key plus one new sharp. Left-to-right order is down four staff degrees, then up five degrees, down four, and up five. Here is a summary of keys with one through four sharps (F♯-C♯-G♯-D♯):

    1 sharp: fifth-line F♯
    2 sharps: fifth-line F♯ + third-space C♯
    3 sharps: fifth-line F♯ & third-space C♯ + above-staff G♯
    4 sharps: fifth-line F♯ & third-space C♯ & above-staff G♯ + fourth-line D♯

Identifying the tonic and naming the key.   You will observe in sharp signatures that the sharp farthest to the right (the new, or last, sharp) is always the seventh tone (or *ti*) of the scale; hence, ascend from the last sharp one staff degree to locate the tonic note (1 or *do*), whose name is also the name of the key. Memorize scale and key names for each signature of one through four sharps and remember the rule for locating the tonic (keynote) from any sharp key signature.

Flat Keys

identification of tonic and key

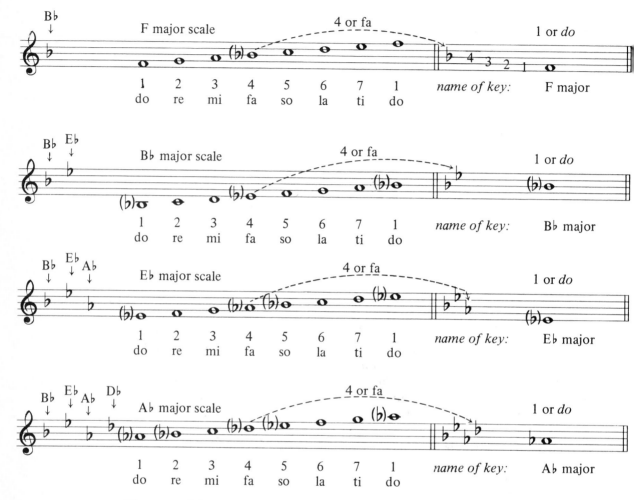

Placement of flats in key signatures. The loop of a flat sign is placed on the line or space representing each flatted pitch in a key signature. Left-to-right order in signatures of one through four flats is up four staff degrees, down five, up four, and down five (Bb-Eb-Ab-Db).

1 flat: third-line Bb
2 flats: third-line Bb + fourth-space Eb
3 flats: third-line Bb & fourth-space Eb + second-space Ab
4 flats: third-line Bb & fourth-space Eb & second-space Ab + fourth-line Db

Identifying the tonic and naming the key. The last flat to the right (the new flat) in flat key signatures is always scale tone number 4 (or *fa*). Start with the line or space occupied by the last flat sign and descend scalewise (4-3-2-1 or *fa-mi-re-do*) on the staff to the keynote (1 or *do*). Give particular attention to the fact that in all flat keys, except one flat, the keynote is one of those flatted in the signature. Flat keys carry names such as F major, B-flat major, and E-flat major.

All possible key signatures, along with staff notation of their keynotes in both a high and low octave, are shown next. C major, of course, has a signature of no sharps or flats. You should memorize the first four or five sharp and flat signatures and continue to practice applying rules for naming a key from the last sharp or flat sign in its signature.

SECONDS AS TONAL INTERVALS

Any interval can be used in music as either a melodic or harmonic interval. *Melodic intervals* are those that occur between one note and the next in linear pitch organization, such as in a melody. *Harmonic intervals* are vertical organizations of pitch in which tones are sounded together and written one above another on a staff, such as in a chord. Interval study in this unit is confined to major and minor seconds sounded and written in melodic form with one note following another in sound and on the staff. Chapter Four introduces harmonic intervals.

Intervals also can be studied and practiced in two different contexts. Thus far, you have worked with *isolated intervals,* which are independent intervals whose two tones are notated as natural, sharped, or flatted pitches without any relation to a key or to other intervals. Intervals, either melodic or harmonic, sounded in the context of a key and written with a key signature can be called *tonal intervals,* for they occur within a tonality and have relationships with other intervals in that tonality. Intervals within a traditional song melody are *tonal melodic intervals.*

You must now learn to accurately identify and name major and minor seconds among tones notated with a key signature. This involves applying sharps or flats in the signature to correctly naming interval tones as natural, sharped, or flatted pitches so that interval quality (major or minor) can be identified. Think through the next notated examples, using the reference keyboard if you need it.

reference
keyboard:

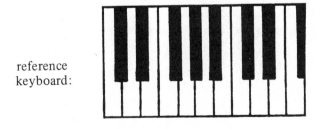

Key: <u>F</u>

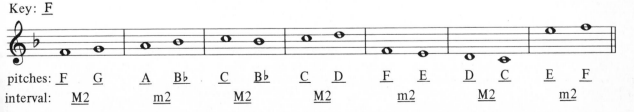

pitches: <u>F</u> <u>G</u>   <u>A</u> <u>Bb</u>   <u>C</u> <u>Bb</u>   <u>C</u> <u>D</u>   <u>F</u> <u>E</u>   <u>D</u> <u>C</u>   <u>E</u> <u>F</u>

interval: <u>M2</u>   <u>m2</u>   <u>M2</u>   <u>M2</u>   <u>m2</u>   <u>M2</u>   <u>m2</u>

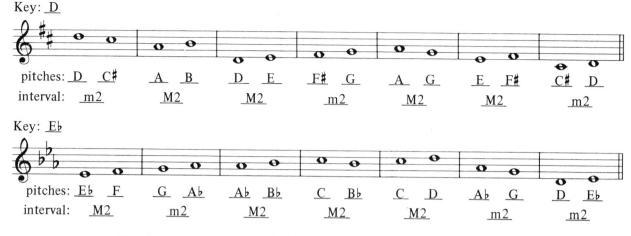

Key: D

pitches: D C# A B D E F# G A G E F# C# D

interval: m2 M2 M2 m2 M2 M2 m2

Key: Eb

pitches: Eb F G Ab Ab Bb C Bb C D Ab G D Eb

interval: M2 m2 M2 M2 M2 m2 m2

Continue your experience in identifying tonal major and minor seconds by observing those found in the following melodic phrases. Can you identify by size only (prime, third, fourth, fifth) some of the other intervals in these phrases?

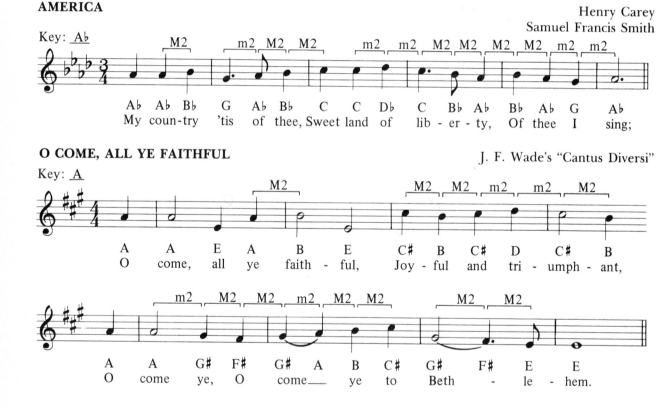

AMERICA

Henry Carey
Samuel Francis Smith

Key: Ab

O COME, ALL YE FAITHFUL

J. F. Wade's "Cantus Diversi"

Key: A

READING AND PERFORMING IN OTHER MAJOR KEYS

Transposition of a Familiar Melody

One meaningful way to begin reading and performing music in major keys other than C major is to play and sing a familiar melody in more than one key. This involves the process of *transposition*, which was explained earlier as performing and/or notating a scale, melody, or piece of music at a higher or lower pitch level—literally, in another key based on another scale. You can easily transpose *Merrily We Roll Along* (learned in C major in Chapter One) to other keys. The melody and basic five-note hand position appear here in the original key of C major and also in D major and F major. Play and sing the melody in all three keys, utilizing these procedures and observations:

1. To play:

    a. Refer to the five-note hand position illustrated for each key in conjunction with the notes each finger will play.

    b. use the same fingering (3-2-1-2-3-3-3, etc.) to play note-to-note melodic patterns in each key.

    c. Observe that the melody sounds exactly the same in each key, although you must play different pitches in each key to produce that sound.

2. To sing:

    a. Sing the familiar melody in each key:

        1) with pitch names in order to have complete awareness of all notated pitches and their relation to the key signature, and

        2) with scale numbers and/or *so-fa* syllables to fully realize location of the tonic in each key and the sameness in each key of relative numbers and syllables, which are transposed along with their corresponding melodic patterns.

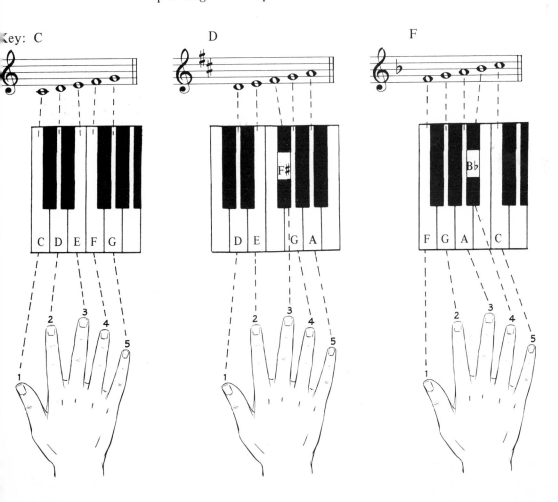

MERRILY WE ROLL ALONG (Keys of C, D, and F)

Reading and Performing a New Melody

You now have enough knowledge and skill to learn a new song through your own efforts, which will include reading rhythm and pitch patterns as you practice playing and singing the melody. *Joyful, Joyful, We Adore Thee* is a hymn that uses a well-known theme from Beethoven's *Symphony No. 9* and words by Henry van Dyke. Here are some suggestions for learning the piece:

1. Interpret the meter signature, scan through the melodic rhythm comprised of patterns learned in Chapter Two, establish a tempo beat, and read the entire melodic rhythm with rhythm syllables (substitute counts if you prefer them).

2. Interpret the key signature, identify the keynote (G), and name the first melodic note (B) along with its scale and key position (3 or *mi*). Scan through the melody and notice a) its four phrases and cadences and b) its pitch patterns, which are based on the first five notes of the G major scale plus a low D at the cadence of phrase three.

3. Study the illustrated five-note (G up to D) hand position in which your thumb, in addition to playing G, can be stretched (left) to play low D.

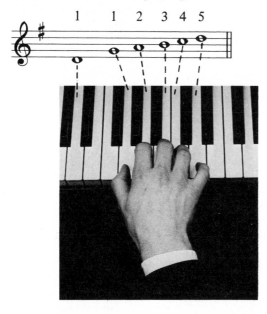

4. Play the melody with correct fingerings and continue to practice until you can play it throughout in accurate rhythm.

5. Sing the melody with *so-fa* syllables (substitute scale numbers if you prefer them), and also sing the song with its text.

JOYFUL, JOYFUL, WE ADORE THEE
Ludwig van Beethoven
Words by Henry van Dyke

1. Ta ta ta ta, *etc.*   ta - i - ti ta - a.
2. Mi mi fa so, *etc.*   mi re re.
3. Joy - ful, joy - ful, we a - dore thee, God of glo - ry, Lord of love.

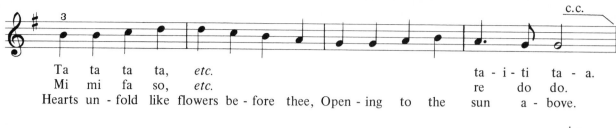

Ta ta ta ta, *etc.*   ta - i - ti ta - a.
Mi mi fa so, *etc.*   re do do.
Hearts un - fold like flowers be - fore thee, Open - ing to the sun a - bove.

Ta ta ta ta ta ti - ti ta ta ta ti - ti ta ta ta ta ta - a.
Re re mi do re mi fa mi do re mi fa mi re do re so.
Melt the clouds of sin and— sad - ness, drive the— dark of doubt a - way.

Ta ta ta ta, *etc.*   ta - i - ti ta - a.
Mi mi fa so, *etc.*   re do do.
Giv - er of im - mor - tal glad - ness, Fill us with the light of day.

Chromatic Tones in Melodies

We have stressed the point that traditional music is based on some kind of scale. Most song melodies in a major key use only notes from that major scale. Some, however, include one or two pitches from outside their key. These nonkey tones, called *chromatic tones,* occur as chromatic alterations to scale tones and are notated with an appropriate *accidental* (sharp, flat, or natural sign) in conjunction with the note whose pitch is being raised or lowered a half step in the melody.

A chromatic tone can add melodic interest in the form of either a *neighboring tone* above or below a scale tone or as a *passing tone* between two scale tones. These kinds of chromatic tones alter neither the fact nor sense of a melody's basic key and tonality. Study *I Heard the Bells on Christmas Day* from these standpoints:

1. The melody is in E-flat major; E-flat is its tonic throughout.
2. The first chromatic tone, F-sharp, is a raising of the second scale tone (F to F-sharp; 2 to +2) and occurs as a *chromatic neighboring tone* below scale note G that precedes and follows it.
3. The second chromatic tone, A-natural, is a raising of the fourth scale tone (A-flat, in the key signature, to A-natural; 4 to +4) and occurs as a *chromatic passing tone* between scale notes A-flat and B-flat.
4. Try playing the melody to confirm points 1, 2, and 3.

I HEARD THE BELLS ON CHRISTMAS DAY

J. Baptiste Calkin
Henry W. Longfellow

Key: E♭

chromatic tones

1 3 +2 3 3 4 3 4 +4 5 1 7 6 6 5 5
I heard the bells on Christ - mas day Their old fa - mil - iar car - ols play,

And   wild   and sweet the   words re - peat Of   peace on earth, good   will   to men;

PRACTICE ACTIVITIES

Page references to relevant *Study Activities* are given in parentheses.

Use, when needed, this reference keyboard in conjunction with making your responses to any of the practice activities.

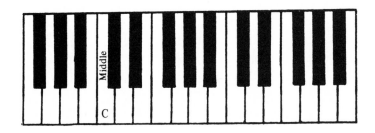

Notating

1. Follow illustrations in the model and write accidentals, as designated, before notes in items *a, b,* and *c.* (53)

Model:

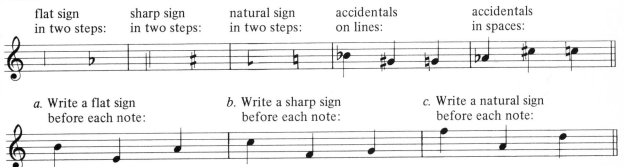

2. Following the open note head given in each item, write a closed note head that would complete an ascending or descending major second (M2) or minor second (m2) as marked—see examples. (57–58)

Examples:

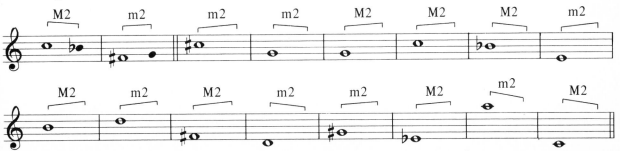

3. Refer to the model and write designated key signatures on the blank staff. Also, write names of sharped or flatted pitches below the signature. (62–65)

Model:

Key: G D   A   E   F   Bb   Eb   Ab

F#   F# C#   F# C# G#   F# C# G# D#   Bb   Bb Eb   Bb Eb Ab   Bb Eb Ab Db

Key: Bb   A   F   Eb   E   G   Ab   D

4. Follow the model given for the scale of F major and complete the scales of D, E-flat, and A to include these components: a) scale tones notated on the staff, written with pitch names on the keyboard, and connected with broken lines between staff and keyboard; b) minor seconds marked at appropriate places between scale tones; c) scale tones labeled with numbers and *so-fa* syllables; and d) the correct key signature written following the scale. (60)

Model:

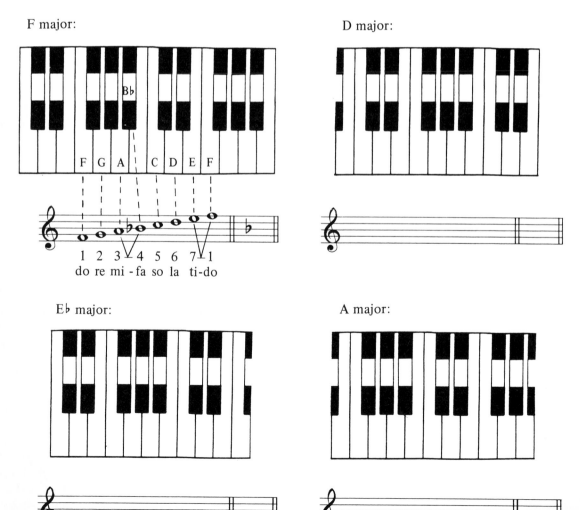

F major:

Bb

F G A C D E F

1 2 3 4 5 6 7 1
do re mi - fa so la ti-do

D major:

Eb major:

A major:

Identifying

5. Indicate the size of each notated melodic interval as illustrated for the first interval. (56)

interval size:

6. Intervals within items *a* and *b* are notated as tonal seconds with key signatures. Follow the pattern illustrated for the first interval and name each interval (M2 or m2) and its two notes. (65–66)

(a)   *(b)*

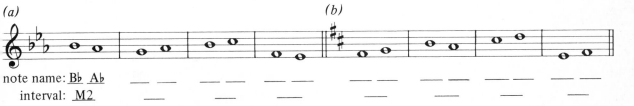

note name: <u>Bb</u> <u>Ab</u> __ __   __ __   __ __   __ __   __ __   __ __

interval: <u>M2</u>   __   __   __   __   __   __

7. Items *a*, *b*, and *c* are phrases from song melodies. Make the following responses in each item:
a. Name the key in the blank above the key signature.
b. In the blank below each note, write either its scale number, *so-fa* syllable, or pitch name as specified for each melody.
c. Above each bracketed interval, write (as specified) either a number to indicate its size or its interval name (M2, m2).
d. Above the final note of each phrase, label the cadence as complete (c.c.) or incomplete (i.c.).

(a)

Key: ____   interval:

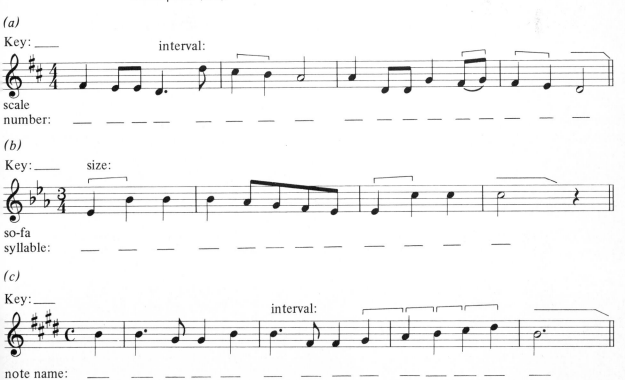

scale number: __ __   __ __   __ __   __ __

(b)

Key: ____   size:

so-fa syllable: __   __   __   __   __

(c)

Key: ____   interval:

note name: __   __   __   __   __

Creating

8. You are given a blank treble staff with a key signature, meter signature, starting note, and bar lines for four complete measures. Your activity is to transcribe the rhythm syllables and *so-fa* syllables into notes of corresponding duration and pitch on the staff; the result will be a short melody you could play and/or sing. (Underlined syllables indicate pitches in the octave below *do*.)

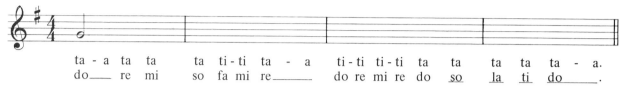

ta - a ta ta   ta ti - ti ta - a   ti - ti ti - ti ta ta   ta ta ta - a.
do____ re mi   so fa mi re_____   do re mi re do <u>so</u>   <u>la</u> <u>ti</u> <u>do</u>___.

9. You are given a blank treble staff with the same key and meter signatures as those in activity 8. Create and notate an original four-measure melody.

Reading

10. The following exercises consist of pitch patterns notated in various keys. Practice reading each exercise in these ways:
    a. Observe the key signature and identify the staff location and name of the keynote (tonic).
    b. Name each note, applying flats or sharps from the signature.
    c. Play the exercise, giving equal duration to each tone.
    d. Sing the exercise with scale numbers and/or *so-fa* syllables.

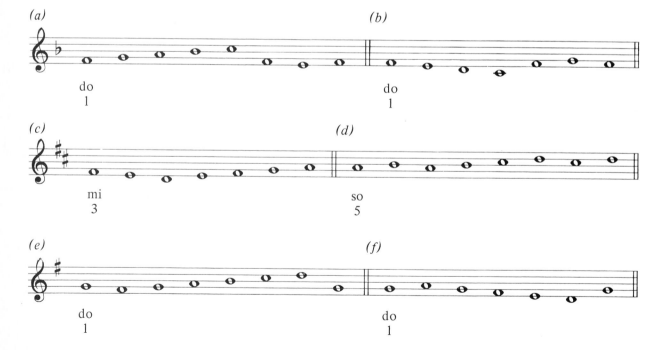

(a)

do
1

(b)

do
1

(c)

mi
3

(d)

so
5

(e)

do
1

(f)

do
1

11. Read and perform *Yankee Doodle* in the following steps:
    a. Read the melodic rhythm with counts or rhythm syllables.
    b. Identify the keynote and sharped pitch in the melody.
    c. Play the melody in correct rhythm and with the fingering given above each note.
    d. Sing the melody with scale numbers and/or *so-fa* syllables.

YANKEE DOODLE   Revolutionary War Song

Performing

12. Continue to practice the following material presented in the *Study Activities:*
    a. Play:
       1) G, D, and F scales
       2) *Merrily We Roll Along* in the keys of D and F
       3) *Joyful, Joyful, We Adore Thee* in the key of G
       4) *Yankee Doodle* in the key of G
    b. Sing with scale numbers and/or *so-fa* syllables:
       1) *Merrily We Roll Along* in D and F
       2) *Joyful, Joyful, We Adore Thee* in G

AFTER YOU HAVE COMPLETED ALL **PRACTICE ACTIVITIES** AND RE-VIEWED **THE OBJECTIVES,** CONTINUE WITH THE **ASSESSMENT OF PROGRESS.**

ASSESSMENT OF PROGRESS

A. *Applied knowledge.* Part A can be completed as a self-administered test without reference to any other material. Write your responses in the blanks beside each item number and, when you have finished all of Part A, check your answers with those in *Keys to Chapter Assessments,* page 249. Correct all of your errors and restudy relevant material in the *Study Activities* and *Practice Activities* before continuing to Chapter Four.

1. Write in the blank above each note the number of the piano key that would produce that notated pitch.

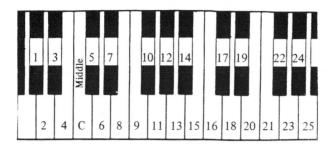

a._____ b._____ c._____ d._____ e._____ f._____ g._____ h._____ i._____ j._____

2. Each set (a, b) of notated pitches is written with a key signature. Write the exact pitch name of each note in the blank below it.

3. Identify each interval as either a major second or minor second and write its abbreviation (M2 or m2) in the blank below. Use, if needed, the reference keyboard that has been provided.

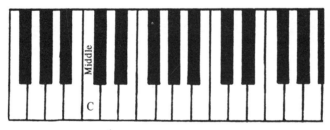

a._____ b._____ c._____ d._____ e._____ f._____ g._____ h._____

4. You are given the staff placement of notes for two (a, b) diatonic scales. Transform each into a major scale by writing sharp or flat signs before notes that need a chromatic alteration, and write the resulting names of all scale tones in blanks below the staff.

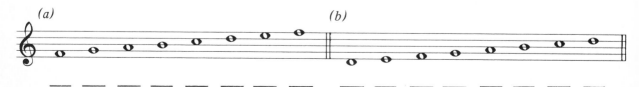

5. Identify the keynote (tonic) from each given key signature and write its name, which is the name of the key, in the blank above.

Key: *a.*_____ *b.*___ *c.*_____ *d.*___ *e.*_____ *f.*_____

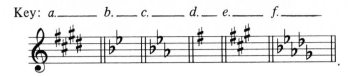

Respond to items 6 through 18 with reference to *Music Alone Shall Live.*

MUSIC ALONE SHALL LIVE

German Round

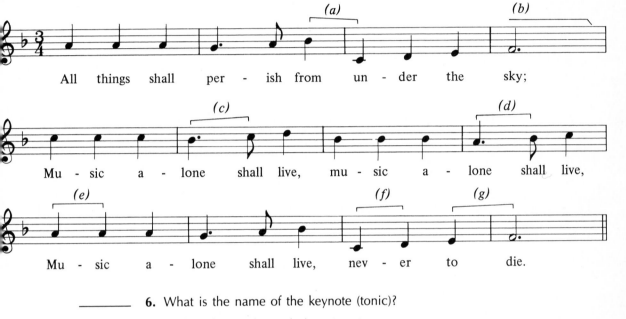

All things shall per - ish from un - der the sky;

Mu - sic a - lone shall live, mu - sic a - lone shall live,

Mu - sic a - lone shall live, nev - er to die.

_____ **6.** What is the name of the keynote (tonic)?

_____ **7.** In what key is the melody written?

_____ **8.** What are the scale numbers of the first and last notes?

_____ **9.** What is the (numerical) size of interval (a)?

_____ **10.** What kind of second (M2 or m2) occurs in interval (c)?

_____ **11.** What kind of second occurs in interval (d)?

_____ **12.** What kind of second occurs in interval (f)?

_____ **13.** What kind of second occurs in interval (g)?

_____ **14.** What is the name of interval (e)?

_____ **15.** What kind of cadence (complete, incomplete) occurs at (b)?

16. Write under each word the *so-fa* syllable for each corresponding note on the first staff.

  "All things shall per - ish from un - der the sky;"

  __ ___ __ __ ___ ___ __ __

17. Write under each word the scale number of each corresponding note on the second staff.

  "Mu - sic a -lone shall live, mu - sic a -lone shall live,"

  __ __ - __ - __ __ __ __ - - __ __ __

18. Write under each word the name of each corresponding note on the third staff.

"Mu - sic a -lone shall live, ne - ver to die."

—   — -   —— —— — —   ——— ——

B. *Skills.* Part B is an assessment of the level of skills you have developed in reading and performing major scales and melodies during the study of this chapter. It should be administered to you by an instructor or student assistant, and you should achieve the minimum acceptable level, or a higher level, before continuing to Chapter Four.

1. Minimum acceptable level of performance
   a. Play, with no more than one error in each endeavor, the following:
      1) G major and F major scales, ascending and descending
      2) *Merrily We Roll Along* in either D or F
      3) *Joyful, Joyful We Adore Thee* in G
   b. Sing the following with either scale numbers or *so-fa* syllables:
      1) Two melodic patterns of your choice selected from item 10 in the *Practice Activities*
      2) *Merrily We Roll Along* in D and F

2. Higher level of performance
   a. Play, with no more than one error in each endeavor, all of the following:
      1) D major, F major, and G major scales, ascending and descending
      2) *Merrily We Roll Along* in D and F
      3) *Joyful, Joyful, We Adore Thee* in G
      4) *Yankee Doodle* in G
   b. Sing all of the following with either scale numbers or *so-fa* syllables:
      1) all melodic patterns in item 10 of the *Practice Activities*
      2) *Merrily We Roll Along* in D and F
      3) *Joyful, Joyful, We Adore Thee* in G

Chapter 4

Harmonic Intervals, Chords, and Chording

INSTRUCTIONS

1. Read the *Objectives* to gain an initial acquaintance with competencies you should have acquired by the end of this chapter. Keep these objectives in mind as you continue through the study and practice activities.

2. Complete all *Study Activities*. Make special efforts to understand major and minor thirds, major triads, and dominant-seventh chords. Try also to develop an ability to play simple chord progressions and chordal accompaniments presented in this unit.

3. Complete all *Practice Activities,* striving for accuracy, to gain experience in applying your knowledge and improving your skills.

4. As soon as you are ready, or when directed by your instructor, complete the *Assessment of Progress*. You should achieve the criterion levels indicated before continuing to Chapter Five.

5. Refer to optional Minichapter C if you desire knowledge of intervals beyond those presented in Chapters Three and Four.

OBJECTIVES

1. Recall and define the following terms and correctly use and interpret them in written or oral communication:

chords	chord structure	harmonic intervals
dominant seventh (V^7)	fifth	major third (M3)
major triad	root	minor third (m3)
seventh chord	seventh	minor seventh (m7)
tonic (I)	third	perfect fifth (P5)
chord progression		perfect octave (P8)
		inversion

2. Identify, name, and notate in treble clef the following harmonic intervals: major third (M3), minor third (m3), perfect fifth (P5), minor seventh (m7), and perfect octave (P8).

3. Identify, name, notate, and play major triads.

4. Identify, name, and notate (root position) tonic (I) and dominant-seventh (V^7) chords in selected major keys.

5. Play from memory, and from rules of finger-pitch movement, the I-V⁷-I chord progression in selected major keys.

6. Read and play selected song melodies (right hand) with chordal accompaniments (left hand) comprised of the I and V⁷ chords.

7. Identify chord skips in melody, and read and sing melodic patterns comprised of chord skips and scale steps.

8. Given choices of notated harmonic intervals or melodic patterns, identify the one heard (played on a piano). This skill involves aural-visual discrimination.

STUDY ACTIVITIES

Chapter Four introduces you to harmonic (vertical) organization of pitch and progresses toward a goal that will enable you to play simple chordal accompaniments with melodies. En route to that goal you will study harmonic intervals contained in primary chords, as well as actual chord structure and identification, and you will develop skill in playing chord patterns comprised of two primary chords—tonic and dominant-seventh—that will provide accompaniments to selected melodies. A third chord (subdominant) is added to these patterns in Chapter Seven, and additional intervals are presented in optional Minichapter C for those who want more knowledge of them.

HARMONIC INTERVALS

Harmonic intervals are pitch relationships between two tones sounded together and notated one above the other. Their sizes and qualities are the same kinds, and identified in the same ways, as those found in melodic intervals, for any interval can occur in either a melodic or harmonic context.

Major and Minor Thirds

Thirds are easy to recognize on the staff, for both notes are either on consecutive lines or consecutive spaces—line to line or space to space. One intervening line or space, or one note, has been skipped over. However, identification of the quality of a third requires determination of the number and kind of steps it contains.

A *major third* (M3) is a third that contains two diatonic whole steps, or two major seconds. A *minor third* (m3) is a half step smaller than a major third; it contains one diatonic whole step plus one diatonic half step, or one major second plus one minor second, for a total one and one-half steps. Study the following isolated major and minor thirds shown notated as harmonic intervals and with keyboard locations of their pitches.

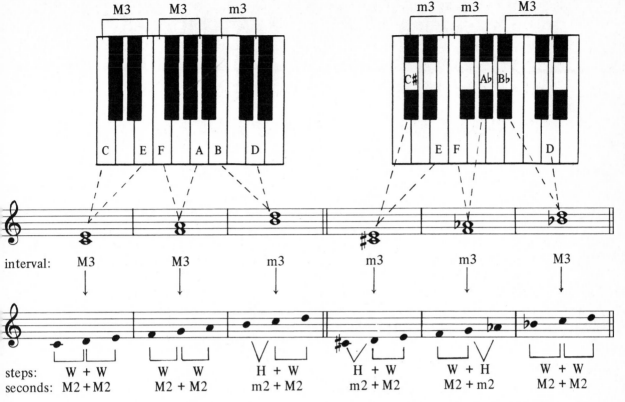

Any major third can be changed to a minor third—made a half step smaller—by either lowering the top note or raising the bottom note by one half step. Conversely, any minor third can be changed to a major third—made a half step larger—by raising the top note or lowering the bottom note by one-half step. Play the notated thirds shown here to compare major and minor qualities.

(a) converting M3 to m3:   *(b)* converting m3 to M3:

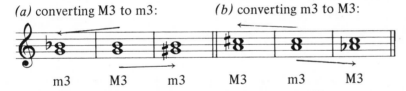

You also must be able to identify thirds notated with a key signature and sounded within a key. Correct labeling of tonal thirds requires naming their two notes, including applied sharps or flats from the signature, and determining whether the third is major or minor (see the next illustration).

reference keyboard:

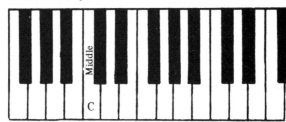

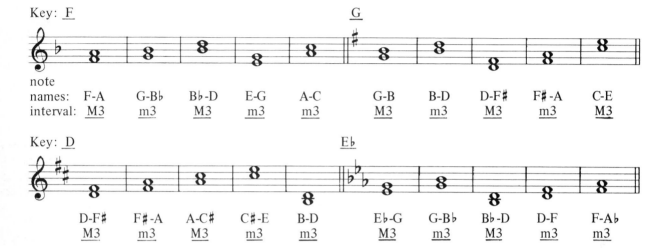

Key: F   G

note names:	F-A	G-B♭	B♭-D	E-G	A-C	G-B	B-D	D-F♯	F♯-A	C-E
interval:	M3	m3	M3	m3	m3	M3	m3	M3	m3	M3

Key: D   E♭

	D-F♯	F♯-A	A-C♯	C♯-E	B-D	E♭-G	G-B♭	B♭-D	D-F	F-A♭
	M3	m3	M3	m3	m3	M3	m3	M3	m3	m3

Perfect Fifths

Fifths encompass five degrees of the staff, including the two tones that comprise the interval. Notated fifths are easily recognized, for they involve distances from a line to the second line above or below and from a space to the second space above or below. In other words, both notes will be on lines with one line between or on spaces with one space between. Fifths, too, can be of different qualities, but we are interested here in only the perfect fifth that occurs in primary chords.

A *perfect fifth* (P5) is a fifth that contains three and one-half steps. (Other kinds of fifths are either one half step smaller or one half step larger than a perfect fifth.) Study the following notated harmonic perfect fifths along with their locations on the keyboard.

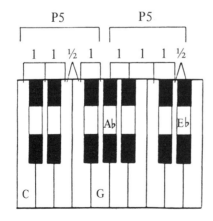

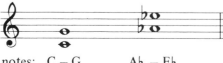

notes: C — G   A♭ — E♭
interval: P5   P5

Another accurate, and sometimes functional, way to view a perfect fifth is to consider it to be the interval that exists between the first and fifth scale tones (1–5 or *do–so*) in any major scale. If, in the case of an isolated fifth, you think of the lower note as a tonic, you can then move up the scale to its fifth tone and establish that note as a perfect fifth above the first. Check out this idea in the next illustrations and compare perfect fifths with other kinds (unnamed for our purposes), whose tones are located on the same staff degrees.

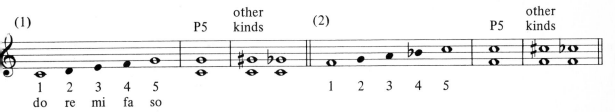

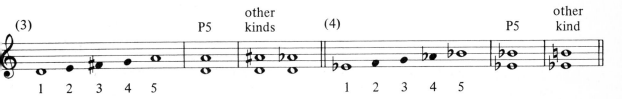

Perfect Octaves and Minor Sevenths

You already are well acquainted with an octave, or eighth, as the interval from any natural, sharped, or flatted note up or down eight tones and staff degrees to a note of the same name. An octave of this quality is called a *perfect octave* (P8); it is the only kind with which you will be involved. Octaves and fifths are called "perfect" since their two pitches have the simplest of all frequency ratios that conform to the first and second overtones in an overtone series: Tones an octave apart have a vibrational ratio of 2:1, and tones a perfect fifth apart have a 3:2 ratio.

Further study of perfect octaves is unnecessary, but octaves are useful in quickly comprehending minor sevenths. A *minor seventh* (m7) is a seventh that is a whole step, or a major second, less than an octave (a major seventh is only one half step less than an octave). Minor sevenths are especially significant, for they are contained in one of the chords you will be constructing and using in this chapter.

Here are some notated harmonic intervals that show minor sevenths compared with octaves:

Comparative octaves and minor sevenths:

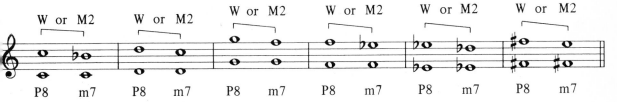

CHORD STRUCTURE

A *chord* is comprised of three or more pitches that sound simultaneously and are notated vertically. Progression through a series of chords provides a musical texture called *harmony*, which in some cases is in the form of an accompaniment to a melody. Most chords used in music contain three, four, or five different notes. We will be using three-note *triads* and four-note *seventh chords*.

Triads

A *triad* is a three-note chord constructed in thirds from a given tone called its *root*. When written in vertical order on a staff, all three notes occupy either consecutive spaces (space-space-space) or consecutive lines (line-line-line). As a member of the chord, each note has its own identity, name, and interval relationship to the other notes. Triads are named from their root. Thus, a triad built upon C is a C triad (or chord), one built upon F is an F triad, and one constructed from E-flat is an E-flat triad. Study the next illustration of a notated triad with each note member named and its interval relationship defined. We can ask and answer questions such as: Which note is the root of the chord? What is the name of the chord? Which chord note is its third, or its fifth? How is the chord "spelled" (with note names vertically from its root)?

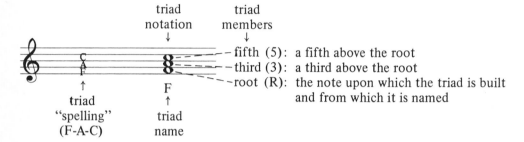

Triads can be built from any natural, sharped, or flatted pitch. The next illustration shows a representative selection of triads that are named, spelled, and notated in whole, half, and quarter values. Observe that all note heads are attached to the same side of a stem, and stems point up from the right side when two or more notes are on or below the middle line and point down when two or more notes are above the middle line. Also, if two or three acccidental signs are necessary to notate chord notes, they are slightly offset in vertical order so as not to overlap.

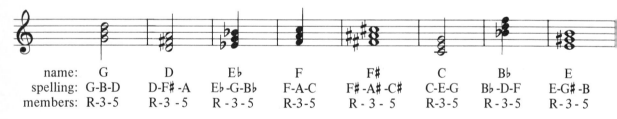

name:	G	D	E♭	F	F♯	C	B♭	E
spelling:	G-B-D	D-F♯-A	E♭-G-B♭	F-A-C	F♯-A♯-C♯	C-E-G	B♭-D-F	E-G♯-B
members:	R-3-5	R-3-5	R-3-5	R-3-5	R-3-5	R-3-5	R-3-5	R-3-5

Inversion of Triads

The three notes of a triad can be sounded and written in three different vertical orders without changing the chord's name, spelling, or quality. Any triad can be arranged in its root position plus two inverted positions. Triads with their root on the bottom are in *root position; first inversion* has the third on the bottom and the root on top; *second inversion* places the fifth on the bottom with the root and third above it. A general concept of inversion, if not a knowledge of all specifics, is important, for some chords you will use in simple accompaniments are inverted to provide greater ease and smoothness in moving from one chord to another.

Study the notated C major triad in its three positions. It retains in all positions the sound of a C major chord, since all arrangements have the same notes (C, E, and G), irrespective of the octave in which they sound.

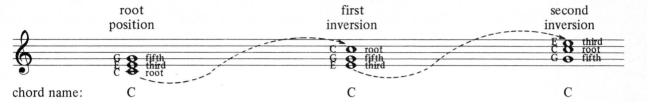

chord name: C   C   C

Major Triads

Triads, like intervals and scales, are of different qualities. Those you will use in chordal accompaniments in major keys are major triads—the only quality introduced in this chapter. A major scale, you will recall, sounds the way it does due to the intervals of which it is constructed. Similarly, quality of sound in a major triad comes from intervals contained within it.

Pitch relations among the three notes of a triad in root position form three intervals within the chord, and these can be analyzed and identified in two ways: 1) as intervals between the root and each of the other notes, or 2) as two vertical thirds—one between the root and third and another between the third and fifth. Study the illustration of both structural views:

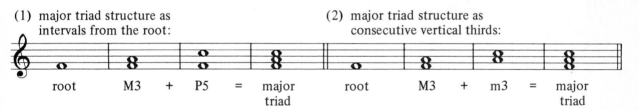

Either illustrated approach to building a major triad is acceptable, but you may find the second way easier, since it deals only with thirds. You must remember that a major triad contains two thirds, the bottom third of which is always major and the top third always minor. Study the illustrations that show several major triads constructed in thirds on both a treble staff and keyboard.

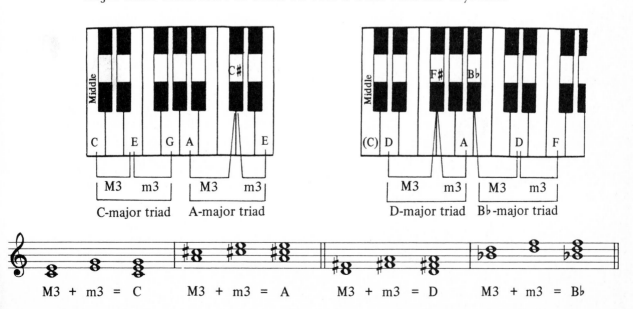

Seventh Chords

A *seventh chord* is a four-note chord comprised of four different pitches. You will use only one kind in this book, and its structure can be analyzed in two ways: 1) as intervals between the root and each of the other three notes, or 2) as a major triad with an added minor seventh above the root. A seventh chord gets its name from the fact that it includes a pitch that is a seventh above the root, and its written and spoken name always includes "seven." Thus, a seventh chord built from G is labeled "G⁷" and spoken "G-seven." Two ways of structuring seventh chords are shown in the next illustration.

(1) seventh-chord structure   (2) seventh-chord structure as a
   as intervals from the root: major triad plus a minor seventh:

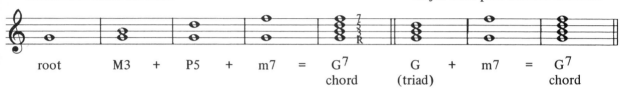

Here are two additional seventh chords, each built as a major triad plus a minor seventh on the staff and keyboard. Inversion of a seventh chord is introduced later in this chapter in conjunction with playing chords.

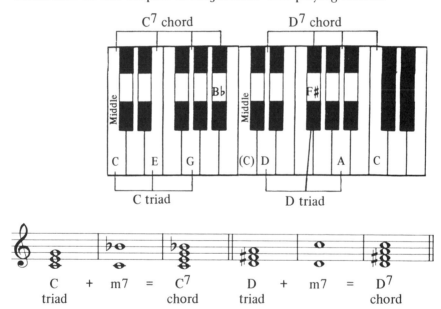

TONAL CHORDS

You have been working with isolated major triads and seventh chords to acquire facility in analyzing chord structures and identifying chords built from various roots. But chords in a piece of music function within a key and tonality. A triad can be built from every tone of a major sale, and the resulting chords have interrelationships corresponding to scale notes that serve as their roots. The tonic chord functions as a harmonic home chord, and other chords are related to it, either directly or indirectly through a second chord. Study the system of numbering and naming functional triads illustrated in the scale and key of C major.

Chord name. Each triad in a key is named with the letter of its root. A C major triad is always composed of the pitches C-E-G, but only in C major is it the tonic chord (in F major, for instance, it functions as the dominant chord). Identification of a tonal chord by name, number, and function is extremely important for purposes of dealing with it in various musical situations.

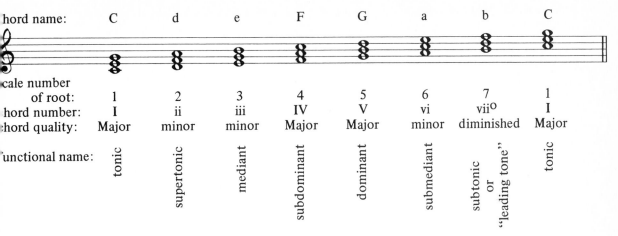

Chord name:	C	d	e	F	G	a	b	C
Scale number of root:	1	2	3	4	5	6	7	1
Chord number:	I	ii	iii	IV	V	vi	vii°	I
Chord quality:	Major	minor	minor	Major	Major	minor	diminished	Major
Functional name:	tonic	supertonic	mediant	subdominant	dominant	submediant	subtonic or "leading tone"	tonic

Chord number. Triads are symbolized with Roman numerals corresponding to scale numbers of their roots. Uppercase is used for major triads, and lowercase represents minor and diminished triads, with a small offset circle added to a diminished-triad symbol.

Functional name. Each tonal chord has a name that identifies its position and function in the key. (Each corresponding scale note carries the same name.) "Tonic" refers to the harmonic home chord; "dominant" is the second most important chord; "mediant" is midway between tonic and dominant; "subdominant" is one tone below the dominant, or it is the same distance (perfect fifth) below the tonic as the dominant is above the tonic; and so forth.

You should be able to interrelate various ways of identifying chords. In C major, for example, we can build a triad upon the fifth scale tone, call it a G major chord, label it with the numeral V, and speak of it as the dominant or "five" chord. No doubt remains about the specific chord to which we refer.

Chord quality. Triads built on each tone of a major scale result in three chords that are major, three that are minor, and one that is diminished. You have worked only with major triads, and major is the only kind you need to understand for now.

Primary chords. Tonic, dominant, and subdominant chords are the most important chords in any major key. These three chords are known as *primary chords* in view of the fact that together they contain all seven scale tones, they are major triads that carry the major harmonic quality of the key, and they provide the main harmonic framework for traditional melodies. You will use only primary chords in this book.

The primary triads:

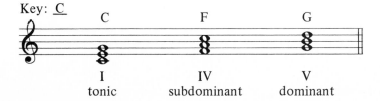

Key: C	C	F	G
	I	IV	V
	tonic	subdominant	dominant

TONIC AND DOMINANT-SEVENTH CHORDS

Simple harmonic accompaniments to most melodies can be done with no more than three primary chords, and only two of these are sufficient to harmonize some melodies. We will confine experiences in this chapter to use of the tonic and dominant-seventh chords and add the subdominant triad in a later chapter.

Western cultures have developed a preference for using the dominant chord in a seventh-chord formation, instead of keeping it in triadic form, in chordal accompaniments. The *dominant-seventh chord* (V^7) in any major key is a seventh chord built from the fifth scale tone and comprised of a dominant triad (V) plus a minor seventh above the root. An offset number indicating the added seventh must accompany both the numeral and name (for example, V^7 and G^7). The *tonic chord* (I), of course, is a triad constructed from the tonic note (or keynote).

Identification

The notated examples illustrate derivations and labelings of tonic and dominant-seventh chords in several keys. Think through each example in these ways:

1. Name the key from its signature.
2. Locate the tonic note (1 or *do*), build a triad from it, give the triad its correct name and number, and name (spell) the notes it contains.
3. Count, inclusively, up the staff to the fifth scale note, build a seventh chord from it, give the chord its correct name and number, and spell the chord notes.
4. Also, locate either or both chords in the next octave (higher or lower) if that octave is more practical from the standpoint of keeping most chord tones on the staff.
5. Finally, practice answering questions such as these: What is the name of the I chord in G major? What is the name of the V^7 chord in F major? What numeral identification goes with the A^7 chord in D major? In what key does the F^7 chord function as the dominant-seventh?

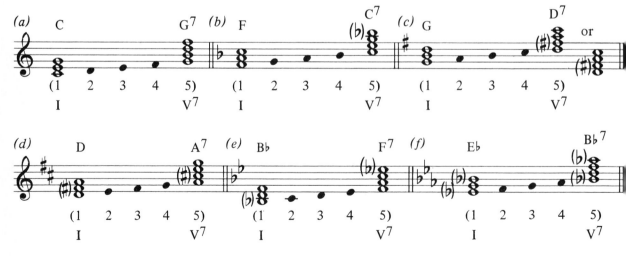

Keyboard Positions

Playing tonic and dominant-seventh chords on a piano requires moving from one chord to the other in a manner that will result in smoothness of sound and ease of finger movement. This is done universally by playing the tonic chord in root position and playing the dominant-seventh in an inverted position with one of its four notes omitted to reduce it to a three-note chord in which each vertical note is in the same position as, or only a half step away from, its corresponding note in the tonic chord.

Conversion of the V^7 from root position to keyboard position:

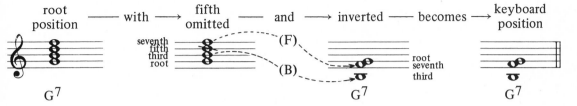

Progressing from I in root position to a reduced and inverted V^7 is better from musical and physical-coordination standpoints than playing both chords in root position (observe the notated illustration in C major).

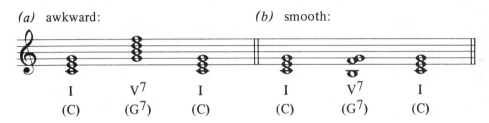

The I to V^7 Progression

Pitch movement from notes in one chord to those in another is called a *chord progression*. Going from tonic to dominant-seventh is the first progression you must become skilled in doing. Application of the following principles and rules makes your task relatively simple.

Chords can be played in either hand, but you will be using only your left hand to play chords and your right hand to play melodies. Fingers of the left hand are numbered from the thumb (1) outward to the little finger (5). Memorize all finger numbers and observe how they are indicated with a notated chord.

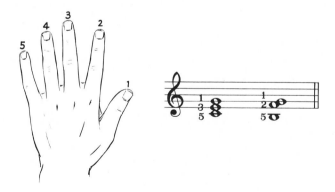

Simple chord progressions can be easily played by rules without having to read the notated chords. However, seeing notated progressions you are initially learning to play is essential for complete understanding of the process. Chord progressions can be written in treble and/or bass clef. We will notate them for comparison in both clefs, although you need not read bass-clef notation in order to accomplish playing the progressions. Since left-hand chords should be played essentially in the octave below Middle C, we will use the standard sign *8va*, followed by a broken line with an upturn, below treble-clef notation to indicate that chords are to be played an octave lower than written. They will actually sound in the octave corresponding to their bass-clef notation.

To execute a I to V^7 progression, finger movement on the keyboard corresponds to pitch movement (note location) on the staff: A pitch that is common to both chords remains in the same position (top to bottom) on both the staff and keyboard, and pitches that change move either up or down one half step on the staff and keyboard. By following some simple rules of finger movement, you can play the progression in any major key without reading notated chords or thinking separate notes:

Top note. Keep the top note—which is common to both chords—the same and play it with the same finger (1 or thumb).

Middle note. Move the middle note up a half step and change from third finger on the tonic-chord note to second finger on the dominant-seventh note.

Bottom note. Move the bottom note down a half step and play it with the same finger (5 or little finger).

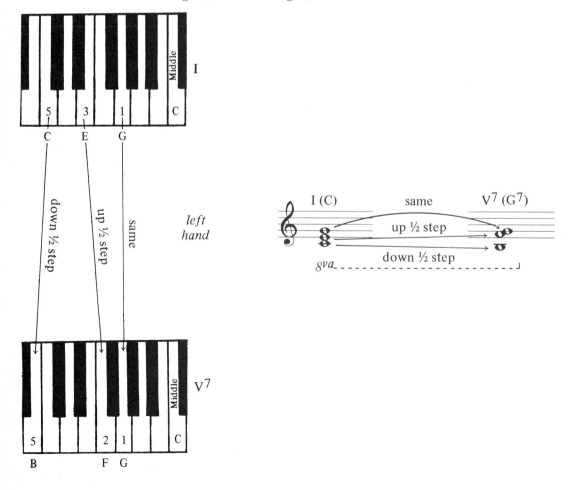

Playing the I–V⁷–I Progression

Whereas the tonic chord, functioning as home chord, provides a stable harmonic sound, the dominant-seventh is an active chord that almost demands a return (*resolution*) to the tonic. Chordal accompaniments require an ability to go from I to V^7 and back to I. The I–V^7–I progression is illustrated in three major keys—C, F, and G. As a prerequisite to playing accompaniments in these keys, practice the chord progressions until you can play them easily and with confidence.

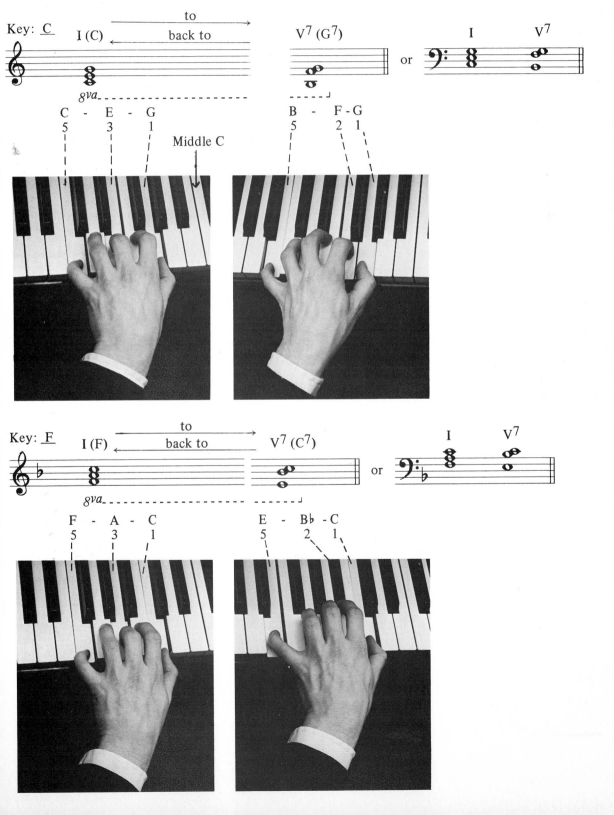

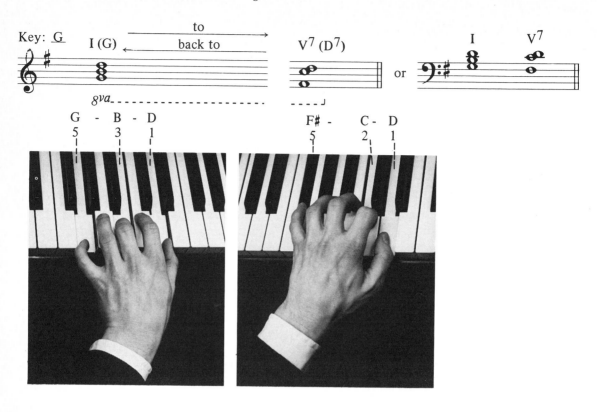

CHORDAL ACCOMPANIMENTS WITH MELODIES

If you can play a melody in your right hand, and if you can play the I–V⁷–I progression in your left hand, only one additional step remains to put the two things together and perform a song melody with accompaniment. Start with *Merrily We Roll Along,* which you played in Chapter One, and learn to play it with accompanying chords in three keys (C, F, and G) by following these procedures:

1. Practice the melody in the key in which it is written until you can play it accurately with your right hand. You should not attempt to add chords until the melody can be performed well by itself. (Start with your third finger, and use right-hand fingerings learned for this melody in Chapter One.)

2. Scan through the chord markings. Many song melodies found in various published sources are marked for chording. The usual system is to identify each chord by name (C, G^7, etc.) above the staff at a point where it is supposed to sound with the melody. You should simultaneously think chord numbers (I or V^7) in that key in order to change chords easily according to rules for finger and pitch movement.

3. Practice playing chords alone with your left hand. Attack each chord in *Merrily We Roll Along* as marked on the first beat of a measure and sustain it (hold down the keys) through the entire measure. If a chord is repeated in the next measure, merely lift your left hand and drop it again on the same keys.

4. Put the right-hand melody and left-hand chords together. Practice until the song has cohesion; so that someone (including yourself) could actually sing it to your accompaniment.

MERRILY WE ROLL ALONG (in C major)

piano chords:

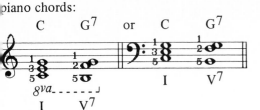

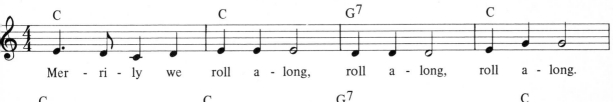

Mer - ri - ly we roll a - long, roll a - long, roll a - long.

Mer - ri - ly we roll a - long o'er the deep blue sea.

MERRILY WE ROLL ALONG (in F major)

piano chords:

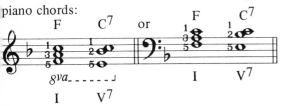

Mer - ri - ly we roll a - long, roll a - long, roll a - long.

Mer - ri - ly we roll a - long o'er the deep blue sea.

MERRILY WE ROLL ALONG (in G major)

piano chords:

Mer - ri - ly we roll a - long, roll a - long, roll a - long.

Mer - ri - ly we roll a - long o'er the deep blue sea.

You now should possess enough skill in playing the I and V⁷ chords in F major and G major to learn the melody and accompaniment for another song in each of those keys. Play *Down in the Valley* in G major. First, practice the melody with right-hand fingerings indicated above the notes and with a sense of underlying tempo beats. Make certain that you give dotted half notes (including the tied ones) their full values. Next, practice left-hand chord progressions, and, finally, put melody and chords together.

Chords used in piano accompaniments are the same ones used in guitar chording. That is to say, a G major chord produced on either instrument will function in the same way. Guitar chord frames for the I and V⁷ in G major are included here as an optional way to accompany *Down in the Valley*. (You can find additional information on guitar chording in optional Minichapter B.)

optional guitar chords:

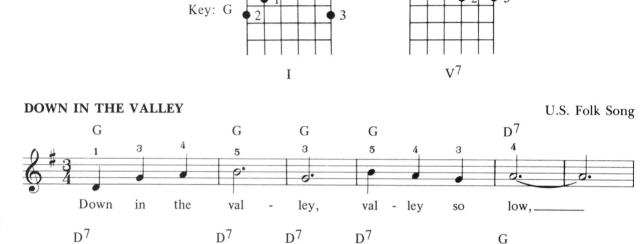

DOWN IN THE VALLEY

U.S. Folk Song

Down in the val - ley, val - ley so low,_____

Hang your head o - ver, hear the wind blow._____

Skip to My Lou is in F major. Reading the melodic rhythm with syllables or counts would be a good starting point for learning the song. Next, try fingering through the melody in rhythm (away from the keyboard) to establish finger coordination. Play the melody alone until all pitches (don't forget the B-flat) and durations are accurate, then add a chording accompaniment.

SKIP TO MY LOU

U.S. Folk Song

Choose your part - ner, skip to my Lou, choose your part - ner, skip to my Lou,

choose your part - ner, skip to my Lou, skip to my Lou, my dar - ling.

CHORD SKIPS IN MELODY

Pitch movement in melody progresses either by steps or skips (Chapter One). Movement up or down by steps follows steps of the scale (Chapter Three), and movement by skips usually is between two or more notes that also belong to a specific chord. Melody, then, essentially moves by scale steps and chord skips, and the most frequent chord skips come from our now familiar I and V⁷ chords.

Visual recognition of chord skips in melodic notation, along with practice in singing such patterns with scale numbers and/or *so-fa* syllables, can improve one's ability to think, read, and sing (also play) correct melodic intervals. To this end, study the chart that shows which scale tones are contained in the I chord (1-*do*, 3-*mi*, 5-*so*) and the V⁷ chord (5-*so*, 7-*ti*, 2-*re*, 4-*fa*) in any and all octaves, and practice singing and playing the melodic pitch patterns that follow.

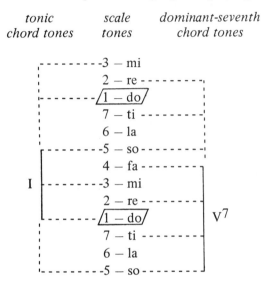

tonic chord tones *scale tones* *dominant-seventh chord tones*

Key to markings for chord skips and scale steps in melody:

I = skips among notes of the tonic chord

V⁷ = skips among notes of the dominant-seventh chord

= scale steps

Tonic chord skips:

(a) C major:

| 1 | 3 | 1 | 3 | 5 | 3 | 5 | 3 | 1 | 1 | 3 | 5 | 3 | 5 | 1̄ | 5 | 1̄ |
| do | mi | do | mi | so | mi | so | mi | do | do | mi | so | mi | so | d̄o | so | d̄o |

(b) F major:

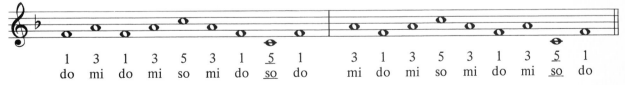

| 1 | 3 | 1 | 3 | 5 | 3 | 1 | 5 | 1 | 3 | 1 | 3 | 5 | 3 | 1 | 3 | 5 | 1 |
| do | mi | do | mi | so | mi | do | so | do | mi | do | mi | so | mi | do | mi | so | do |

(c) G major:

| 1 | 5 | 1 | 3 | 1 | 5 | 1 | 3 | 5 | 1 | 1 | 3 | 5 | 1 | 5 | 3 | 1 |
| do | so | do | mi | do | so | do | mi | so | do | do | mi | so | do | so | mi | do |

Tonic and dominant-seventh chord skips:

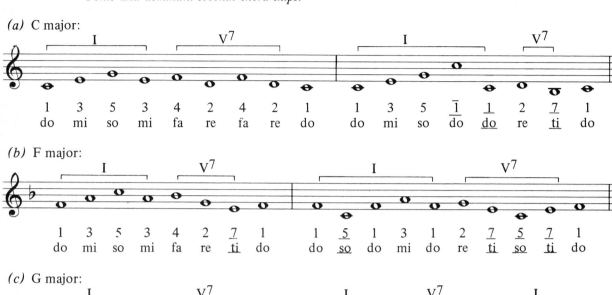

Chord skips and scale steps:

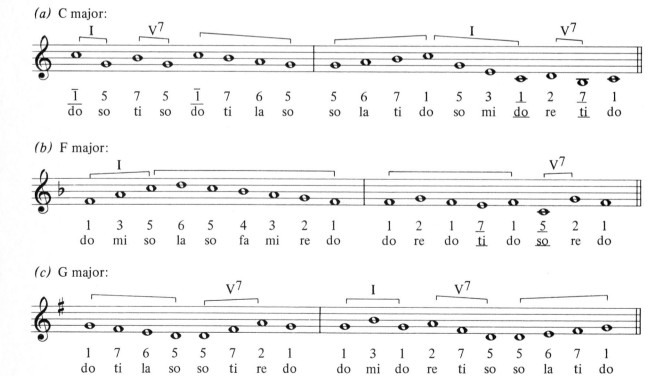

Melody grows out of harmony in most traditional songs; melody often implies underlying chords, even when none are present. Sing *Skip to My Lou* and *Down in the Valley* with scale numbers and/or syllables in order to observe that chord skips at any point in the melody actually follow notes of the chord used at that point in the accompaniment.

SKIP TO MY LOU

3	3	1	1	3	3	3	5,	2	2	7	7	2	2	2	4,
mi	mi	do	do	mi	mi	mi	so,	re	re	ti	ti	re	re	re	fa,
Choose	your	part -	ner,	skip	to	my	Lou,	choose	your	part -	ner,	skip	to	my	Lou,

3	3	1	1	3	3	3	5,	2	3	4	3	2	1	1.
mi	mi	do	do	mi	mi	mi	so,	re	mi	fa	mi	re	do	do.
choose	your	part -	ner,	skip	to	my	Lou,	skip	to	my	Lou,	my	dar -	ling.

DOWN IN THE VALLEY

5	1	2*	3	1,	3	2	1	2,
so	do	re	mi	do,	mi	re	do	re,
Down	in	the	val -	ley,	val -	ley	so	low,___

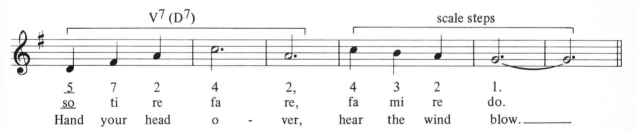

5	7	2	4	2,	4	3	2	1.
so	ti	re	fa	re,	fa	mi	re	do.
Hand	your	head	o -	ver,	hear	the	wind	blow.___

*This note is a passing scale tone between two chord tones.

PRACTICE ACTIVITIES

Page references to relevant *Study Activities* are given in parentheses.

reference
keyboard:

Notating and Naming

1. Write above the given note a second note that would create either a major third (M3) or minor third (m3) as designated below the staff. (80–81).

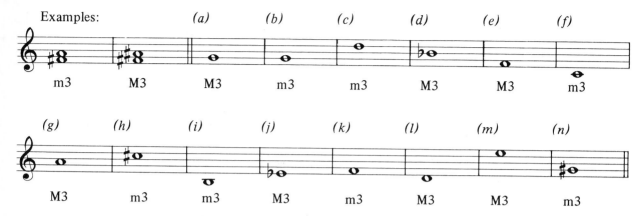

2. Write above the given note a second note that would create either a perfect fifth (P5), minor seventh (m7), or perfect octave (P8) as designated. (82–83).

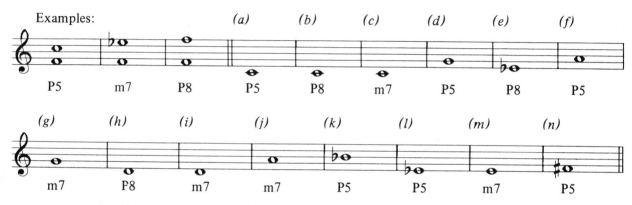

3. You are given one note identified as either the root, third, or fifth of a major triad. To the right of the given note, notate a complete triad in root position and place its name in the blank below the staff. (84)

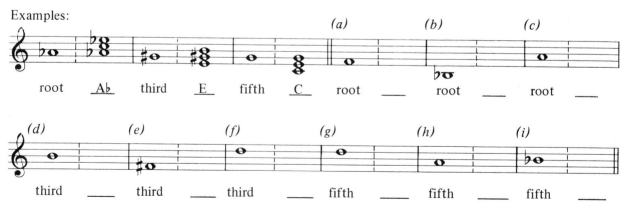

4. For each given key signature a) notate in root position the I and V⁷ chords in that key, b) write the name of each chord in the blank above it, and c) "spell" each chord with names of its notes. (88)

Example:
  name: _Eb_   _Bb_7   *(a)* ___   ___   *(b)* ___   ___

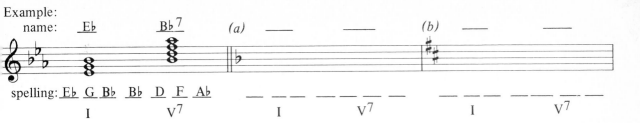

spelling: _Eb G Bb_ _Bb D F Ab_ ___ ___ ___ ___ ___ ___ ___ ___ ___ ___ ___ ___
          I   V7   I   V7   I   V7

Identifying

5. Write the name of each harmonic interval in the blank below it.

Examples: *(a)* *(b)* *(c)* *(d)* *(e)* *(f)*

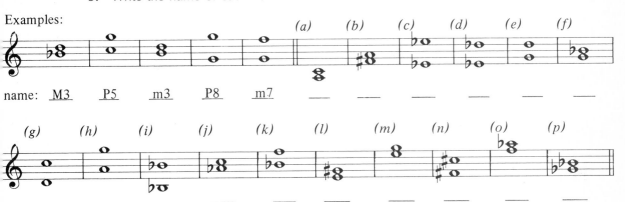

name: _M3_   _P5_   _m3_   _P8_   _m7_   ___   ___   ___   ___   ___   ___

(g) *(h)* *(i)* *(j)* *(k)* *(l)* *(m)* *(n)* *(o)* *(p)*

___ ___ ___ ___ ___ ___ ___ ___ ___ ___

6. Follow the example and complete exercises *a, b,* and *c* in which you are given
a blank staff with key signature and a keyboard segment. Notate the I and V7
chords in the position in which they would be played in a I to V7 progression in
that key, write the names of chord notes on the keyboard, and label the keyboard chords with both their numeral and name. Apply rules for pitch movement in a I–V7 progression to achieve both staff notation and keyboard location of the chords. (90)

Example: *(a)*

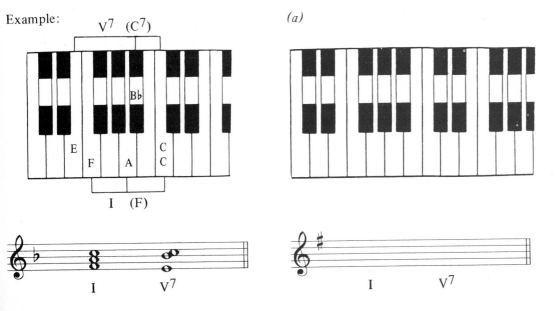

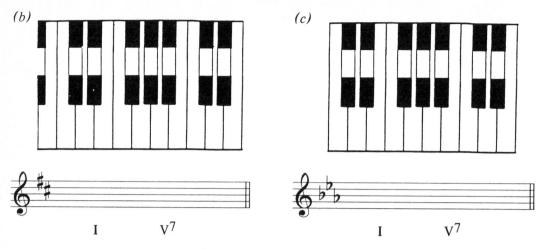

I   V⁷   I   V⁷

7. You are given three excerpts (*a, b,* and c) from familiar songs, each notated in a certain key. Following the model at the beginning of the first excerpt, write either syllable names or scale numbers in the blanks below the notes, then label each bracketed pattern as chord skips or scale steps. Mark chord skips with both the chord numeral and name, and merely write "steps" to identify scale-step patterns. (95–97)

Creating

8. You are given a blank staff with a key signature for G major and a four-four meter signature. Create and notate an original four-measure melody that con-

tains both scale steps and chord skips, as well as durations consisting of quarter, eighth, and half notes. Restudy the melodies in activity 7 to obtain some initial ideas.

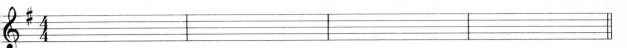

Discriminating (Aural-Visual)

Practice activities 9, 10, and 11 should be presented by an instructor.

9. In each item you see three different intervals, each of which is melodically and harmonically notated and named. You will hear one of these intervals played; draw a circle around the number of the interval that was played.

10. Each item (a through f) has three pitch patterns written in the same key and starting on the same scale tone (marked with number and syllable), but each pattern contains different intervals comprised of scale tones and/or scale steps. One of the three patterns will be played; circle the number of the pattern played.

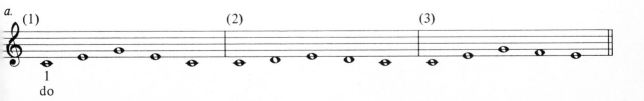

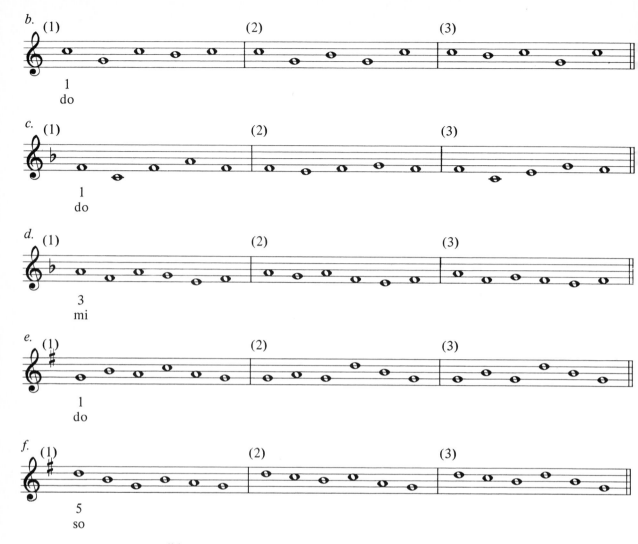

11. You will hear a chord progression played on a piano. Circle the number of the progression played.

	(a)		(b)		(c)
(1)	I–V⁷–I–I	(1)	I–V⁷–I–V⁷–I	(1)	I–V⁷–I
(2)	I–V⁷–V⁷–I	(2)	I–V⁷–V⁷–I–I	(2)	I–I–V⁷
(3)	I–I–V⁷–I	(3)	I–I–V⁷–V⁷–I	(3)	V⁷–V⁷–I

Reading and Performing

12. Continue to practice the following material presented in the *Study Activities:*
   a. Sing with *so-fa* syllables and/or scale numbers:
     1) All melodic exercises based on chord skips and scale steps
     2) *Down in the Valley* in G
     3) *Skip to My Lou* in F
   b. Play the melody with chordal accompaniment:
     1) *Merrily We Roll Along* in C, F, and G
     2) *Down in the Valley* in G
     3) *Skip to My Lou* in F

AFTER YOU HAVE COMPLETED ALL **PRACTICE ACTIVITIES** AND RE-VIEWED THE **OBJECTIVES,** CONTINUE WITH THE **ASSESSMENT OF PROGRESS.**

ASSESSMENT OF PROGRESS

A.   *Applied knowledge.* Part A can be completed as a self-administered test without reference to any other material. Write your responses in the blanks provided and, when you have finished all of Part A, check your answers with those in *Keys to Chapter Assessments,* page 249. Correct all of your errors and restudy relevant material in the *Study Activities* and *Practice Activities* before continuing to Chapter Five.

reference keyboard:

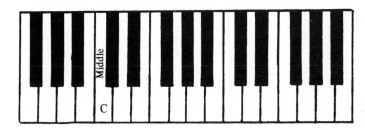

1.   Identify each harmonic interval and write its name in the blank below the staff: M3 = major third, m3 = minor third, P5 = perfect fifth, m7 = minor seventh, P8 = perfect octave.

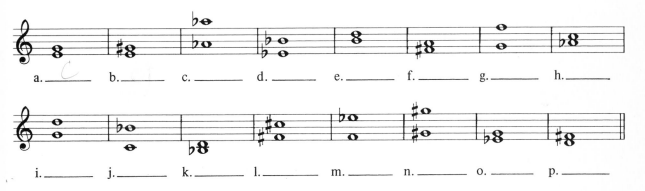

Respond to items 2 through 12 with coordinated reference to the keyboard with numbered keys and the four (*a, b, c, d*) notated key signatures, for which you are given chord numbers (I, V⁷) and the first chord name. Prior to answering the questions, fill in the remaining chord names for each key. You may use the blank staff for thinking or notating chord tones if you find it necessary or helpful to do so.

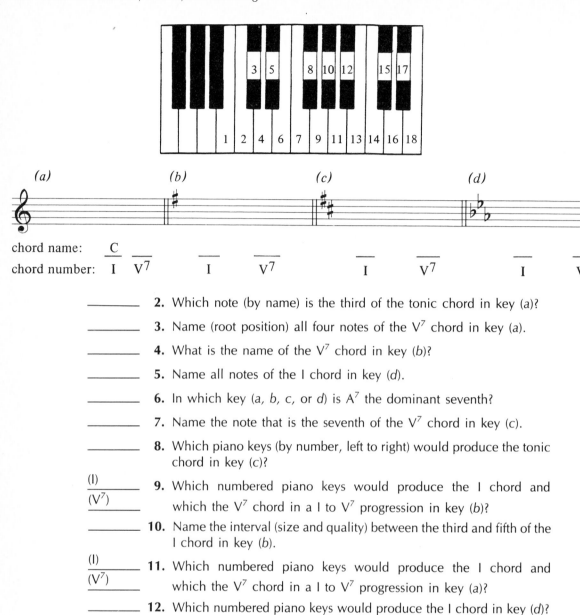

chord name: <u> C </u>   _____   _____   _____   _____   _____   _____   _____

chord number: I   V⁷   I   V⁷   I   V⁷   I   V⁷

_____ **2.** Which note (by name) is the third of the tonic chord in key (a)?

_____ **3.** Name (root position) all four notes of the V^7 chord in key (a).

_____ **4.** What is the name of the V^7 chord in key (b)?

_____ **5.** Name all notes of the I chord in key (d).

_____ **6.** In which key (a, b, c, or d) is A^7 the dominant seventh?

_____ **7.** Name the note that is the seventh of the V^7 chord in key (c).

_____ **8.** Which piano keys (by number, left to right) would produce the tonic chord in key (c)?

(I) _____
(V⁷) _____ **9.** Which numbered piano keys would produce the I chord and which the V^7 chord in a I to V^7 progression in key (b)?

_____ **10.** Name the interval (size and quality) between the third and fifth of the I chord in key (b).

(I) _____
(V⁷) _____ **11.** Which numbered piano keys would produce the I chord and which the V^7 chord in a I to V^7 progression in key (a)?

_____ **12.** Which numbered piano keys would produce the I chord in key (d)?

Respond to items 13 through 20 with reference to the notated melody of *Some Folks Do.*

SOME FOLKS DO   Stephen C. Foster

_____ **13.** In what key is the melody written?

_____ **14.** What are the names of the I and V^7 chords in this key?

_____ **15.** To which chord (I or V^7) do the notes in pattern (a) belong?

_____ **16.** Name the interval between the two notes in pattern (a).

_____ **17.** To which chord do the notes in pattern (b) belong?

_____ **18.** Which chord should be played in the accompaniment during pattern (c)?

_____ **19.** Which chord should be played in the accompaniment during pattern (d)?

(I)
_____ **20.** Which numbered piano keys (see numbered keyboard) would
(V^7)
_____   produce the I chord and the V^7 chord in a chordal accompaniment to _Some Folks Do?_

B. _Skills._ Part B is an assessment of the level of skills in playing chord progressions and chordal accompaniments, as well as reading melodic patterns based on chord skips, that you have developed during the study of this chapter. It should be administered to you by an instructor or student assistant, and you should achieve the minimum acceptable level, or a higher level, before continuing to Chapter Five.

1. Minimum acceptable level of performance
 a. Play with no uncorrected errors:
   1) I–V^7–I progression in C, F, and G
   2) _Merrily We Roll Along_ (melody and chordal accompaniment) in C and in either F or G
 b. Sing with either scale numbers or _so-fa_ syllables:
   1) one exercise of your choice in each key (C, F, G) on pages 95–96
   2) the melody of either _Down in the Valley_ or _Skip to My Lou_

2. Higher level of performance
 a. Play with no uncorrected errors:
   1) I–V^7–I progression in C, F, and G, plus two additional major keys of your choice
   2) melody and chordal accompaniment for the following songs:
    a) _Merrily We Roll Along_ in C, F, and G
    b) _Down in the Valley_ in G
    c) _Skip to My Lou_ in F
 b. Sing with either scale numbers or _so-fa_ syllables:
   1) any melodic exercises selected by your instructor from pages 95–96
   2) the melodies of _Down in the Valley_ and _Skip to My Lou_

Chapter 5

Subdivision, Triplet Division, and Off-Beat Syncopation

INSTRUCTIONS

1. Read the *Objectives* to gain an initial acquaintance with competencies you should have acquired by the end of this chapter. Keep these objectives in mind as you continue through the study and practice activities.

2. Complete all *Study Activities*. Give special attention to developing your skill in recognizing, reading, and performing new rhythm patterns in Chapter Five.

3. Complete with accurate responses all *Practice Activities* before proceeding to the assessment of progress.

4. As soon as you are ready, or when directed by your instructor, complete the *Assessment of Progress*. You should achieve the criterion levels that are indicated before continuing to Chapter Six.

OBJECTIVES

1. Recall and define the following new terms and correctly use and interpret them in oral or written communication:

off-beat
subdivision
   equal
   unequal

syncopation
triplet

2. Recognize from their notation subdivided patterns, syncopated patterns, and triplet patterns introduced in this chapter, and identify or write rhythm syllables and rhythm counts used to vocalize (chant) these patterns.

3. Given notated rhythm comprised of mixed patterns, indicate where each metric beat falls in relation to the patterns and/or place bar lines at appropriate places in accordance with the meter signature.

4. Given choices of notated rhythm patterns, identify the one you hear performed by an instructor or student assistant (aural-visual discrimination).

5. Read, with rhythm syllables or counts to a clapped tempo beat, the rhythm exercises and melodic rhythms included in this chapter.

6. Play the melody of at least two songs contained in this chapter, and add a I–V^7 chordal accompaniment to at least one melody.

7. Sing, with the words of their texts, and with or without the aid of a piano or second person, at least two songs from this chapter.

STUDY ACTIVITIES

Chapter Five will extend your experiences with organizations of rhythm. It will do so through a continuing use of what you learned in Chapter Two at the same time you are learning to read and perform new patterns. By the end of this chapter, you should be able to understand and read almost any melodic rhythm encountered in traditional music in simple meters with a quarter-note beat unit.

Chapter Two dealt with melodic rhythm in meters of two-four, three-four, and four-four in situations where a quarter note functions as the beat unit and represents a one-beat duration. Patterns of duration included: beat patterns (quarter notes or rests), combined patterns (whole, half), divided patterns (eighths), elongated patterns (dotted half, dotted quarter), and tied patterns. Chapter Five presents subdivided patterns, triplet patterns, and syncopated patterns in the same meters you have been using and with a quarter note still functioning as the beat unit.

SUBDIVISION

A divided beat, you will recall, splits the duration of a beat into two equal and even parts notated with two eighth notes (two eighth values = one quarter value). *Subdivision* is a second division of a beat (a division of the divided beat) into four equal and even parts represented by four sixteenth notes (one quarter = two eighths = four-sixteenths).

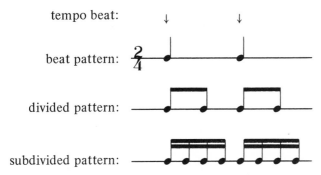

Additional patterns are derived from the basic subdivision by tieing together two or three of the four sixteenth notes and replacing the tied values with one note. An eight replaces two tied sixteenths, and a dotted eighth replaces either three tied sixteenths or one eighth tied to one sixteenth. Such patterns have an effect of *unequal division:* one longer sound plus two shorter sounds, two shorts plus one long, or one elongated (dotted) sound and one short sound. Any pattern that contains one or more sixteenths is related to subdivision. Here are subdivided patterns most frequently encountered in melodic rhythm:

Common subdivided patterns:

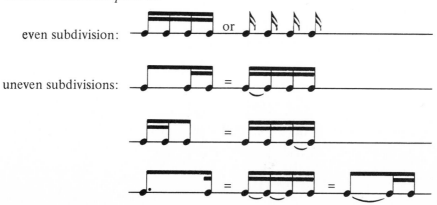

Reading Subdivided Patterns

Chapter Two introduced you to two systems of vocalizing rhythm patterns superimposed upon a clapped tempo beat. We will continue to use these systems in learning to read all new patterns in this chapter. In subdivided patterns, rhythm syllables form two-, three-, and four-syllable words to a beat and provide a natural and accurate sense of each discrete pattern. Chanting with subdivided counts makes one aware of where in the beat and measure various sounds (and silences) occur.

Common patterns. Study the chart of common subdivided patterns (*a, b, c, d*), and practice chanting each with a clapped beat until your vocal articulation of correct syllables or counts is an automatic response to seeing the notated pattern.

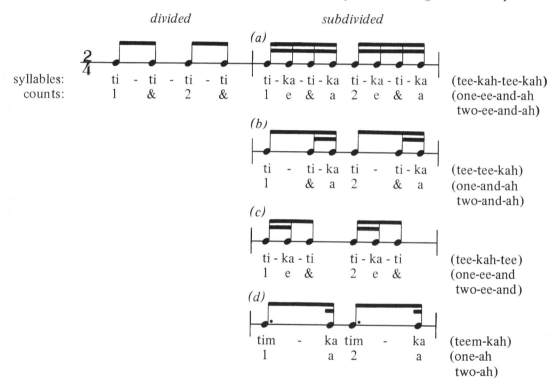

Rhythm exercises 1 through 8 contain mixed patterns comprised of all common subdivisions. Tempo beats are marked with downward arrows above each pattern so that you can visually relate beat and pattern. Clap a moderate tempo beat and vocally read each exercise until you are confident of your accuracy.

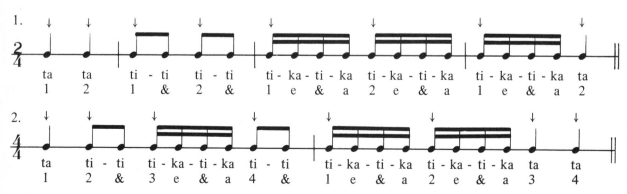

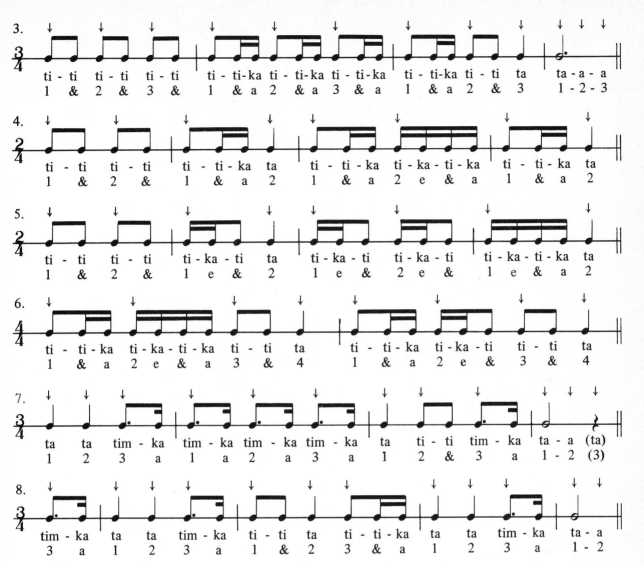

Anacrusis, tie, and rest. Music sometimes involves subdivided patterns in conjunction with ties and rests. The first note of a subdivided pattern can be tied to the preceding note, or an elongation dot might be used instead of a tie, and any note of a pattern can be replaced with a rest. Numerous possibilities exist, but we will focus on only the most common cases, shown in the next illustration, which also shows the off-beat half of a subdivided pattern as an *anacrusis*. Practice chanting each notated pattern to a clapped beat until it is performed correctly. You also will encounter some of these situations in melodies found in the next section.

(a) off-beat anacrusis:

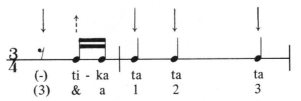

(b) on-beat tie plus
off-beat subdivision:

(c) elongation dot plus
off-beat subdivision:

(d) on-beat rest plus
off-beat subdivision:

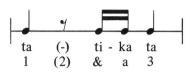

Reading and Performing Melodic Rhythm

Melodic rhythm, of course, is made up of a series of mixed patterns through which sounds and silences move in continuation from beginning to end. A great many melodies contain a mixture of divided and subdivided patterns, plus beat durations and combined durations. The next four traditional songs are typical examples. You might follow this sequence of activities to learn each song: (1) Start by reading the melodic rhythm with syllables and/or counts to a clapped beat at the tempo indicated. (2) Chant the words of the text in the same rhythm. (3) Sing and/or play the melody in correct rhythm.

Hush, Little Baby is a beautiful American lullaby notated here in G major. Once you have learned its melodic rhythm, you will find the song relatively easy to play with right-hand fingerings that are given. A chordal accompaniment (Chapter Four) can be provided with the I–V^7–I progression. Try it!

HUSH, LITTLE BABY

U.S. Lullaby

Moderately slow

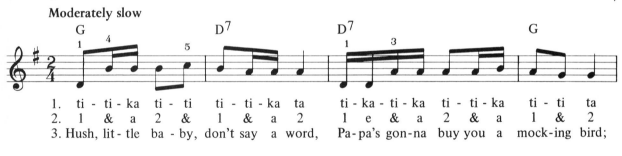

What Shall I Do with a Drunken Sailor? is a great song to sing; you might need to learn its melody with the aid of a piano and/or group singing. This song carries a key signature of no sharps or flats, but the melody is not in C major. The tonic is D (final note), and the melody is based on an old scale form called Dorian mode (see optional Minichapter D for additional information on modes). The fact that this sea chanty is not in a major key should be no deterrent to reading its rhythm and singing or playing its melody, but do not attempt to add a chordal accompaniment.

WHAT SHALL I DO WITH A DRUNKEN SAILOR?

Sea Chantey

Moderately

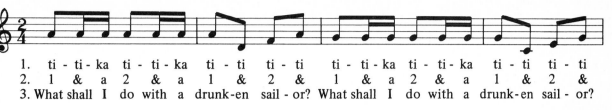

1. ti - ti - ka ti - ti - ka ti - ti ti - ti ti - ti - ka ti - ti - ka ti - ti ti - ti
2. 1 & a 2 & a 1 & 2 & 1 & a 2 & a 1 & 2 &
3. What shall I do with a drunk-en sail - or? What shall I do with a drunk-en sail - or?

ti - ti - ka ti - ti - ka ti - ti ti - ti ti - ti ti - ti ta ta
1 & a 2 & a 1 & 2 & 1 & 2 & 1 2
What shall I do with a drunk-en sail - or ear - ly in the morn - ing?

Chorus:

ta tim - ka ti - ti ti - ti ta tim - ka ti - ti ti - ti
1 2 a 1 & 2 & 1 2 a 1 & 2 &
Yo - ho, and up she ris - es. Yo - ho, and up she ris - es,

ta tim - ka ti - ti ti - ti ti - ti ti - ti ta ta
1 2 a 1 & 2 & 1 & 2 & 1 2
Yo - ho, and up she ris - es ear - ly in the morn - ing.

You might call *Ol' Texas* a cowboy lament; therefore read its melodic rhythm and perform it at a moderately slow tempo. Observe that each two-measure phrase starts on the off-beat (last half) of count one, sometimes with a divided pattern (eighth note) and sometimes with a subdivided pattern (two sixteenth notes). To which chord (tonic or dominant-seventh) do the melodic skips in phrase one belong?

OL' TEXAS

Cowboy Song

Slowly

1. (-) ti ti - ti ta - a (-) ti - ka ti - ti ta - a
2. (1) & 2 & 1 - 2 (1) & a 2 & 1 - 2
3. I'm goin' to leave Ol'___ Tex - as now,

(-) ti ti - ti ta - a (-) ti - ka ti - ti ta - a - a a
(1) & 2 & 1 - 2 (1) & a 2 & 1 - 2 - 1 - 2
They have no use for the long-horned cow._____

Many people incorrectly perform the melodic rhythm in *Battle Hymn of the Republic*. Their problem is a failure to discriminate between values of two kinds of notes (eighth and sixteenth) that follow two kinds of dotted notes (dotted quarter and dotted eighth). But you should be able to establish accurate durations by perceiving complete patterns—ones you have previously read and practiced—as you chant them with syllables and/or counts to a clapped beat.

BATTLE HYMN OF THE REPUBLIC

Moderately quick

Music by William Steffe
Words by Julia Ward Howe

1. ta - i - ti tim - ka tim - ka ta - a ta (-) ta - i - ti tim - ka tim - ka ta - a ta (-)
2. 1 - 2 & 3 a 4 a 1 - 2 3 (4) 1 - 2 & 3 a 4 a 1 - 2 3 (4)
3. Glo - ry, glo - ry, hal - le - lu - jah! Glo - ry, glo - ry, hal - le - lu - jah!

ta - i - ti tim - ka tim - ka ta - a ta ta ta ta ta ta ta - a (- -)
1 - 2 & 3 a 4 a 1 - 2 3 4 1 2 3 4 1 - 2 (3 - 4)
Glo - ry, glo - ry, hal - le - lu - jah! His truth is march - ing on.

TRIPLET DIVISION

Our system of notating rhythm is based on halving numerical values. Thus, one quarter is halved into two eighths, and two eighths are halved into four sixteenths; or, to put it another way, a beat in simple meter is first divided into two equal parts and again into four equal parts. But what about three (or five) equal parts?

Duration of a beat can be divided into any practical number of even sounds. However, divisions other than normal ones (two and four) require special notation. Such is the case of a triple division, which is illustrated among comparative divisions of a quarter-note beat into two, three, and four equal parts. A *triplet* is generally defined as three notes in the same duration as two notes of the same kind, and its notated pattern usually has both a number 3 and a bracket encompassing its three notes, although the bracket is sometimes omitted. Other kinds of notes, such as quarters and sixteenths, also can be grouped as triplets, but our concern here is with the pattern that divides a quarter-note beat into triplet eighths.

Comparative divisions of the beat:

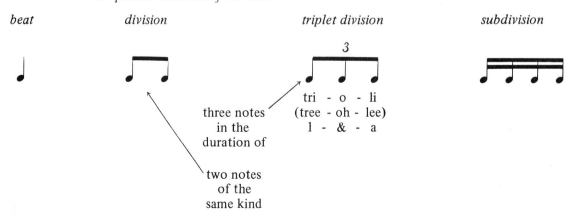

beat

division

three notes
in the
duration of

two notes
of the
same kind

triplet division

3

tri - o - li
(tree - oh - lee)
1 - & - a

subdivision

Reading Triplet Patterns

Triplet patterns are easy to read accurately if you 1) evenly distribute the three sounds over the entire duration of a beat, and 2) shift smoothly to and from the triplet pattern as it occurs among other patterns in melodic rhythm. Exercises 1 through 5 provide experiences in reading triplets in various contexts of mixed patterns. Correct practice will improve your skill in accurate discrimination among the patterns.

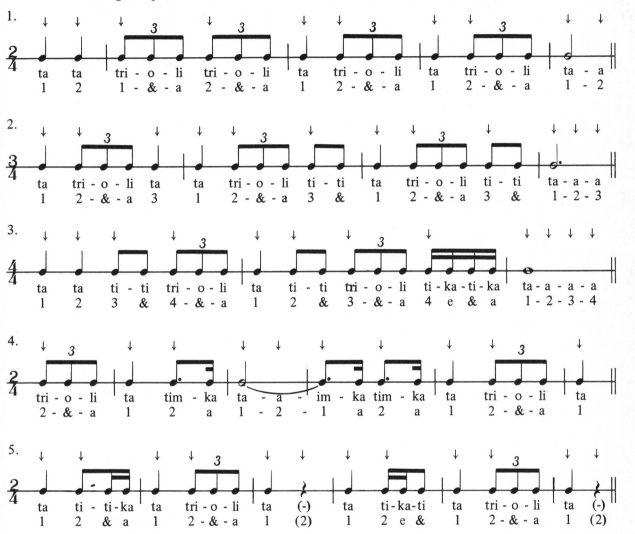

Reading and Performing Melodic Rhythm

If you have successfully read the preceding exercises, you should have no trouble reading the melodic rhythm in *Sing, Sing Together*. This is a song you can both sing and play.

SING, SING TOGETHER

English Round

Quickly

1. ta   ti - ti   ta   ta   tri - o - li   tri - o - li   ta - a
2. 1   2   &   1   2   1 - & - a   2 - & - a   1 - 2
3. Sing,   sing   to - geth - er,   Mer - ri - ly,   mer - ri - ly   sing;

ta	ti	ti	ta	ta	tri	o	li	tri	o	li	ta	a
1	2	&	1	2	1	-	& - a	2	-	& - a	1	- 2
Sing,	sing	to	geth	er,	Mer	ri	ly,	mer	ri	ly	sing;	

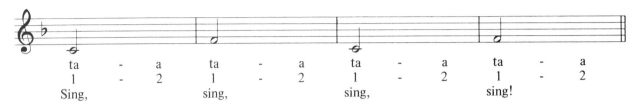

ta	-	a	ta	-	a	ta	-	a	ta	-	a
1	-	2	1	-	2	1	-	2	1	-	2
Sing,			sing,			sing,			sing!		

Performing accurate rhythm patterns in *Swinging Along* will depend, first of all, on your ability to maintain a steady, moderate (walking) tempo beat. Make certain that the triplet patterns (tri-o-li) are exactly even and that the dotted patterns (tim-ka) are decidedly uneven. Extract the first two measures and practice them alone with syllables and/or counts until all durations fit the tempo beat.

SWINGING ALONG

Traditional

Moderately

1.	tri	o	li	ta	a	im	ka	tim	ka	ta	a	a	tri	o	li	ta	a	ta	a	ta	a	a
2.	4	&	a	1	2	3	a	4	a	1 - 2 - 3	4	& - a	1	2	3	4	1	2	3		
3.	Swing-ing	a	long	the	o	pen	road	un	der	a	sky	that's	clear.								

tri	o	li	ta	a	im	ka	tim	ka	ta	a	a	tim	ka	ta	ta	a	ta	ta	a	a
4	&	a	1	2	3	a	4	a	1 - 2 - 3	4	a	1	2	3	4	1	2	3		
Swing-ing	a	long	the	o	pen	road	in	the	fall	of	the	year.								

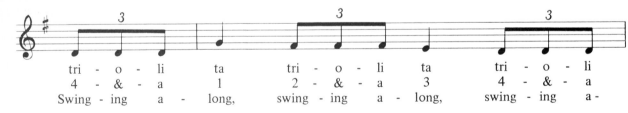

tri	o	li	ta	tri	o	li	ta	tri	o	li
4	&	a	1	2	&	a	3	4	&	a
Swing	ing	a	long,	swing	ing	a	long,	swing	ing	a

tim	ka	tim	ka	ta	a	ta	tim	ka	ta	tim	ka	ta	a	a
1	a	2	a	3 - 4	1	2	a	3	4	a	1 - 2 - 3		
long	the	o	pen	road	All	in	the	fall	of	the	year.		

SYNCOPATION

Normally, certain beats in a measure have a rhythmic stress, or accent, that makes sound at these points somewhat heavier in comparison with other beats. Beat one is usually stressed in duple and triple meters, and beats one and three are stronger in quadruple meter. Also, an on-beat sound often receives slightly more stress than an off-beat sound in divided patterns. Rhythmic syncopation happens when these norms of rhythmic stress are deliberately disturbed.

Syncopation occurs when rhythmic stress or accent is displaced—when it is shifted to a normally unaccented beat of a measure or to the off-beat in divided patterns. We will limit our consideration here to off-beat syncopated patterns, for they are most commonly found in songs, especially American folk songs.

Study the illustration that shows how the basic syncopated pattern is derived and notated (eighth-quarter-eighth). This three-note pattern has relative durations of short-long-short distributed over two beats. The quarter-note sound, which starts on an off-beat, receives greater stress (accent) by virtue of the fact that it is of longer value than the eighth notes that precede and follow it. Practice chanting the basic pattern and its two variations (*a* and *b*) against a clapped tempo beat until each pattern is accurate and, also, expressive of the syncopated effect of an off-beat accent.

Derivation of syncopation:

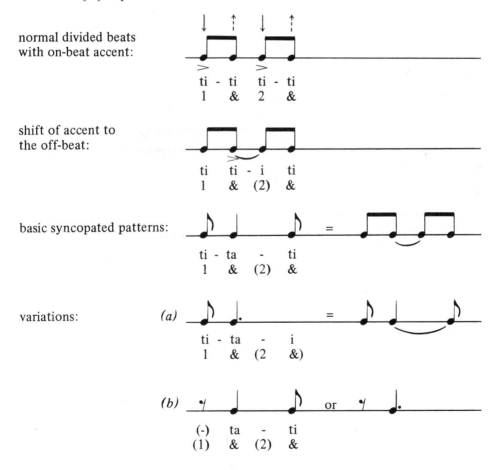

normal divided beats
with on-beat accent:

    ti - ti   ti - ti
    1 & 2 &

shift of accent to
the off-beat:

    ti ti - i ti
    1 & (2) &

basic syncopated patterns:

    ti - ta - ti
    1 & (2) &

variations: *(a)*

    ti - ta - i
    1 & (2 &)

    (b)   or

    (-) ta - ti
    (1) & (2) &

Reading Syncopated Patterns

Rhythm exercises 1 through 5 include off-beat syncopated patterns in a context of mixed patterns. First, analyze each exercise by identifying patterns of duration that occur in relation to the beats (downward arrows). Second, clap a moderate tempo beat and chant the pattern with syllables and/or counts. Repeat each exercise until its rhythmic continuity is both accurate and expressive.

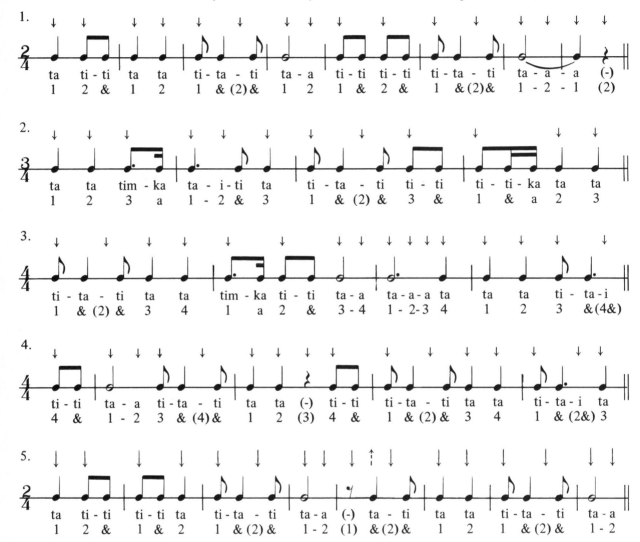

Reading and Performing Melodic Rhythm

Various forms of syncopation appear in many kinds and styles of music—including classical music, popular music, jazz, American folk songs, and music of some other cultures. Syncopation generates a degree of rhythmic vitality in any melody in which it occurs. *Go Tell It On the Mountain* has both the basic syncopated pattern and variation *a* (see page 115). Read its melodic rhythm with syllables and/or counts, then chant its text in the same rhythm. You can play, as well as sing, this melody; right-hand fingerings are indicated.

GO TELL IT ON THE MOUNTAIN
Chorus: Spiritual

1. ta - a tim - ka tim - ka   ta - a ta - a   ti - ta - ti   ta   ta   ti - ti   ta   ti - ta - i
2. 1 - 2 3   a   4   a   1 - 2 3 - 4   1 & (2) & 3   4   1 & 2   3 & (4)
3. Go   tell it on the moun - tain,   O - ver the hills and ev - 'ry - where; __

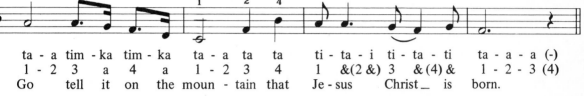

ta - a tim - ka tim - ka   ta - a ta   ta   ti - ta - i ti - ta - ti   ta - a - a (-)
1 - 2 3   a   4   a   1 - 2 3   4   1 &(2 &) 3 & (4) &   1 - 2 - 3 (4)
Go   tell it on the moun - tain that Je - sus   Christ __ is   born.

You're a Grand Old Flag uses the basic syncopated pattern in several measures. Rhythm syllables and counts have been omitted so that you can practice
sight reading the melodic rhythm. Scan the notated melody and identify its
various patterns, all of which are familiar to you. Read its rhythm in your usual
way with syllables or counts to a clapped marching beat, then try singing and/or
playing the melody. Observe two *acccidentals* (Chapter Three) that occur as an
E-flat and an F-sharp toward the end.

YOU'RE A GRAND OLD FLAG
Words and Music by George M. Cohan

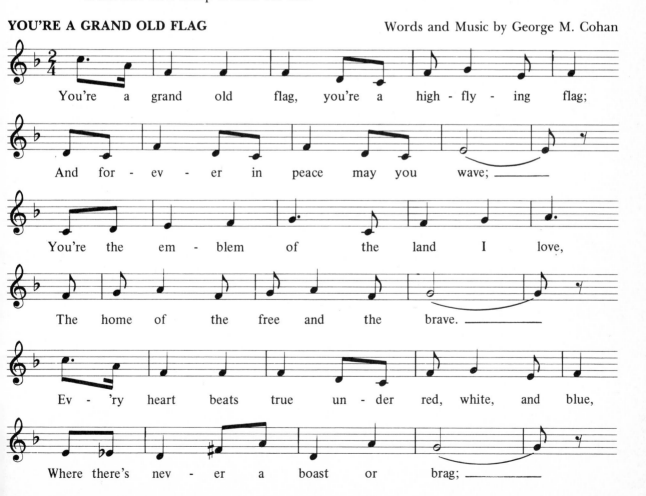

You're   a   grand   old   flag,   you're   a   high - fly - ing   flag;

And   for - ev - er   in   peace   may   you   wave; _____

You're   the   em - blem   of   the   land   I   love,

The   home   of   the   free   and   the   brave. _____

Ev - 'ry   heart   beats   true   un - der   red,   white,   and   blue,

Where there's nev - er   a   boast   or   brag; _____

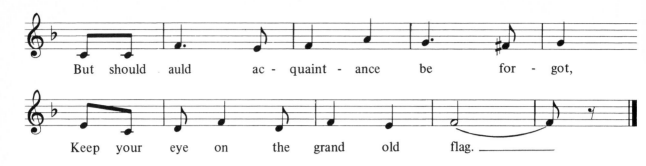

But should auld ac - quaint - ance be for - got,

Keep your eye on the grand old flag. _____

PRACTICE ACTIVITIES

Notating

1. You are given a model of notated patterns with corresponding syllables and counts, all with a meter signature of two-four. On the blank rhythm lines, correctly notate in each measure the pattern that is indicated.

Model:

(a) Notate from syllables:

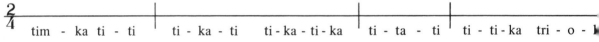

(b) Notate from counts:

2. You are given three lines of notated patterns, each with a meter signature. Draw bar lines at appropriate points to create complete measures.

Identifying

3. You are given four melodic excerpts from actual song melodies. Follow the example given for the first measure of excerpt *a* and in all excerpts: a) mark the onset of each beat with a downward arrow, b) write rhythm syllables for all patterns in the top line of blanks, and c) write counts for all patterns in the bottom line of blanks.

(a)

beats: ↓   ↓

syllables: ti - ka - ti - ka ti - ti - ka __ __ __ __ __ __ __ __ __ __ __ __ __

counts: 1   e   &   a   2   &   a   __ __ __ __ __ __ __ __ __ __ __ __ __

(b)

(c)

(d)

4. You are given four choices of rhythm patterns (*a, b, c, d*) from which to select one pattern that would complete each of the incomplete measures (1 through 6) in four-four meter. Actually notate at the end of each measure the pattern you have chosen (a pattern may be used more than once).

(a)   *(b)*   *(c)*   *(d)*

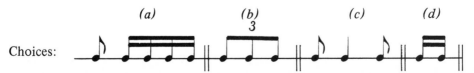

Choices:

Notate the pattern (*a, b, c,* or *d*) that completes each measure:

Creating

5. You are given the first phrase of each of two (*a, b*) incomplete melodies, including key and meter signatures. Play the given phrase in order to become acquainted with its rhythm patterns and pitch movement. Create an original second phrase that would incorporate the designated elements and satisfactorily complete the melody. Notate your phrase in the blank measures.

(a) F Major: Complete the second two-measure phrase, ending on the tonic note and using one triplet and one subdivided pattern.

(b) G Major: Complete the second three-measure phrase, ending on the tonic note and using either one syncopated or one subdivided pattern.

Reading

6. Continue to practice reading the rhythm in all exercises and song melodies presented in the *Study Activities*.

7. Read with rhythm syllables or counts the melodic rhythm of each excerpt in activity 3 (page 119).

8. Sight-read with rhythm syllables and/or counts the melodic rhythm of *Shoo Fly*. Try playing the melody with the fingerings indicated (the Refrain is repeated following the Verse). You also can use I (F) and V⁷ (C⁷) chords to accompany this melody.

SHOO FLY
U.S. Folk Song

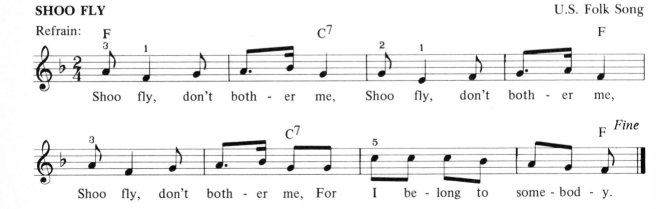

I feel, I feel, I feel like a morn-ing star,

I feel, I feel, I feel like a morn-ing star.

Discriminating (Aural-Visual)

Activity 9 should be administered by an instructor or student assistant.

9. In each notated item (a through f) you see three different rhythm patterns, each occupying a complete measure in the same meter. You will hear one of the patterns chanted on a neutral syllable (*lah*) with an accompanying beat. Circle the number of the pattern you hear performed.

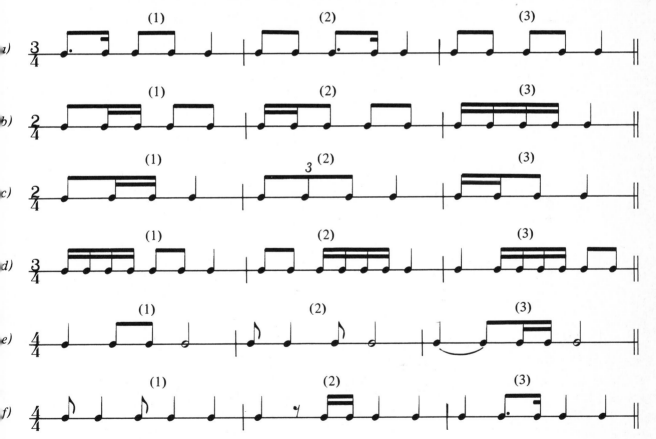

Performing

10. Sing with their texts at least three of the following songs:
a. *Hush, Little Baby*
b. *What Shall I Do with a Drunken Sailor?*

    c. *Ol' Texas*
    d. *Sing, Sing Together*
    e. *Battle Hymn of the Republic*
    f. *Go Tell It on the Mountain*
    g. *You're a Grand Old Flag*
    h. *Shoo Fly*

11. Play at least two song melodies chosen from those listed in activity 10.

12. Play one, or both, of the following song melodies with a chordal accompaniment comprised of the tonic and dominant-seventh chords.
    a. *Hush, Little Baby*
    b. *Shoo Fly*

AFTER YOU HAVE COMPLETED ALL **PRACTICE ACTIVITIES** AND REVIEWED THE **OBJECTIVES,** CONTINUE WITH THE **ASSESSMENT OF PROGRESS.**

ASSESSMENT OF PROGRESS

A. *Applied knowledge.* Part A can be completed as a self-administered test without reference to any other material. Write your responses in the blanks beside item numbers and, when you have finished all of Part A, check your answers with those in *Keys to Chapter Assessments,* page 249. Correct all of your errors and restudy relevant material in the *Study Activities* and *Practice Activities* before continuing to Chapter Six.

Answer questions 1 through 4 with reference to *Do, Lord, Remember Me.*

DO, LORD, REMEMBER ME
                                                               Spiritual

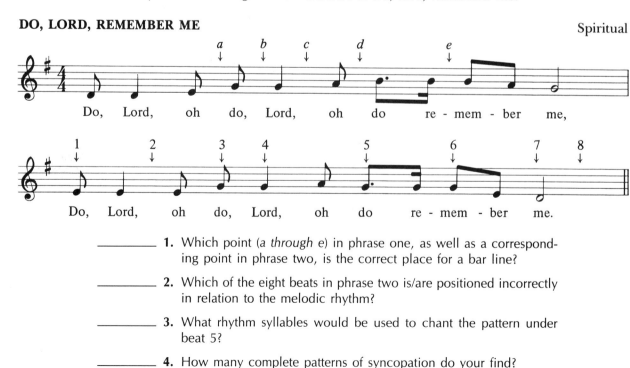

_____ **1.** Which point (*a* through *e*) in phrase one, as well as a corresponding point in phrase two, is the correct place for a bar line?

_____ **2.** Which of the eight beats in phrase two is/are positioned incorrectly in relation to the melodic rhythm?

_____ **3.** What rhythm syllables would be used to chant the pattern under beat 5?

_____ **4.** How many complete patterns of syncopation do your find?

Answer questions 5 through 11 with reference to *Camptown Races*.

CAMPTOWN RACES   Stephen Foster

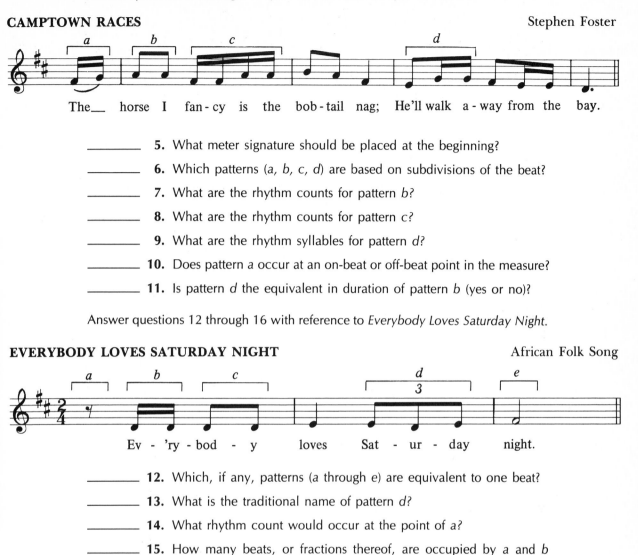

The__ horse I fan-cy is the bob-tail nag; He'll walk a-way from the bay.

_____ **5.** What meter signature should be placed at the beginning?

_____ **6.** Which patterns (*a, b, c, d*) are based on subdivisions of the beat?

_____ **7.** What are the rhythm counts for pattern *b*?

_____ **8.** What are the rhythm counts for pattern *c*?

_____ **9.** What are the rhythm syllables for pattern *d*?

_____ **10.** Does pattern *a* occur at an on-beat or off-beat point in the measure?

_____ **11.** Is pattern *d* the equivalent in duration of pattern *b* (yes or no)?

Answer questions 12 through 16 with reference to *Everybody Loves Saturday Night*.

EVERYBODY LOVES SATURDAY NIGHT   African Folk Song

Ev - 'ry - bod - y   loves   Sat - ur - day   night.

_____ **12.** Which, if any, patterns (*a* through *e*) are equivalent to one beat?

_____ **13.** What is the traditional name of pattern *d*?

_____ **14.** What rhythm count would occur at the point of *a*?

_____ **15.** How many beats, or fractions thereof, are occupied by *a* and *b* together?

_____ **16.** On what count of the measure does pattern *d* occur?

   B. *Skills.* Part B is an assessment of the level of skills in reading and performing rhythm patterns you developed during the study of this chapter. It should be administered to you by an instructor or student assistant, and you should achieve the minimum acceptable level, or a higher level, before continuing to Chapter Six.

   1. Minimum acceptable level of performance:
   a. Chant, with either rhythm syllables or counts to a clapped beat, at least two exercises of your choice from each of these pages: 108–09, 113, 116.
   b. Chant in the same way the melodic rhythm of one song of your choice from each group:
   1) *Hush, Little Baby* or *Ol' Texas*
   2) *Sing, Sing Together* or *Swinging Along*
   3) *Go Tell It On the Mountain* or *Shoo Fly*

      c. Play and/or sing the melody of one of these songs:
         1) *Hush, Little Baby*
         2) *Go Tell It On the Mountain*

2. Higher level of performance:
    a. Chant, with either rhythm syllables or counts to a clapped beat, any exercises selected by the instructor from these pages: 108–09, 113, 116.
    b. Chant, with rhythm syllables or counts to a clapped beat, the melodic rhythm of the following songs:
      1) *What Shall I Do with a Drunken Sailor?*
      2) *Ol' Texas*
      3) *Swinging Along*
      4) *Battle Hymn of the Republic*
      5) *You're a Grand Old Flag*
      6) *Go Tell It On the Mountain*
    c. Sing with accurate rhythm at least two songs listed under 2*b*.
    d. Play with accurate rhythm the melody and chordal accompaniment of either *Hush, Little Baby* or *Shoo Fly*.

Chapter 6
Other Beat Units

INSTRUCTIONS

1. Read the *Objectives* to gain an initial acquaintance with competencies you should have acquired by the end of this chapter.

2. Complete all *Study Activities*. Give priority to developing your skills in recognizing, reading, and performing familiar rhythm patterns written with new meter signatures introduced in this chapter.

3. Complete with accurate responses all *Practice Activities* before proceeding to the assessment of progress.

4. As soon as you are ready, or when directed by your instructor, complete the *Assessment of Progress*. You should achieve the criterion levels that are indicated before continuing to Chapter Seven.

OBJECTIVES

1. Give both *absolute* and *applied* meanings for all of these meter signatures:

2 or ¢	3	4
2	2	2

2	3	4
8	8	8

2. Define *true beat* and *alle breve* and give a second applied meaning, relevant to very fast tempos, for these signatures: $\frac{4}{4}$ or **C** $\frac{3}{4}$ $\frac{3}{8}$

3. *Transcribe* (rewrite) a given melodic rhythm, using another meter signature that has the same top number but a different bottom number—for example, from $\frac{3}{4}$ to $\frac{3}{8}$.

4. Identify: a) various kinds of notated patterns written with meter signatures listed in objective 1, b) patterns found in sextuple meter with a signature of $\frac{6}{8}$, c) correct placement of bar lines, d) complete and incomplete measures of notation, and e) the appropriate meter signature for a given melodic rhythm.

5. Read, with rhythm syllables and/or counts to a clapped beat, exercises and melodic rhythms included in this chapter.

6. Given choices of different notated rhythm patterns, identify the one you hear performed.

7. Play the melody of at least two songs contained in this chapter.

8. Sing with words of their texts, and with or without the aid of a piano or second person, at least two songs from this chapter.

STUDY ACTIVITIES

Thus far, all rhythm you have read and performed has been written in simple meters in which a quarter note functioned as the beat unit, and all of the various patterns (divided, subdivided, syncopated, triplet) were written with notes of appropriate related values. Now, we come to an interesting factor with regard to notating and reading rhythm: In simple meters, the same patterns are encountered over and over, but they are not always written with the same note values, due to the fact that different kinds of notes can be used to represent one beat.

Theoretically, any basic note—whole, half, quarter, eighth, or sixteenth—can be employed as a *beat unit* by composers and others who notate music. Practically, however, we find only quarter, half, and eighth notes commonly used. You will continue in this chapter to read the same patterns previously experienced, but you will see them notated with meter signatures of $\frac{2}{2}$, $\frac{3}{2}$ and $\frac{4}{2}$ in which the half note is the beat unit, and with signatures of $\frac{2}{8}$, $\frac{3}{8}$, $\frac{4}{8}$, and $\frac{6}{8}$ in which an eighth note receives one beat. Finally, you will be introduced to some additional *applied meanings* of a few familiar signatures such as $\frac{4}{4}$ and $\frac{3}{4}$.

THE HALF NOTE AS BEAT UNIT

Meter Signatures

Half notes are probably next to quarter notes in frequency of use as beat units in simple meters. Their commonality necessitates familiarity with three meter signatures, shown here with both their *absolute* and *applied* meanings.

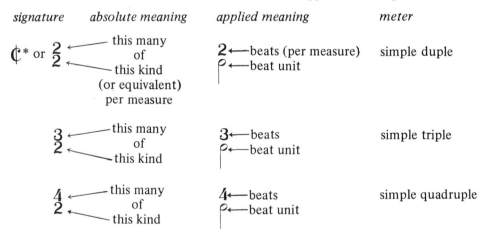

signature	absolute meaning	applied meaning	meter
¢ * or $\frac{2}{2}$	this many of this kind (or equivalent) per measure	2←beats (per measure) / ♩←beat unit	simple duple
$\frac{3}{2}$	this many of this kind	3←beats / ♩←beat unit	simple triple
$\frac{4}{2}$	this many of this kind	4←beats / ♩←beat unit	simple quadruple

*This signature, called *alla breve* or *cut time*, is a traditionally optional way of writing $\frac{2}{2}$ and has exactly the same interpretation.

Patterns

The three meter signatures cited represent *simple meters* based on a half-note beat unit. Patterns of duration that you have previously dealt with are now to be derived from combining or dividing the half note instead of the quarter note. Study comparative measures, one above another, and observe that they contain the same pattern of sound (and silence) notated differently. Chant, with rhythm syllables and/or counts to a clapped beat, each familiar pattern (each measure) from its notation in four-two.

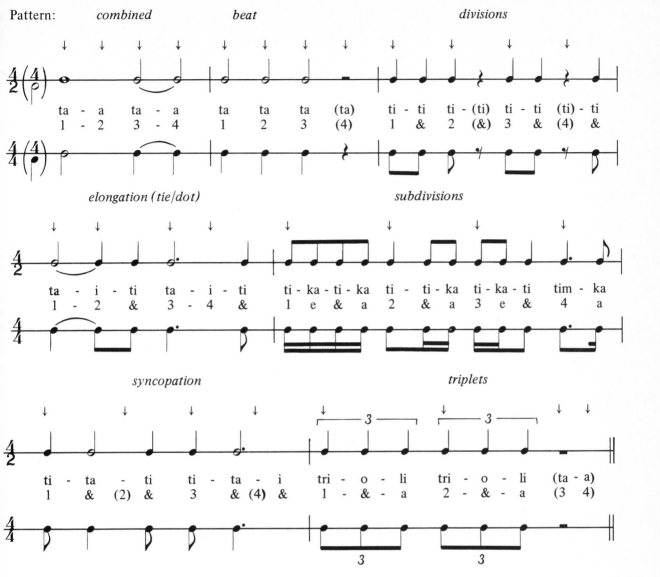

Another productive way to develop comprehension of patterns based on different beat units is through *rhythm transcription*, which is a process of rewriting music with a meter signature that has the same top number (meter) but a different bottom number (beat unit). The rewritten melodic rhythm will sound exactly like the original, but it will appear differently in notation. Here is a basic rule of transcription: To go from a bottom number of one value to a bottom number double that value requires doubling the value of every note and rest in the piece, or, to go from a bottom number of one value to a bottom number of half that value requires halving the value of every note and rest.

Observe the first four measures of *Hush, Little Baby,* written in two-four (the way you learned it in Chapter Five) and rewritten in two-two. The bottom number has been changed from four (quarter note) to two (half note), and each note, therefore, has been doubled in value—an eighth becomes a quarter, etc. Assuming the same tempo, this melody will sound exactly the same played or sung from either version. Whoever writes a piece of music chooses the beat unit (bottom number). Sometimes the choice is based on particular musical reasons, but in other cases it is somewhat arbitrary. Our job as readers of music notation is to interpret correctly what we see.

HUSH, LITTLE BABY

original rhythm:

Hush, lit - tle ba - by, don't say a word, Pa - pa's gon-na buy you a mock-ing bird.

transcribed rhythm:

Hush, lit - tle ba - by, don't say a word, Pa - pa's gon-na buy you a mock-ing bird.

Reading Patterns

By way of preparation for reading melodic rhythms, practice chanting each exercise with syllables or counts to a clapped beat until you have acquired a strong aural-visual-kinesthetic response to familiar patterns in two-two, three-two, and four-two. Make sure that you attain skill in reading from the notated patterns instead of merely following the written syllables or counts.

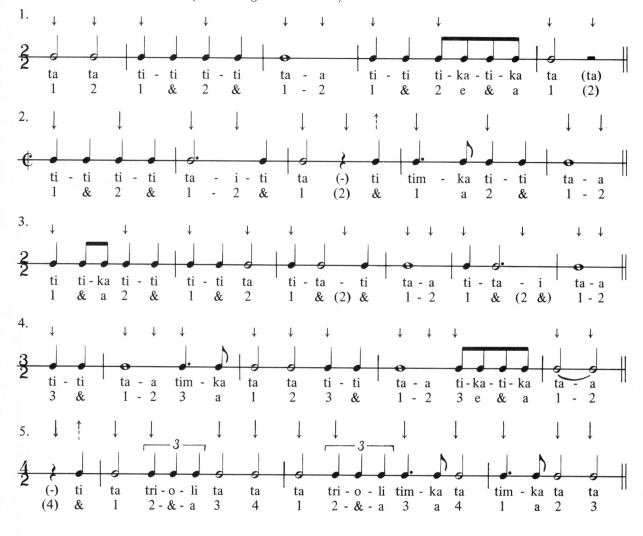

Reading and Performing Melodic Rhythm

Pieces written with meter signatures that set a half-note beat unit are fairly common; the next four songs are representative. Learn each song by chanting its melodic rhythm with syllables or counts to a clapped tempo beat followed by singing and/or playing the melody in that same rhythm. Three melodies have right-hand fingerings given and are easy to play. Can you identify various kinds of patterns, such as on-beat and off-beat anacruses, syncopation, triplets, divided patterns, subdivided patterns, and tied values?

EV'RY NIGHT WHEN THE SUN GOES IN

U.S. Folk Song

Blues tempo

YELLOW ROSE OF TEXAS

U.S. Folk Song

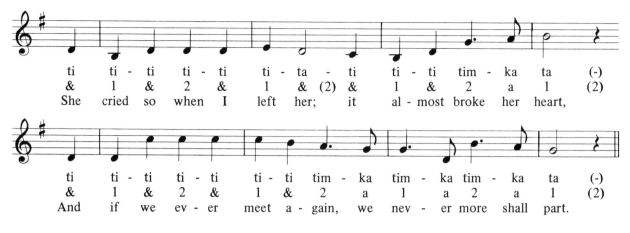

ti ti ti ti ti ti - ta - ti ti - ti tim - ka ta (-)
& 1 & 2 & 1 & (2) & 1 & 2 a 1 (2)
She cried so when I left her; it al - most broke her heart,

ti ti - ti ti - ti ti - ti tim - ka tim - ka tim - ka ta (-)
& 1 & 2 & 1 & 2 a 1 a 2 a 1 (2)
And if we ev - er meet a - gain, we nev - er more shall part.

ONCE TO EVERY MAN AND NATION

Music by T. J. Williams
Words by James Russell Lowell

Moderately

1. ta tri - o - li ta ta ta tri - o - li tim - ka ta
2. 1 2 - & - a 3 4 1 2 - & - a 3 a 4
3. Once to ev - 'ry man and na - tion

ta tri - o - li tim - ka ta tim - ka ta ta - a
1 2 - & - a 3 a 4 1 a 2 3 - 4
Comes the mo - ment to de - cide,

ta tri - o - li ta ta ta tri - o - li tim - ka ta
1 2 - & - a 3 4 1 2 - & - a 3 a 4
In the strife of truth with false - hood,

ta tri - o - li tim - ka ta tim - ka ta ta - a
1 2 - & - a 3 a 4 1 a 2 3 - 4
For the good or e - vil side.

WHEN THE SAINTS GO MARCHING IN

New Orleans Processional

March

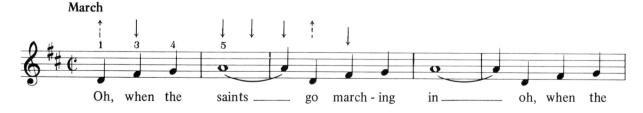

Oh, when the saints go march - ing in oh, when the

saints   go   march-ing   in, _____ how   I   want   to   be   in   that

num - ber, _____ when   the   saints   go   march - ing   in. _____

THE EIGHTH NOTE AS BEAT UNIT

Cases in which an eighth note functions as the true beat unit are less common than those in which quarter or half notes are beat units. However, some pieces, including traditional songs, have signatures with eight as their bottom number, and an eighth note actually represents one felt tempo beat. In the signatures shown, you will observe familiar duple (2), triple (3), and quadruple (4) meters plus one new meter called *sextuple* (6).

signature	absolute meaning	applied meaning	meter
$\frac{2}{8}$	this many of this kind (or equivalent) per measure	2 ←—beats (per measure) ♪ ←—beat unit	duple
$\frac{3}{8}$	this many of this kind	3 ←—beats ♪ ←—beat unit	triple
$\frac{4}{8}$	this many of this kind	4 ←—beats ♪ ←—beat unit	quadruple
$\frac{6}{8}$	this many of this kind	6 ←—beats ♪ ←—beat unit	sextuple

Patterns

Theoretically, all patterns you have read in music with quarter- and half-note beat units could be notated in meter signatures with an eight on the bottom. Actually, subdivided patterns (and even triplets and syncopation) are uncommon for practical reasons. Subdivision, for example, would require use of thirty-second notes that have three beams or flags, and these tend to appear more complex than they are. Persons who write music usually choose another meter signature—such as three-four instead of three-eight—if more unusual patterns are involved. Common patterns with which you need familiarity are illustrated here in three-eight. Practice chanting each pattern to a clapped beat.

Common patterns based on an eighth-note beat unit:

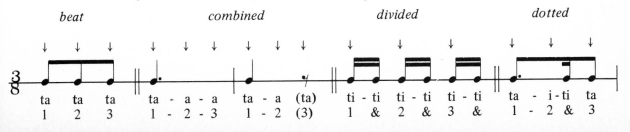

beat	combined	divided	dotted
ta ta ta	ta - a - a ta - a (ta)	ti - ti ti - ti ti - ti	ta - i-ti ta
1 2 3	1 - 2 - 3 1 - 2 (3)	1 & 2 & 3 &	1 - 2 & 3

Rhythm transcription, introduced earlier, also can be demonstrated by changing the bottom number from four to eight in a meter signature and rewriting the melodic rhythm with notes (and rests) of half their original values. This is shown with the first phrase of *America.*

AMERICA

Music by Henry Carey
Words by Samuel Francis Smith

original rhythm:

My coun-try, 'tis of thee, Sweet land of lib-er-ty, Of thee I sing;

transcribed rhythm:

Reading and Performing Melodic Rhythm

Traditional melodies written in two-eight or four-eight are so rare that we need not concern ourselves with examples. A few melodies in triple meter are notated in three-eight, and a few others are cast in sextuple meter (a multiple of triple meter) with a signature of six-eight. *We Three Kings of Orient Are* has a melodic rhythm comprised of only beat values and combined values (two- and three-beat notes). Read its rhythm to a clapped beat, then try playing the melody with the fingerings that are given. *The Alphabet Song,* also in three-eight, is a well-known tune by Mozart. Its melodic rhythm includes one-beat silences (eighth rests) and divided-beat patterns represented by sixteenth notes.

WE THREE KINGS OF ORIENT ARE

J. H. Hopkins

Moderately

1. ta - a ta ta - a ta ta ta ta ta - a - a ta - a ta
2. 1 - 2 3 1 - 2 3 1 2 3 1 - 2 - 3 1 - 2 3
3. We three kings of Or - i - ent are, Bear - ing

ta - a ta ta ta ta ta - a - a ta - a ta ta - a ta
1 - 2 3 1 2 3 1 - 2 - 3 1 - 2 3 1 - 2 3
gifts we trav - el a - far, Field and foun - tain

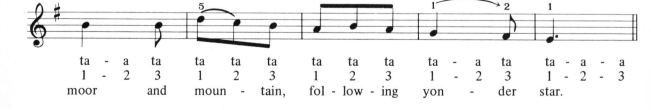

ta - a ta ta ta ta ta ta ta ta - a ta ta - a - a
1 - 2 3 1 2 3 1 2 3 1 - 2 3 1 - 2 - 3
moor and moun - tain, fol - low - ing yon - der star.

THE ALPHABET SONG
Mozart

Moderately fast

```
1. ta - a - a   ta - a - a   ta - a - a   ta - a - a   ta  ta  ta   ta  ta  ta
2. 1 - 2 - 3    1 - 2 - 3    1 - 2 - 3    1 - 2 - 3    1   2   3    1   2   3
3. A            B            C            D            E   F   G    H   I   J
```

```
ti - ti  ta  ta   ta - a (ta)   ti - ti  ta  ta   ta  ta  ta   ti - ti  ta  ta
1   &  2  3        1 - 2 (3)     1   &  2  3        1   2   3    1   &  2  3
K   L  M  N        O,            K   L   M   N      O   P   Q,   K   L   M   N
```

```
ta  ta  ta   ta  ta  ta   ta  ta  ta   ti - ti  ti - ti  ti - ti   ta - a (ta)
1   2   3    1   2   3    1   2   3    1   &  2  &  3  &            1 - 2 (3)
O   P   Q    R   S   T    U   V   W    X___     Y___     and___    Z.
```

SEXTUPLE METER

Six-eight is one of the most common meter signatures in music. But six-eight is a signature with two functional applied meanings, each of which requires special interpretation and perception of its notated patterns. One application places six-eight in a category of metric organization referred to as compound duple meter, which is by far its most frequent use and one that is fully presented in Chapter Nine. At this point, we are interested in six-eight only in those relatively few cases where it results in *sextuple meter*, which is a metric grouping of six beats—actually felt and clapped—per measure.

You should realize that sextuple meter is really a combination of two triple metric groups, and that you will find the same patterns occuring in both six-eight and three-eight—measures in six-eight are merely twice as long. (A similar relation exists between quadruple and duple meters.) *Home On the Range* contains a good variety of basic patterns in sextuple meter. Accuracy in performing them can be acquired best by chanting the melodic rhythm with syllables or counts to a moderately quick beat. Of course, you should also sing and/or play this melody.

HOME ON THE RANGE
U.S. Folk Song

Verse

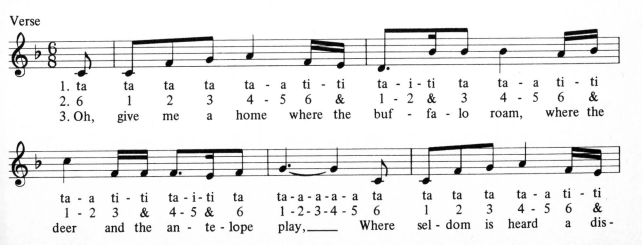

```
1. ta    ta  ta  ta   ta - a  ti - ti   ta - i - ti  ta   ta - a  ti - ti
2. 6     1   2   3    4 - 5 6  &         1 - 2 & 3    4 - 5 6  &
3. Oh,   give me  a    home   where the  buf - fa - lo roam,    where the
```

```
ta - a  ti - ti  ta - i - ti  ta   ta - a - a - a - a  ta   ta  ta  ta   ta - a  ti - ti
1 - 2   3  &  4 - 5  &  6      1 - 2 - 3 - 4 - 5  6     1    2   3   4 - 5 6  &
deer    and the  an - te - lope play,___    Where      sel - dom is heard a  dis-
```

ta - i - ti ta	ta - a ti - ti	ta - i - ti ta	ta - i - ti ta	ta - a - a - a
1 - 2 & 3	4 - 5 6 &	1 - 2 & 3	4 - 5 & 6	1 - 2 - 3 - 4 - 5
cour - ag - ing word,	And the skies	are not cloud - y	all	day._____

TRUE BEAT AND OTHER APPLIED MEANINGS

In Chapter Two we defined beat as the regular, recurring pulsation that is felt underlying all traditional music. We now will call this sensed pulsation the *true beat:* the beat we naturally feel, clap, or tap our foot to when we hear music, and the same beat that a musician perceives, or a conductor "beats," as he or she performs music. A type of paradox arises when we attempt to generalize a relation between the kind of note that represents one beat and the bottom number of a meter signature. In a vast majority of cases in simple meters—the only situations you have experienced so far—the *true beat unit* does correspond to the bottom number. In certain other cases, usually resulting from very fast or very slow tempos, a note of larger or smaller value than the bottom number functions as the true beat unit. In other words, the meter signature takes on a new applied meaning and is interpreted differently. We will illustrate only common situations in which signatures of four-four, three-four, and three-eight have different meanings in pieces that move at a very fast tempo. You will notice that absolute meaning of a given signature remains the same, that fast four-four becomes the same as *cut time* (or two-two), and that a dotted note becomes the beat unit in fast triple meter.

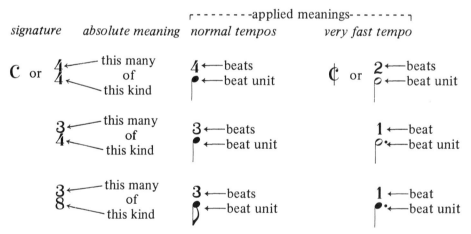

Excerpts from three familiar songs will demonstrate the meaning of *true beat* and its relation to signatures and melodic rhythms. Chant, then sing, each excerpt to a clapped (true) beat. You will feel two half-note beats per measure in *Old MacDonald,* one dotted-half-note beat per measure in *Sidewalks of New York,* and one dotted-eighth-note beat per measure in *Du, Du Liegst Mir im Herzen.*

OLD MACDONALD HAD A FARM

U.S. Folk Song

SIDEWALKS OF NEW YORK
Charles B. Lawler

East side, west side, All a - round the town,_____

DU, DU LIEGST MIR IM HERZEN
German Folk Song

Du, du liegst mir im Herz - en, Du, du liegst mir im Sinn,
You, you live in my heart,— You, you live in my mind,

PRACTICE ACTIVITIES

Page references to relevant *Study Activities* are given in parentheses.

Notating

1. You are given a model of common rhythm patterns written, along with their syllables and counts, in two-two. On the blank rhythm lines, correctly notate in each measure the pattern that is indicated below line *a* with syllables and below line *b* with counts. (127)

Model:

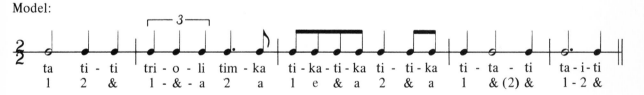

a. notate from syllables:

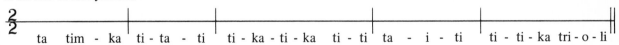

b. notate from counts:

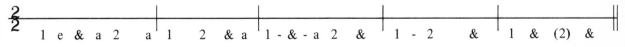

2. Follow the same instructions given in activity 1 and notate the indicated patterns in three-eight. (131)

Model:

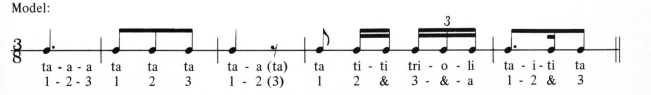

a. notate from syllables:

ta   ti - ti   ta   ta - i - ti   ta   ta - a   tri - o - li   ta - a - a   ta - a (ta)

b. notate from counts:

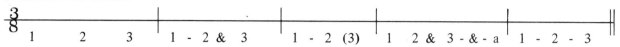

1   2   3   1 - 2 & 3   1 - 2 (3)   1   2 & 3 - & - a   1 - 2 - 3

3. You are given an excerpt from the familiar melody *Skip to My Lou* written in two-four. On the blank staff, transcribe (rewrite) the melody in two-two so that it will sound like the original. (127–28)

SKIP TO MY LOU

original:

Choose your part - ner,   skip   to   my Lou,   Skip   to   my Lou, my   dar - ling.

rewrite in $\frac{2}{2}$:

Choose your part - ner,   skip   to   my Lou,   Skip   to   my Lou, my   dar - ling.

Identifying

4. You are given excerpts from five song melodies notated with appropriate meter signatures but without bar lines. Follow the example worked out at the beginning of the first melody and complete these tasks in sequence:
   a. Draw *bar lines* at appropriate places to form complete measures in keeping with the meter signature.
   b. Write in the lower line of blanks rhythm *counts* that correspond to the notated melodic patterns.
   c. Write in the upper line of blanks rhythm *syllables* that correspond to the notated melodic patterns.

SANTA LUCIA   Neapolitan Boat Song

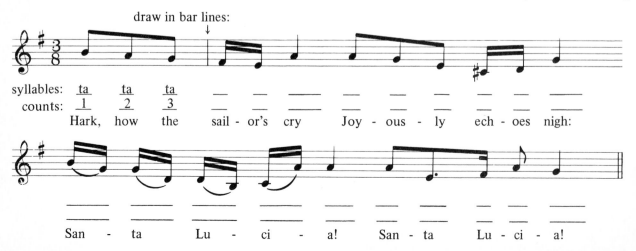

draw in bar lines:

syllables: ta   ta   ta   __   __   __   __   __   __
counts: 1   2   3   __   __   __   __   __   __
           Hark, how the sail - or's cry Joy - ous - ly ech - oes nigh:

San - ta   Lu - ci - a!   San - ta   Lu - ci - a!

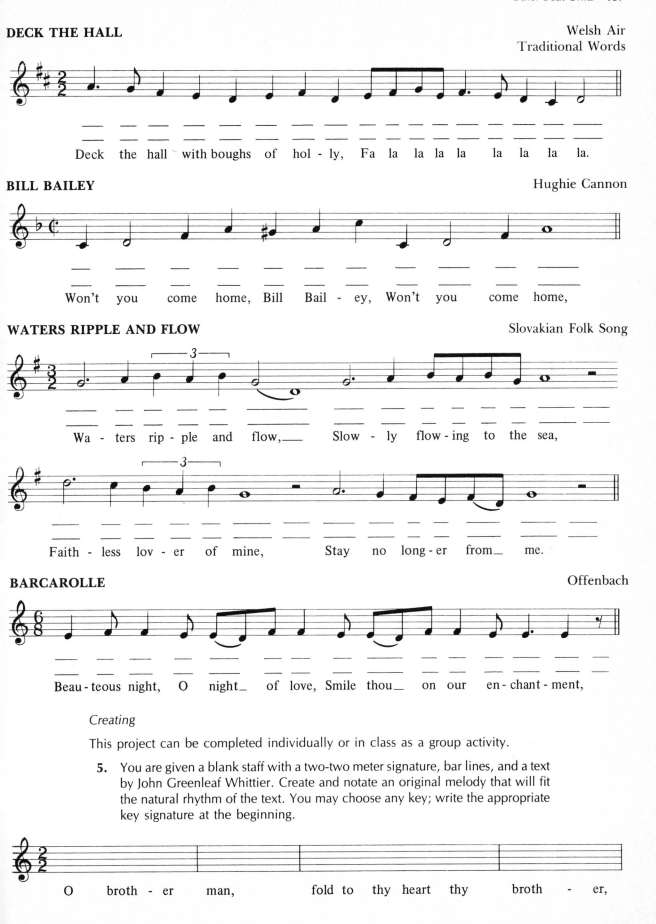

DECK THE HALL

Welsh Air
Traditional Words

Deck the hall with boughs of hol - ly, Fa la la la la la la la la.

BILL BAILEY

Hughie Cannon

Won't you come home, Bill Bail - ey, Won't you come home,

WATERS RIPPLE AND FLOW

Slovakian Folk Song

Wa - ters rip - ple and flow,___ Slow - ly flow - ing to the sea,

Faith - less lov - er of mine, Stay no long - er from_ me.

BARCAROLLE

Offenbach

Beau - teous night, O night_ of love, Smile thou_ on our en - chant - ment,

Creating

This project can be completed individually or in class as a group activity.

5. You are given a blank staff with a two-two meter signature, bar lines, and a text by John Greenleaf Whittier. Create and notate an original melody that will fit the natural rhythm of the text. You may choose any key; write the appropriate key signature at the beginning.

O broth - er man, fold to thy heart thy broth - er,

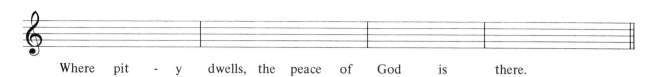

Where pit - y dwells, the peace of God is there.

Reading

6. Continue to practice reading the rhythm in all exercises and songs presented in the *Study Activities*.

7. Read with rhythm syllables or counts each melodic excerpt in activity 4.

8. Sight read the melodic rhythm of each of the following song melodies. Maintain an appropriate tempo beat and chant the patterns with either rhythm syllables or counts.

DEEP IN THE HEART OF TEXAS

Don Swander
June Hershey

BELIEVE ME, IF ALL THOSE ENDEARING YOUNG CHARMS

Irish Air
Words by Thomas Moore

Discriminating (Aural-Visual)

Activity 9 should be administered by an instructor or student assistant.

9. In each notated item (a through i) you see three different rhythm patterns that occupy a complete measure with the same meter signature. Circle the number of the pattern you hear chanted on the syllable *lah* to an accompanying beat.

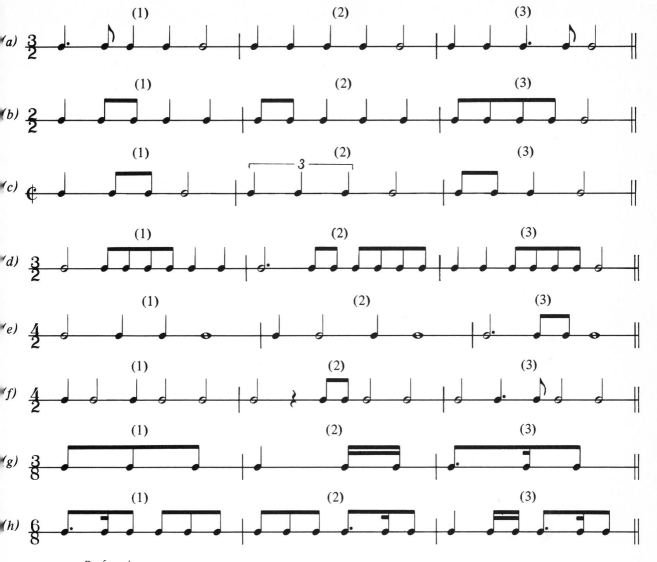

Performing

10. Sing with the words of their texts at least three songs presented in the *Study Activities*, and play the melody of at least two of them.

AFTER YOU HAVE COMPLETED ALL **PRACTICE ACTIVITIES** AND RE-VIEWED THE **OBJECTIVES,** CONTINUE WITH THE **ASSESSMENT OF PROGRESS.**

ASSESSMENT OF PROGRESS

A. *Applied knowledge.* Part A can be completed as a self-administered test without reference to any other material. Write your responses in the blanks beside item numbers and, when you have finished all of Part A, check your answers with those in *Keys to Chapter Assessments*, page 249. Correct all of your errors and restudy relevant material in the *Study Activities* and *Practice Activities* before continuing to Chapter Seven.

Answer questions 1 through 8 with reference to your selection of the correct note (choice 1, 2, 3, or 4) to complete each incomplete measure (*a* through *h*). Observe the meter signature given for each measure.

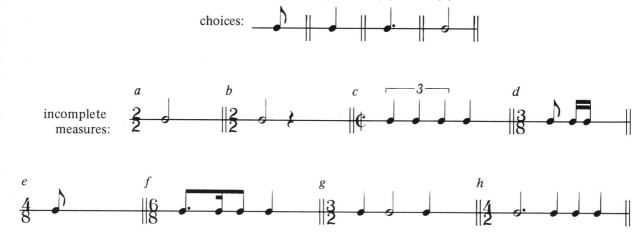

1. Which note (choice 1, 2, 3, or 4) would complete measure *a*?

2. Which note would complete measure *b*?

3. Which note would complete measure *c*?

4. Which note would complete measure *d*?

5. Which note would complete measure *e*?

6. Which note would compete measure *f*?

7. Which note would complete measure *g*?

8. Which note would complete measure *h*?

Answer questions 9 through 15 with reference to the excerpt from *Li'l 'Liza Jane,* which is notated without bar lines in two-two.

LI'L 'LIZA JANE

U.S. Folk Song

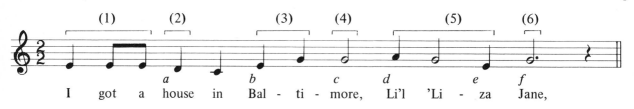

9. Which numbered note (2, 4, or 6) functions as the beat unit?

10. At which lettered points (*a* through *f*) should bar lines be drawn to form complete measures in the given signature?

11. What are the rhythm syllables for pattern (1)?

12. How would you count pattern (3)?

13. Which numbered pattern represents syncopation?

14. How many beats are occupied by pattern (1)?

15. How many beats are occupied by pattern (5)?

Answer questions 16 through 21 with reference to the excerpt from *When Jesus Wept,* which is notated correctly but without a meter signature.

WHEN JESUS WEPT   William Billings

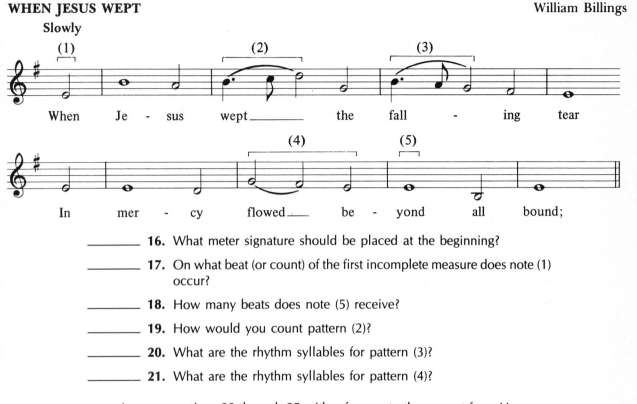

_____ **16.** What meter signature should be placed at the beginning?

_____ **17.** On what beat (or count) of the first incomplete measure does note (1) occur?

_____ **18.** How many beats does note (5) receive?

_____ **19.** How would you count pattern (2)?

_____ **20.** What are the rhythm syllables for pattern (3)?

_____ **21.** What are the rhythm syllables for pattern (4)?

Answer questions 22 through 25 with reference to the excerpt from *Home on the Range* in sextuple meter.

HOME ON THE RANGE

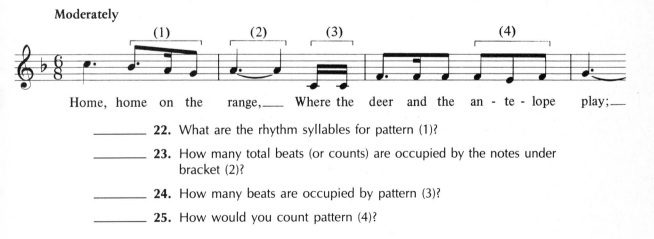

_____ **22.** What are the rhythm syllables for pattern (1)?

_____ **23.** How many total beats (or counts) are occupied by the notes under bracket (2)?

_____ **24.** How many beats are occupied by pattern (3)?

_____ **25.** How would you count pattern (4)?

B. *Skills.* Part B is an assessment of the level of skills you have developed in reading and performing rhythm patterns based on half- and eighth-note beat units. It should be administered to you by an instructor or a student assistant, and you should achieve the minimum acceptable level, or a higher level, before continuing to Chapter Seven.

1. Minimum acceptable level of performance:
   a. Chant, with either rhythm syllables or counts to a clapped beat, the following:
      1) at least two exercises on page 128
      2) the melodic rhythm of at least one song of your choice from group a and one from group b:
         a) *Ev'ry Night When the Sun Goes In*
            Yellow Rose of Texas
            Once to Every Man and Nation
            When the Saints Go Marching In
         b) *We Three Kings of Orient Are*
            The Alphabet Song
            Home on the Range
   b. Play and/or sing with its text the melody of at least one song of your choice from the following:
      1) *Ev'ry Night When the Sun Goes In*
      2) *Once to Every Man and Nation*
      3) *When the Saints Go Marching In*
      4) *We Three Kings of Orient Are*

2. Higher level of performance:
   a. Chant, with either rhythm syllables or counts to a clapped beat, the following:
      1) any exercises or melodic excerpts selected by your instructor from these pages: 128, 136–38
      2) the melodic rhythm of any songs selected by your instructor from the following list:
         a) *Yellow Rose of Texas*
         b) *Once to Every Man and Nation*
         c) *When the Saints Go Marching In*
         d) *The Alphabet Song*
         e) *Home on the Range*
         f) *Believe Me, If All Those Endearing Young Charms*
   b. Play and sing (either separately or simultaneously) the melody of any four songs of your choice from the preceding list.

Chapter 7

The Subdominant Chord in Harmony and Melody

INSTRUCTIONS

1. Read the *Objectives* to obtain an initial acquaintance with competencies you should have acquired by the end of this chapter. Keep these objectives in mind as you continue through the study and practice activities.

2. Complete all *Study Activities*. Your primary concern should be to understand the subdominant chord and to develop minimal skills in incorporating it into playing primary chord progressions and chordal accompaniments.

3. Complete all *Practice Activities,* striving for accuracy in your responses, in order to gain experience in applying your knowledge and improving your skills.

4. As soon as you are ready, or when directed by your instructor, complete the *Assessment of Progress*. You should achieve the criterion levels indicated before continuing to Chapter Eight.

5. If you want to try some styles of accompaniment other than the block-chord style used in this chapter, refer to optional Minichapter A. Also, you might want additional information on guitar chording found in optional Minichapter B.

OBJECTIVES

1. Identify, name, number, and notate (in root and keyboard positions) the subdominant (IV) chord in various major keys.

2. Identify, name, number, notate, and locate on the keyboard the three primary chords (I, IV, V^7) in representative major keys.

3. Play from memory (and from rules of finger-pitch movement) in selected major keys these chord progressions: I–IV–I, I–V^7–I, I–IV–V^7–I.

4. Read and play selected song melodies with a left-hand chordal accompaniment comprised of the I, IV, and V^7 chords.

5. Read and sing melodies that contain skips among notes of the primary chords.

6. Given a notated melody with chord markings, identify chord tones and nonchord tones in the melody.

7. Given a notated melody without chord markings, determine from a study of the melody which chords and progressions could be used to accompany it.

8. Given choices of either notated melodic intervals or symbolized chord progressions, identify the one you hear played (aural-visual discrimination).

STUDY ACTIVITIES

Chapter Four introduced you to concepts of vertical organization of pitch into harmonic intervals and chords. You learned how to identify chords by name (C, G), number (I, V), and function (tonic, dominant). More particularly, you dealt with the tonic (I) and dominant-seventh (V^7) chords, learning to identify them, play them in a I–V^7–I progression, and use them in creating chordal accompaniments with melodies. In the intervening units you have increased your knowledge of, and skill in reading, rhythm. Now is a good time to utilize those previous experiences and increase your repertory of chord progressions and melodies with accompaniments. The main new ingredient is a third chord to be added to the two with which you are familiar.

THE SUBDOMINANT (IV) CHORD

Identification

Since we are specifically interested in what have been called the three *primary chords* in any major key, we will illustrate in C major how these chords are constructed, named, and numbered. The *subdominant chord*, you will observe, is a major triad built from the fourth scale tone (4 or *fa*) and numbered with an upper-case numeral (IV). In C major the IV chord is an F-major triad whose *root* is F, whose *third* is A, and whose *fifth* is C. (You should also recall from Chapter Four that a major triad contains two harmonic thirds of which the bottom one is major and top one is minor.)

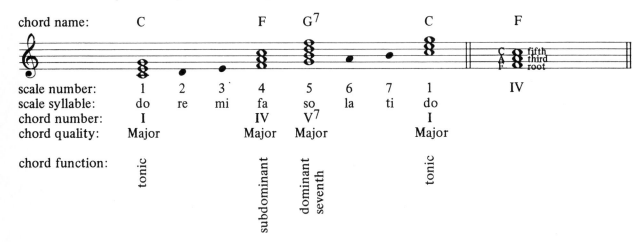

chord name:	C			F	G^7			C		F
scale number:	1	2	3	4	5	6	7	1		IV
scale syllable:	do	re	mi	fa	so	la	ti	do		
chord number:	I			IV	V^7			I		
chord quality:	Major			Major	Major			Major		
chord function:	tonic			subdominant	dominant seventh			tonic		

The I and IV chords are shown notated in root position in four additional common major keys to provide further illustration of how the subdominant chord is identified by numeral and name in a given key. Also, you should "spell" each chord with names of its pitches and realize that a major third (M3) exists between the triad's root and third, and a minor third (m3) occurs between its third and fifth.

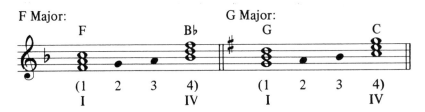

F Major: G Major:

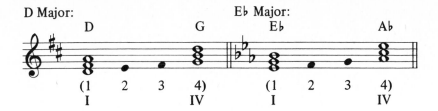

Inversion and Keyboard Position

You will recall from Chapter Four that the dominant-seventh in a I to V^7 progression is inverted so as to keep its notes in proximity to notes of the tonic chord. For the same reason, a I to IV chord progression employs an inverted subdominant chord (see illustration).

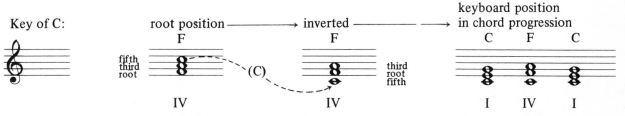

PRIMARY CHORD PROGRESSIONS

Most traditional melodies can be harmonized in a basic, if not the most colorful, way with no more than three primary chords from which three functional progressions are possible. You have played the first progression in chordal accompaniments in the keys of C, F, and G. Now you must practice the second and third progressions before attempting additional accompaniments.

1. $I–V^7–I$
2. $I–IV–I$
3. $I–IV–V^7–I$

The I to IV Progression

A chord progression, you will remember, can be played by applying rules of left-hand finger movements that correspond to note (pitch) changes and repetitions between chords. Here are rules for finger and pitch movement in going from the tonic to the subdominant chord *in any major key:*

> *Bottom note.* Keep the bottom note—which is common to both chords—the same and play it with the same finger (5 or little finger).
> *Middle note.* Move the middle note up a half step and change from third finger on the tonic-chord note to second (index) finger on the subdominant-chord note.
> *Top note.* Move the top note up a whole step and play it with the same finger (1 or thumb).

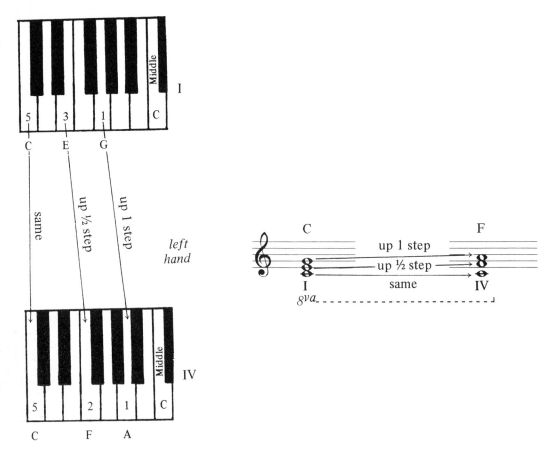

The I–IV–I and I–IV–V⁷–I Progressions

The next illustrations capture all factors involved in playing the three primary-chord progressions in C, F, and G. Carefully study them from standpoints of chord identifications, chord notations (treble and bass clefs), left-hand fingerings, and patterns of movement (relatively the same in each key). Practice each of the three progressions indicated below the keyboard photographs: I–IV–I, I–V⁷–I, and I–IV–V⁷–I. Your immediate objective should be to be able to play all progressions by simply thinking them, without reference to either the notated chords or keyboard pictures.

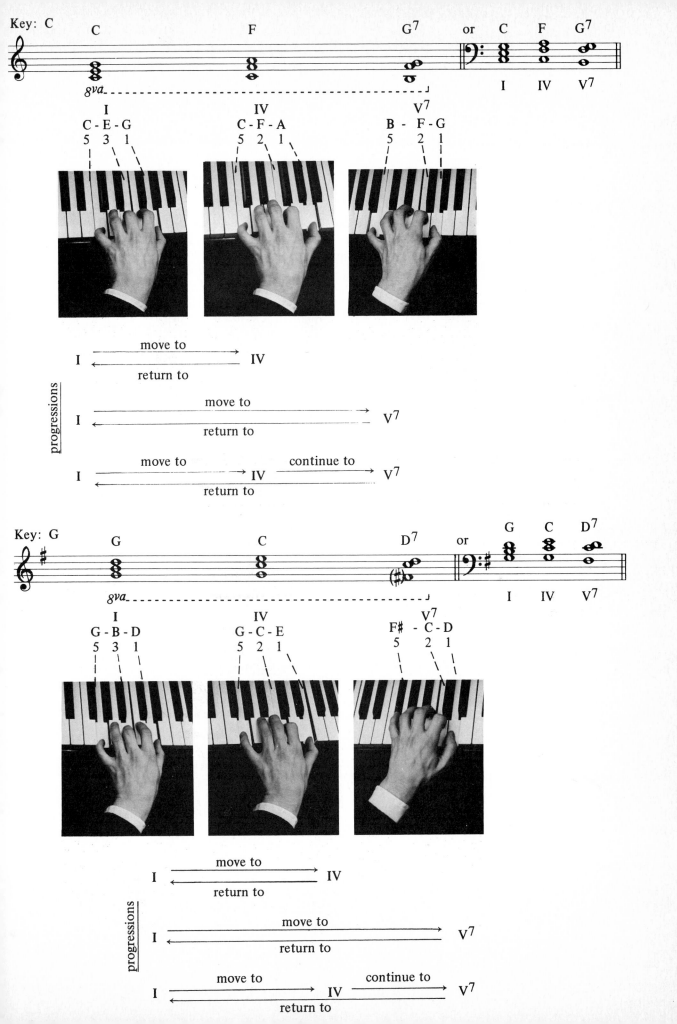

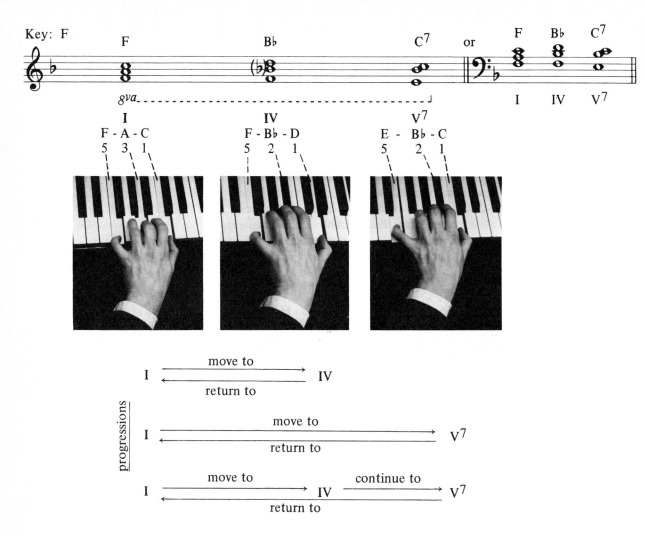

CHORDAL ACCOMPANIMENTS

Can you play the preceding primary chord progressions in C, F, and G? If so, you are ready to use them in chordal accompaniments to melodies in the same keys. Approach learning to play the next songs in the following ways:

1. Read the melodic rhythm with syllables or counts to a tempo beat.
2. Practice playing the melody alone until it can be performed in strict rhythm and with correct fingering.
3. Play the left-hand chord progressions as they occur at points indicated by their letter names above the staff. Realize which chord (I, IV, or V^7) you are going from and to, and apply the corresponding rules of finger-pitch movement.
4. Put melody and accompaniment together and practice until the song could be sung with your accompaniment.

By way of preview (and review), the three chords used in each key are shown as *block chords* notated in both treble (*8va*) and bass clefs for piano. In addition, guitar chord frames for the same chords are given for optional use. Styles of keyboard accompaniments other than block chords are illustrated in optional Minichapter A, and more information on guitar chording can be found in optional Minichapter B.

Accompaniments in C

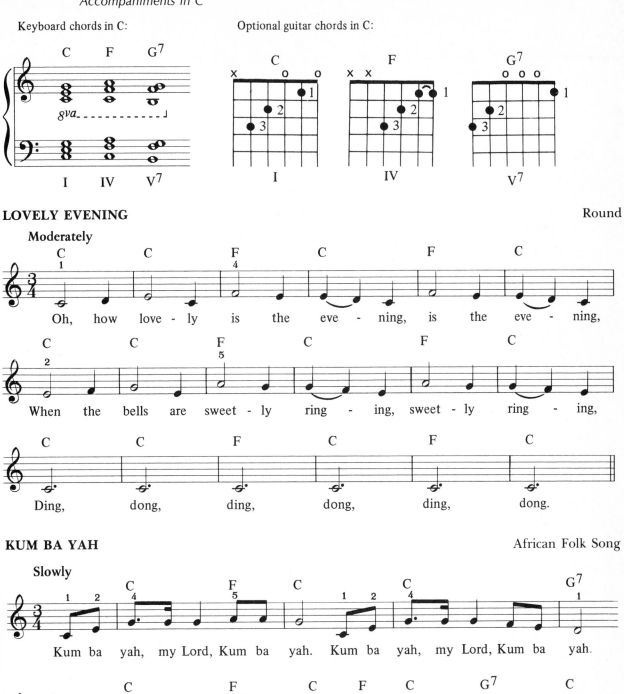

LOVELY EVENING   Round

Moderately

Oh, how love - ly   is   the   eve - ning,   is   the   eve - ning,

When   the   bells   are   sweet - ly   ring - ing, sweet - ly   ring - ing,

Ding,   dong,   ding,   dong,   ding,   dong.

KUM BA YAH   African Folk Song

Slowly

Kum ba   yah,   my Lord, Kum ba   yah.   Kum ba   yah,   my Lord, Kum ba   yah.

Kum ba   yah,   my Lord, Kum ba   yah.   Oh   Lord,___   Kum ba   yah.

Accompaniments in F

Keyboard chords in F:

Optional guitar chords in F:

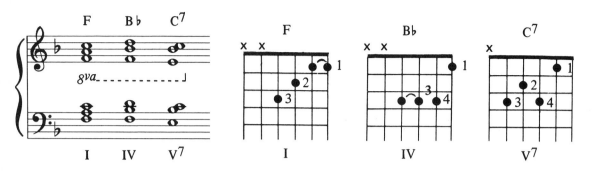

THE WATER IS WIDE

U.S. Folk Song

The wa - ter is wide, _____ I can - not get o'er,

And nei - ther have I _____ wings _____ to fly.

Give me a boat _____ that can car - ry two,

And both shall row, _____ my love and I.

MICHAEL, ROW THE BOAT ASHORE

Work Spiritual

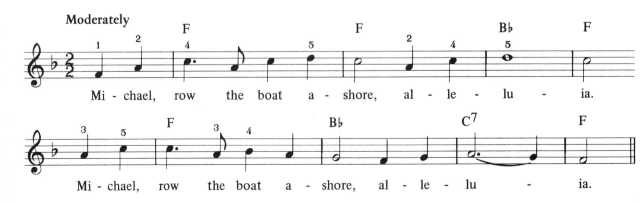

Mi - chael, row the boat a - shore, al - le - lu - ia.

Mi - chael, row the boat a - shore, al - le - lu - ia.

Accompaniments in G

Keyboard chords in G:

Optional guitar chords in G:

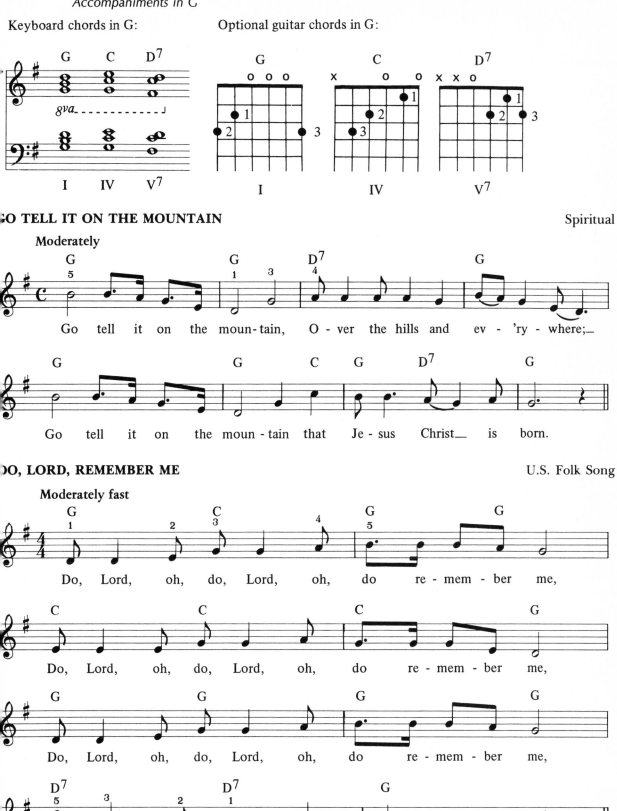

GO TELL IT ON THE MOUNTAIN

Spiritual

Moderately

Go tell it on the moun-tain, O - ver the hills and ev - 'ry - where;—

Go tell it on the moun - tain that Je - sus Christ— is born.

DO, LORD, REMEMBER ME

U.S. Folk Song

Moderately fast

Do, Lord, oh, do, Lord, oh, do re - mem - ber me,

Do, Lord, oh, do, Lord, oh, do re - mem - ber me,

Do, Lord, oh, do, Lord, oh, do re - mem - ber me,

Do, Lord, re - mem - ber me.

Accompaniments in Other Major Keys

Patterns of finger and pitch movement in the three primary-chord progressions are relatively the same in all major keys. A practical implication of this statement is that you should be able to play chordal accompaniments essentially as easily in one key as another, albeit some practice in other keys may be necessary. Demonstrate this proposition to yourself by *transposing* the familiar *Michael, Row the Boat Ashore*—melody and chords—to D major as notated here. Also, practice chord progressions in still other keys (for example, B-flat, E-flat, and E) by merely following the rules.

MICHAEL, ROW THE BOAT ASHORE   Work Spiritual

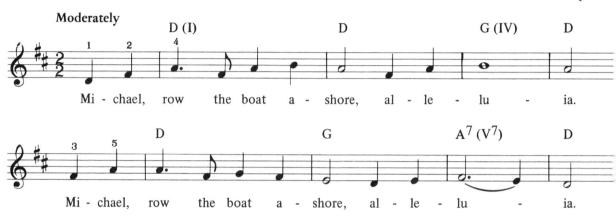

Mi - chael, row   the boat   a - shore,   al - le - lu - ia.

Mi - chael, row   the boat   a - shore,   al - le - lu - ia.

MELODY AND HARMONY

Melody and harmony are integrally related; melody grows out of harmony in traditional songs. Chapter Four introduced the idea that skips in melody are usually skips among notes of primary chords. Recognition of the specific chord from which melodic intervals arise can be an aid in accurately reading and singing the melody as well as in determining which chord is appropriate in the accompaniment. Study the chart of scale tones that are members of the I, IV, and V^7 chords in any major key, including tones common to two chords.

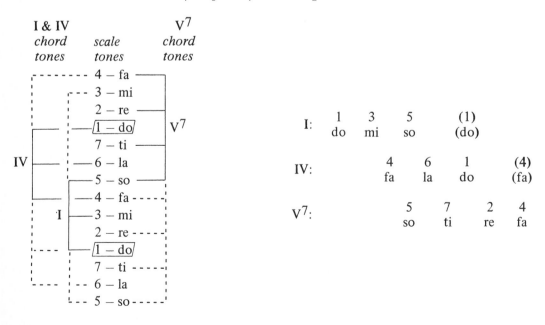

I: 1   3   5   (1)
     do   mi   so   (do)

IV: 4   6   1   (4)
               fa   la   do   (fa)

V^7:   5   7   2   4
               so   ti   re   fa

Reading Melodic Skips

The next illustrations show melodic skips written on the top treble staff and chords to which these notes belong notated on the bottom treble staff. Chord notes in parentheses are merely extensions of that chord into a higher or lower octave. Sing each melodic pattern while playing the chord as harmonic background. You will have a keen awareness of a relation between melodic intervals and harmony that should enable you to improve your ability to think and read chord skips.

Models of melodic chord skips in C, F, and G:

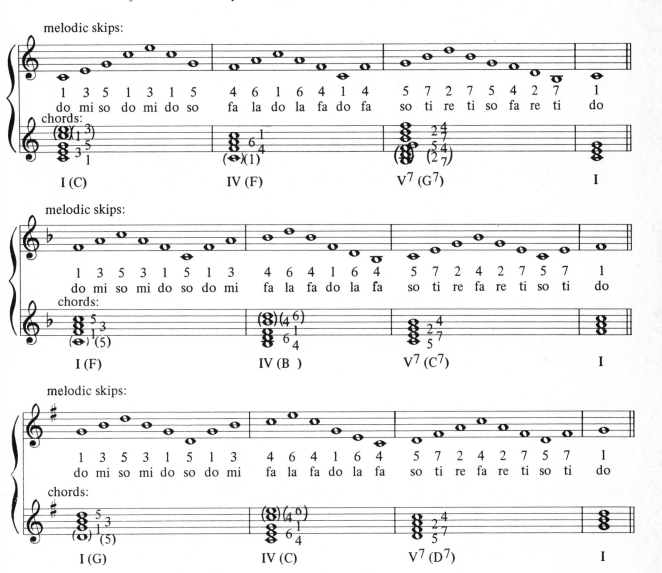

Harmonization of a Melody

Your experience in playing chordal accompaniments should provide a basis for determining which chords to use in harmonizing a melody and at which points to use them. You can create your own accompaniment from the melody alone by following these principles:

1. Simple chording should be economical. The same chord should be sustained or repeated so long as it sounds correct with the melody. Progression to another chord should be made only at points where a change in harmony is necessary to sound right with the melody.

2. Determine from an analysis of the melody which chord (I, IV, or V^7) will most likely sound best in each measure, or half measure. The most probable chord is the one that contains either all melodic notes it will underlie, or most of those notes, or the most important of those notes.

3. Some melodic notes that occur during a specific harmonizing chord may not belong to that chord, yet the accompaniment will sound acceptable with them. These *nonchord tones* do not ordinarily require a change of harmony at that point.

4. Aural confirmation is the final criterion for selecting correct chords. Do they individually sound well with the melody, and do they together create acceptable overall chord progressions?

Additional knowledge of *nonchord* (nonharmonic) *tones* will be useful before harmonizing a melody. They are mostly of two basic types: (1) A *passing tone* (P) is a note that occurs between two chord notes in a melody. (2) A *neighboring tone* (N), also called an auxiliary tone, is a note that lies a step either above or below a chord note and its repetition. Study the two melodic phrases that have labeled chord notes (arrows) and nonchord notes (N or P). Play the melodic phrases with chords that are indicated to confirm whether or not the harmonization is satisfactory, even though other harmonizations might be possible.

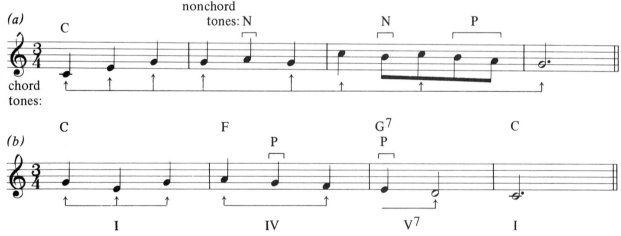

Now, study the melody of *On Top of Old Smoky* (C major) and improvise your own chordal accompaniment. Write in each blank above the staff the name of the primary chord that you believe should be used to harmonize the melody from that point to the point of the next chord, which can be either a repetition of the previous chord or a different one. Play the melody with chordal accompaniment and either confirm your selections or make corrections.

ON TOP OF OLD SMOKY U.S. Folk Song

PRACTICE ACTIVITIES

Page references to relevant *Study Activities* are given in parentheses.

Notating and Identifying

1. Follow the example, and for each given key signature:
   a. Notate in root position on the blank staff the I, IV, and V⁷ chords. You may write the IV and V⁷ either higher or lower than the tonic chord, whichever location places more notes on the staff.
   b. Write each chord name in the blank above it.
   c. "Spell" each chord with names of its notes.

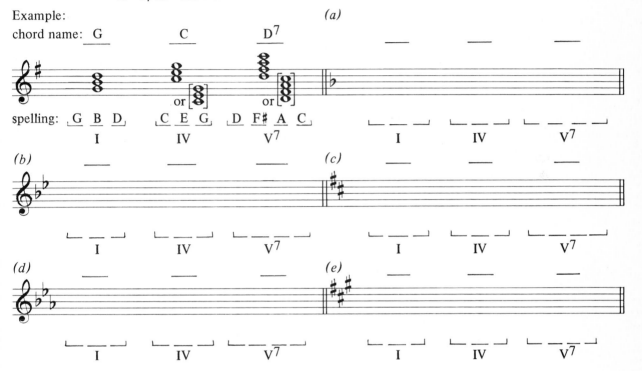

2. Follow the model and complete activities (a) and (b) as follows:
   a. Notate each primary chord in *keyboard position* above its numeral.
   b. Write chord names in the blanks above the staff.
   c. Write the name of each chord note (tone), along with the left-hand finger number, on the piano key that would produce it.

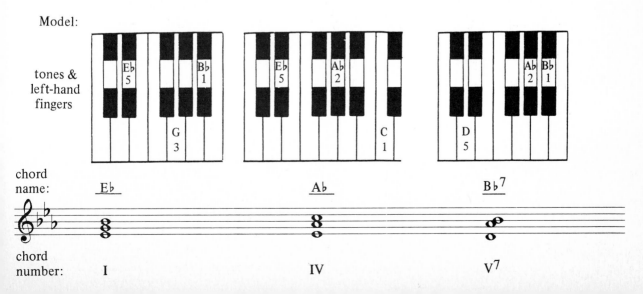

(a)

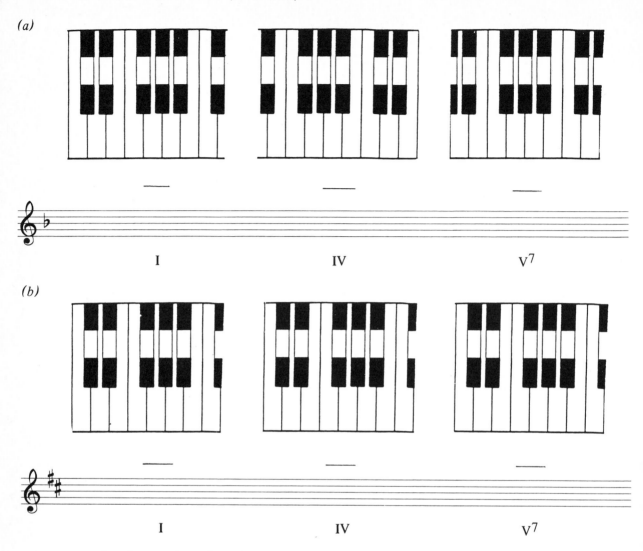

I   IV   V⁷

(b)

I   IV   V⁷

Identifying and Reading

3. You are given three song melodies for which you should complete the following activities:
   a. Read the melodic rhythm with rhythm syllables or counts.
   b. Read the melody with scale numbers or *so-fa* syllables.
   c. Name the key and fill in all parenthetical blanks so that chord names and numbers are indicated.
   d. Mark bracketed *nonchord notes* as to type: passing tone (P) or neighboring tone (N).
   e. As an optional activity according to your ability, play any or all melodies with chordal accompaniment.

ALL NIGHT, ALL DAY   Spiritual

Key: ___

G (_) ... D⁷ (_) ... G (_)

All night, all_____ day, An - gels watch-ing o - ver me.

EARLY ONE MORNING

English Folk Song

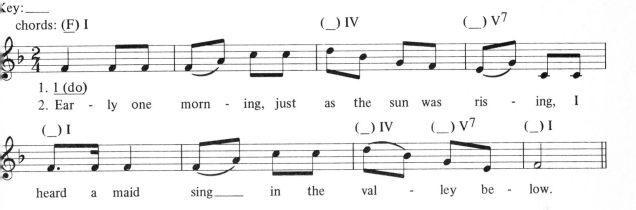

Key:___

chords: (F) I ... (_) IV ... (_) V⁷

1. 1 (do)
2. Ear - ly one morn - ing, just as the sun was ris - ing, I

(_) I ... (_) IV ... (_) V⁷ ... (_) I

heard a maid sing_____ in the val - ley be - low.

CAMPTOWN RACES

Stephen Foster

Key:_____

chords: (— —) ... (— —) ... (— —)

1. 1 (do)
2. Goin' to run all night, Goin' to run all day. The__

(— —) ... (— —) ... (— —)

horse I fan - cy is the bob - tail nag; He'll walk a - way from the bay.

Creating

4. Make your own chordal accompaniment for *Silent Night.* First, notate the primary chords so that you will have in mind the scale tones each chord contains. Second, study the melodic notes that occur over the duration of each chord to determine which chord will sound best with those notes; write the name of that chord in the blank above the staff. Finally, play the melody and chords to confirm your decisions. (153–54)

SILENT NIGHT

Franz Gruber

notate primary chords in root position:

I IV V⁷

chord names: __ ... __ ... __

Si - lent night! Ho - ly night! All is calm, all is bright.

'Round yon vir - gin moth - er and child! Ho - ly in - fant, so ten - der and mild,

Sleep in heav - en - ly peace,____ Sleep__ in heav - en - ly peace.____

Discriminating (Aural-Visual)

Activities 5 and 6 should be presented by an instructor.

5. Each item (a through e) has three patterns of melodic intervals containing skips among notes of the tonic, subdominant, and dominant-seventh chords. Each of the three patterns is in the same key and starts on the same scale tone (marked with number and syllable). One pattern will be played; circle the number of the pattern you hear performed.

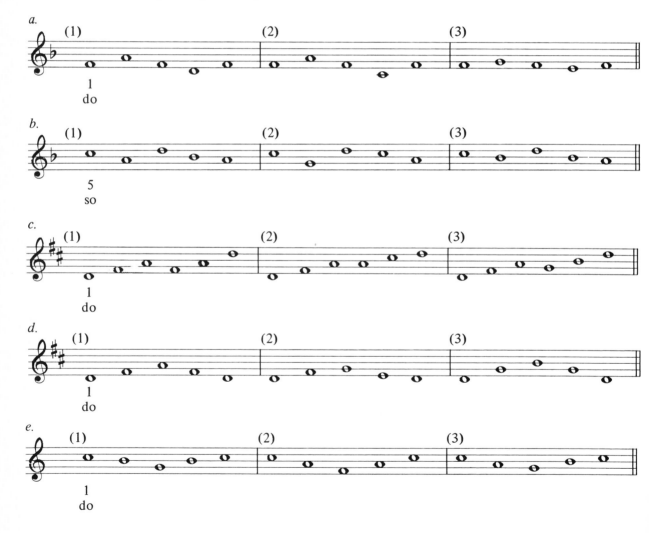

6. One of three chord progressions will be played on a piano. Circle the number of the progression played.

(a)
(1) I–I–IV–I
(2) I–V⁷–V⁷–I
(3) I– IV–V⁷–I

(b)
(1) I–IV–I–IV–I
(2) I–V⁷–I–V⁷–I
(3) I–IV–I–V⁷–I

(c)
(1) I–IV–V⁷–V⁷–I
(2) I–IV–I–V⁷–I
(3) I–V⁷–I–IV–I

Performing

7. Continue to practice playing song melodies and chordal accompaniments presented in the *Study Activities.*

AFTER YOU HAVE COMPLETED ALL **PRACTICE ACTIVITIES** AND RE-VIEWED THE **OBJECTIVES,** CONTINUE WITH THE **ASSESSMENT OF PROGRESS.**

ASSESSMENT OF PROGRESS

A. *Applied knowledge.* Part A can be completed as a self-administered test without reference to any other material. Write your responses in blanks beside item numbers and, when you have finished all of Part A, check your answers with those in *Keys to Chapter Assessments,* page 250. Correct all of your errors and restudy relevant material in the *Study Activities* and *Practice Activities* before continuing to Chapter Eight.

Respond to questions 1 through 10 with coordinated references to the keyboard with numbered keys and the six (a through f) notated key signatures for which you are given the tonic chord and either the name or number of a second chord. You may, at your option, notate the second chord in *keyboard position* and name or number it. Apply your knowledge of finger-pitch movement in primary chord progressions to answering the questions.

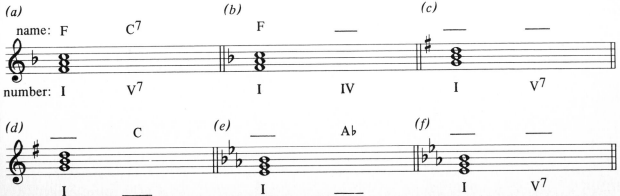

_____ 1. Which numbered piano keys would produce the V⁷ chord in a I to V⁷ progression in key (a)?

_____ 2. What is the name of the IV chord in key (b)?

_____ 3. Which piano keys would produce the IV chord in a I to IV progression in key (b)?

_____ 4. What are the names of the I and V⁷ chords in key (c)?

_____ 5. Which piano keys would produce the V⁷ chord in a I to V⁷ progression in key (c)?

_____ 6. Which piano keys would produce the C chord in progressing to it from the I chord in key (d)?

_____ 7. What is the name of the i chord in key (e)?

_____ 8. What is the number of the A-flat chord in key (e)?

_____ 9. Which piano keys would produce the I chord in key (f)?

_____ 10. Which piano keys would produce the V⁷ chord in a I to V⁷ progression in key (f)?

Respond to questions 11 through 19 with reference to the following melodic phrase:

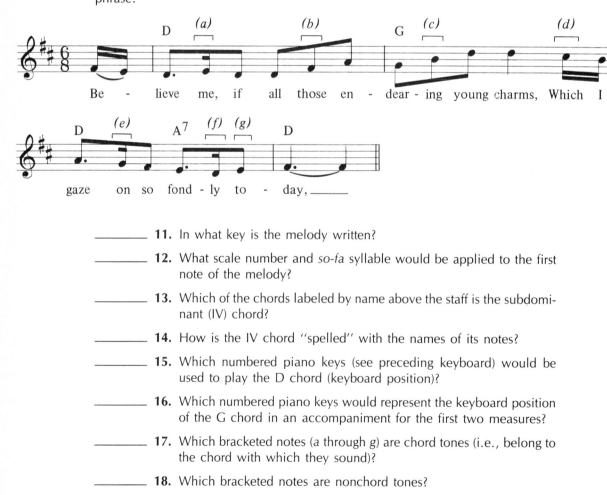

_____ 11. In what key is the melody written?

_____ 12. What scale number and _so-fa_ syllable would be applied to the first note of the melody?

_____ 13. Which of the chords labeled by name above the staff is the subdominant (IV) chord?

_____ 14. How is the IV chord "spelled" with the names of its notes?

_____ 15. Which numbered piano keys (see preceding keyboard) would be used to play the D chord (keyboard position)?

_____ 16. Which numbered piano keys would represent the keyboard position of the G chord in an accompaniment for the first two measures?

_____ 17. Which bracketed notes (a through g) are chord tones (i.e., belong to the chord with which they sound)?

_____ 18. Which bracketed notes are nonchord tones?

_____ 19. Which bracketed notes are neighboring tones?

Respond to questions 20 through 24 with reference to the following melody, in which skips on notes of primary chords are characteristic. You may notate on the blank staff the primary chords of this key in both their root and keyboard positions if this will assist you in answering the questions.

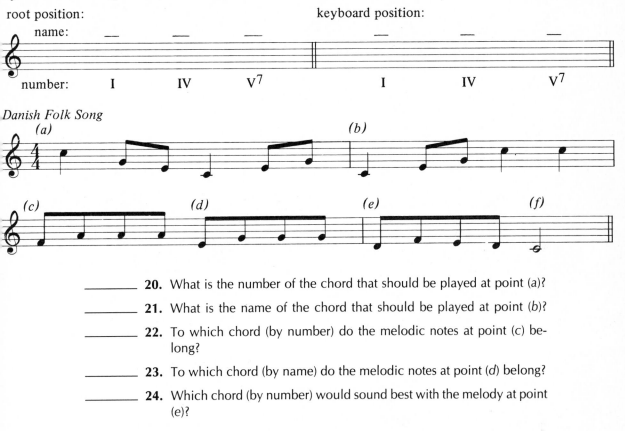

Optional notation of chords

root position: keyboard position:

Danish Folk Song

_____ **20.** What is the number of the chord that should be played at point (a)?

_____ **21.** What is the name of the chord that should be played at point (b)?

_____ **22.** To which chord (by number) do the melodic notes at point (c) belong?

_____ **23.** To which chord (by name) do the melodic notes at point (d) belong?

_____ **24.** Which chord (by number) would sound best with the melody at point (e)?

B. *Skills.* Part B is an assessment of the level of skills you have developed in playing chord progressions and accompaniments involving all three primary chords. Skills in reading and singing chord skips in melody are also included. An instructor or a student assistant should administer this part, and you should achieve the minimum acceptable level, or a higher level, before continuing to Chapter Eight.

1. Minimum acceptable level of performance
  a. Play the following chord progressions in the keys of C, F, and G:
  1) I–IV–I
  2) I–V⁷–I
  3) I–IV–V⁷–I
  b. Play at least two of the following song melodies with their chordal accompaniments. The songs should be in different keys.
  1) *Lovely Evening* (C)
  2) *Kum Ba Yah* (C)
  3) *Michael, Row the Boat Ashore* (F)
  4) *The Water Is Wide* (F)
  5) *Go Tell It On the Mountain* (G)
  6) *Do, Lord, Remember Me* (G)

    c. Sing with scale numbers or *so-fa* syllables at least one of the following songs:
  1) *All Night, All Day*
  2) *Early One Morning*
  3) *Camptown Races*

2. Higher level of performance
  a. Play the following chord progressions in the keys of C, F, and G, and in two additional major keys of your choice:
    1) I–IV–I
    2) I–V⁷–I
    3) I–IV–V⁷–I
  b. Play the melody and chordal accompaniment for all songs, or any selected by the instructor, from those listed in 1b.
  c. Sing with scale numbers or *so-fa* syllables the melody of each of the songs listed in 1c.

Chapter 8

Compound Meters

INSTRUCTIONS

1. Read the *Objectives* to gain an initial acquaintance with competencies you should have acquired by the end of this chapter.

2. Complete all *Study Activities*. Give particular attention to development of your skills in recognizing, reading, and performing common rhythm patterns encountered in the compound meters introduced in this chapter.

3. Complete with accurate responses all *Practice Activities* before proceeding to the assessment of progress.

4. As soon as you are ready, or when directed by your instructor, complete the *Assessment of Progress*. You should achieve the criterion levels indicated before continuing to Chapter Nine.

5. Through combined experiences provided in Chapters Two, Five, Six, and Eight, you will have studied in considerable depth rhythmic organizations in the simple and compound meters most widely found in traditional music. At your option, and in accord with your interest, you can find information about more unusual rhythmic organizations in optional Minichapter E.

OBJECTIVES

1. Define *compound meter* and compare its organization with that of *simple meter*.

2. Give both the *absolute meaning* and *applied meaning* for each of the following compound meter signatures: $\frac{6}{8}$ $\frac{9}{8}$ $\frac{12}{8}$ $\frac{6}{4}$ $\frac{9}{4}$

3. Identify the *true beat unit* and *common patterns* found in music with any meter signature listed in Objective 2.

4. Given incomplete measures of notated rhythm with a compound meter signature, select and write appropriate notes or rests to complete each measure. Given complete measures of rhythm notated without meter signatures in either simple or compound meter, identify and write the appropriate meter signature for each measure.

5. Read with either rhythm syllables, or the neutral syllable *lah,* exercises and melodic rhythms contained in this chapter.

6. Sing with their texts, and with or without the aid of a piano or second person, at least two songs presented in this chapter.

7. Play in correct rhythm at least two song melodies from those introduced in the *Study Activities*.

8. Given choices of different notated patterns in compound meter, identify the one you hear performed (aural-visual discrimination).

STUDY ACTIVITIES

COMPARATIVE METERS

You have previously learned to read and perform what amounts to a rather large number and variety of rhythm patterns, and, consequently, you can interpret all factors of rhythmic organization and notation found in many pieces of music. Yet, your experience is still limited to melodic rhythm in *simple meters* whose signatures have top numbers of 2, 3, or 4 and bottom numbers of 2, 4, or 8. A significant amount of music is in another temporal organization called *compound meter*. You can make an initial discovery of differences between simple and compound meters through singing each of the following melodic excerpts while clapping what you naturally feel to be the *true tempo beat* and comparing notated patterns that fall to each beat.

JINGLE BELLS (simple meter)   James Pierpont

WHAT CAN THE MATTER BE (compound meter)   Traditional

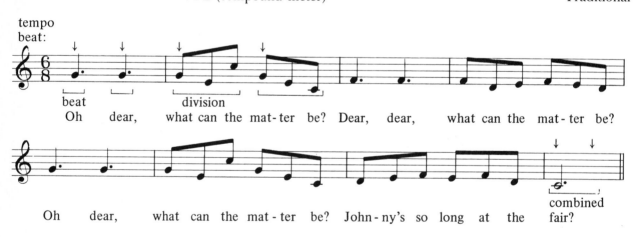

COMPOUND METERS

We can generalize comparative definitions of simple and compound meters from what has been observed about the previous two melodic rhythms. In *simple meters* a basic note (eighth, quarter, or half) functions as the beat unit, and its division is into two equal and even parts, represented by two notes of a kind that is half the value of a beat unit. *Compound meters* have a dotted-note (dotted quarter or dotted half) beat unit, and this divides into three equal and even parts represented by three notes of a kind that together equal the value of one beat unit.

Meter	Beat Unit	Division	Examples
			(a)　　　(b)
Simple:	a basic note	duple (two equal parts)	♩ or ♩ ♪♪ ♩♩
Compound:	a dotted note	triple (three equal parts)	♩. or ♩. ♪♪♪ ♩♩♩

COMPOUND METER SIGNATURES

You must get used to seeing and interpreting meter signatures employed with music in compound meter. Here are some features that should be remembered:

Top numbers. The top number in a compound meter signature is either 6, 9, or 12. Each number is divisible by 3, and the quotient of this computation is the *metric group,* which corresponds to the number of beats per measure. 6 divided by 3 equals 2 (duple meter), 9 divided by 3 equals 3 (triple meter), and 12 divided by 3 equals 4 (quadruple meter).

Bottom number. The bottom number in a compound meter signature represents a divided-beat note, not the true beat unit. The *true beat,* therefore, is represented by a dotted note three times the value of a note corresponding to the bottom number. A bottom number 8 implies a dotted-quarter (value of three eighth notes) beat unit, and 4 on the bottom results in a dotted-half (value of three quarter notes) beat unit.

Applied meaning. The applied meaning of a specific meter signature in a specific piece of music in compound meter is comprised of the quotient top number over the dotted note that functions as the beat unit. For example, applied meanings for nine-eight and six-four are:

Signature	Computation	Applied Meaning
9 ------→ 9 8 ------→ ♪	÷ 3 x 3 = 3. ♩.	3 ←-- beats per measure ♩. ←-- true beat unit
6 ------→ 6 4 ------→ ♩	÷ 3 x 3 = 2. ♩.	2 ←-- beats per measure ♩. ←-- true beat unit

Absolute meaning. Absolute meanings of compound meter signatures are the same as for all meter signatures. Each complete measure contains the quantity indicated by the top number of the kind of note represented by the bottom number, or notes and rests of a total equivalent value. Six-eight, for instance, always means there are six eighth notes or the equivalent in each complete measure. The next chart presents a comprehensive summary of compound meter signatures.

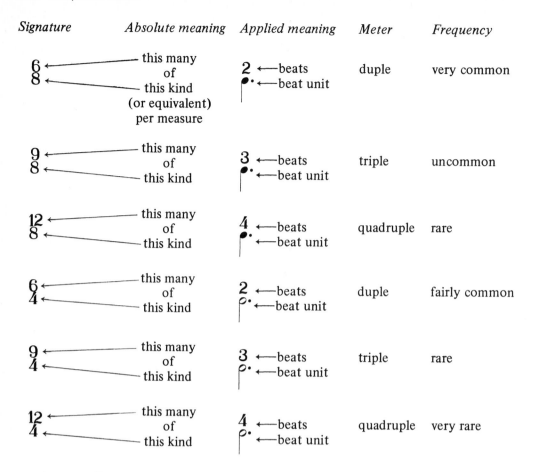

Signature	Absolute meaning	Applied meaning	Meter	Frequency
6/8	this many / of / this kind / (or equivalent) / per measure	2 ←beats / ♪·←beat unit	duple	very common
9/8	this many / of / this kind	3 ←beats / ♪·←beat unit	triple	uncommon
12/8	this many / of / this kind	4 ←beats / ♪·←beat unit	quadruple	rare
6/4	this many / of / this kind	2 ←beats / ♩·←beat unit	duple	fairly common
9/4	this many / of / this kind	3 ←beats / ♩·←beat unit	triple	rare
12/4	this many / of / this kind	4 ←beats / ♩·←beat unit	quadruple	very rare

THE DOTTED QUARTER NOTE AS BEAT UNIT

Identification of Patterns

Reading patterns in either compound or simple meter involves the same kinds of mental processes and neuromuscular responses. However, patterns of sound and silence, along with their notation, differ between the two kinds of meter. Your next responsibility is to become very familiar with common patterns and their notation in six-eight, nine-eight, and twelve-eight—all of which have a dotted-quarter beat unit. Also, the systems used in simple meters for reading rhythm with syllables and counts will be extended, so far as practical, into compound meter.

    Basic patterns. Basic patterns of duration in compound meters include beat patterns, combined-beat patterns, and divided-beat patterns, which together comprise the majority of patterns found in melodic rhythm. Specific basic patterns are few in number and consist of those shown illustrated in six-eight. These same patterns also occur in nine-eight and twelve-eight—in all compound meters with a bottom number 8, which translates into a dotted-quarter beat unit that divides into three eighths.

    You should practice reading separately, and in various alternations and combinations, the basic patterns illustrated in six-eight. Clap a tempo beat and chant the patterns with their rhythm syllables. Syllables probably work better than counts for vocally reproducing sounds in compound meter. Whereas syllables actually form specific patterns that are easily articulated, counts really represent divisions of the two true beats in each measure and, therefore, seem to be a contradiction in what is perceived as the relation of pattern and beat. If counts are used, 1 and 4 should be accented to represent the onset of each true (dotted quarter) beat.

Common patterns:

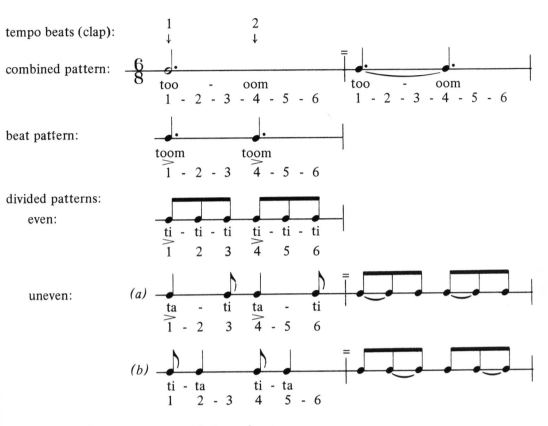

Common patterns with ties and rests:

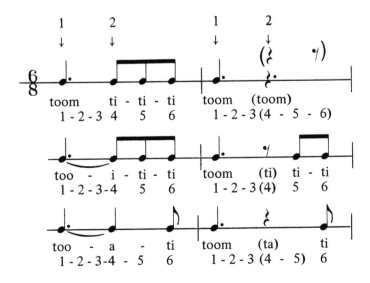

Subdivided patterns. A dotted-quarter beat unit divides into a pattern of three equal parts represented by eighth notes and subdivides into six equal parts represented by sixteenth notes. Still other patterns can be derived from this full subdivision so that we can say any pattern containing one or more sixteenth notes is a subdivided pattern. Study and practice the most common and representative of these patterns illustrated in six-eight.

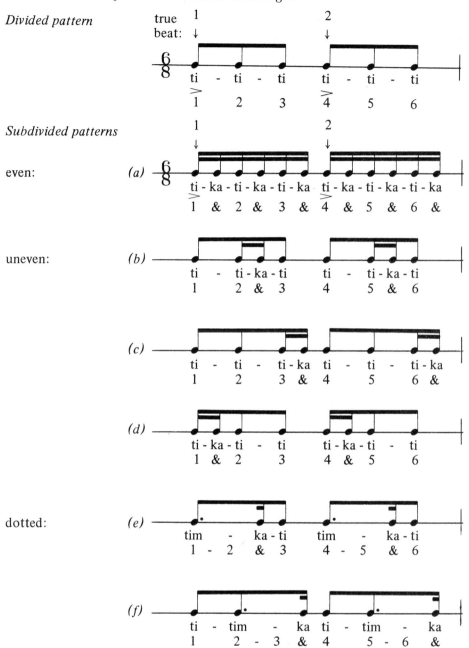

Reading Patterns

Once you are familiar with the kinds of patterns expected in music notated with a dotted-quarter beat unit, you can acquire, through further experience, skill in reading the flow of those patterns in a variety of organizations. Practice exercises 1 through 12 in the following ways:

1. Establish and clap a moderate tempo beat through each exercise as you think (silently) the patterns that fall to each beat whose onset is marked with an arrow.

2. Chant each exercise with the rhythm syllables that are given—they will stimulate your sense of exactness and continuity of ongoing patterns.

3. Repeat chanting each exercise, still maintaining the beat, with a single syllable (such as *lah*) on each note in order to gain independence from rhythm syllables, which, after all, are only an aid to your initial learning of accurate patterns; you should not retain a permanent dependence on them.

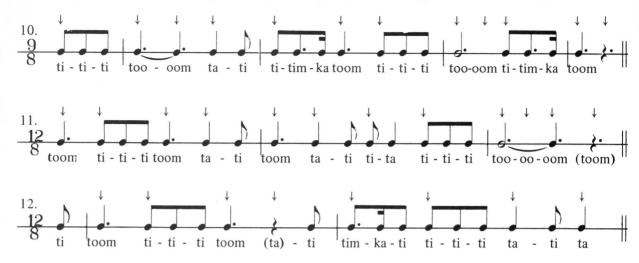

Reading Melodic Rhythm

Reading melodic rhythm in compound meter differs little, if at all, from reading the previous exercises, for the same kinds of patterns are involved. The next three examples are representative of song melodies written in six-eight and nine-eight.

When Johnny Comes Marching Home is in minor tonality (presented in Chapter Nine), but this feature has no bearing on its rhythm. Read the melodic rhythm, which begins with an eighth-note *anacrusis,* with either rhythm syllables or *lah* as you clap two dotted-quarter beats per measure. Sing and/or play the melody in the same rhythm.

WHEN JOHNNY COMES MARCHING HOME

Louis Lambert
(Civil War Song)

Blow the Man Down also begins with an eighth-note anacrusis, and its melodic rhythm includes one of the dotted patterns (tim-ka-ti). After you have correctly read its rhythm, try playing the melody with right-hand fingerings that are given. You can add a chordal accompaniment with the I and V^7 chords in F major (see chord symbols above the staff).

Down in the Valley is written in nine-eight and begins with an anacrusis consisting of a complete divided pattern (three eighth notes) on beat 3 of an incomplete measure. You can accompany this melody with the I and V^7 chords in G.

BLOW THE MAN DOWN

Sea Chanty

Come all ye young fel - lows that fol - low the sea,
Yeo - ho, blow the man down, And please pay at - ten - tion and
lis - ten to me, Give us some time to blow the man down.

DOWN IN THE VALLEY

U.S. Folk Song

Down in the val - ley, the val - ley so low,
Hang your head o - ver, hear the winds blow.
Hear the winds blow, dear, hear the winds blow,
Hang your head o - ver, hear the winds blow.

THE DOTTED HALF NOTE AS BEAT UNIT

You will recall from your previous experiences with simple meters that the same patterns are encountered regardless of whether the beat unit is a quarter or half note; only the notation is different. If the beat unit is of double value—half versus quarter—each note and rest must be doubled in value. The same principle holds true in compound meters with different beat units. Signatures of six-four and nine-four, which have a dotted-half beat unit, require notes double the value of those in the same patterns in six-eight or nine-eight. Study the chart that shows corresponding patterns notated in six-four and six-eight. Practice chanting each familiar pattern while following its notation in six-four.

Comparative patterns in compound meter: dotted-half and dotted-quarter beat units:

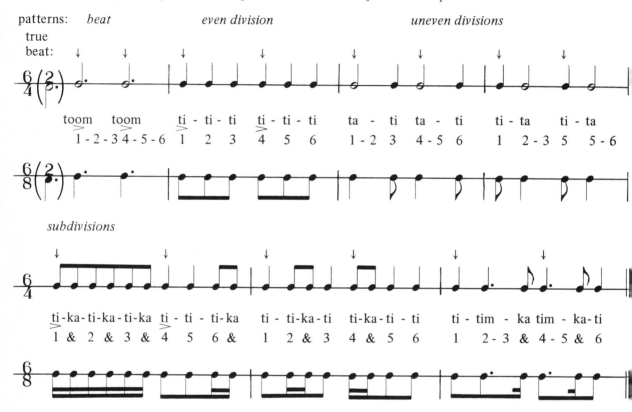

Reading Patterns and Melodic Rhythm

Read the next five exercises with rhythm syllables and repeat them on the syllable *lah*. When you have achieved accuracy in the exercises, continue to the two songs. *In Dulci Jubilo* is in six-four and starts with a single-note anacrusis on the last part of beat two of an incomplete measure. Read the melodic rhythm with either syllables or *lah*, then sing the song and also play the melody. Melodic rhythm in *Morning Has Broken* is comprised of simple basic patterns in nine-four. Read the rhythm, sing the song, and, at your option, play the melody.

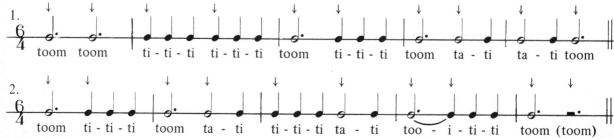

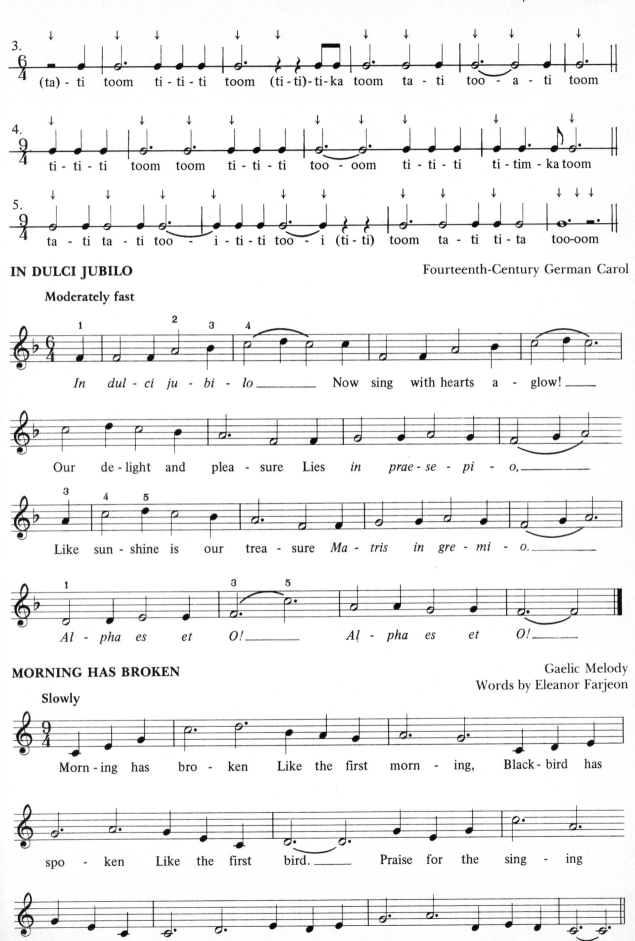

3.
(ta) - ti toom ti - ti - ti toom (ti - ti) - ti-ka toom ta - ti too - a - ti toom

4.
ti - ti - ti toom toom ti - ti - ti too - oom ti - ti - ti ti - tim - ka toom

5.
ta - ti ta - ti too - i - ti - ti too - i (ti - ti) toom ta - ti ti - ta too-oom

IN DULCI JUBILO

Fourteenth-Century German Carol

Moderately fast

In dul - ci ju - bi - lo _____ Now sing with hearts a - glow! _____

Our de - light and plea - sure Lies in prae - se - pi - o, _____

Like sun - shine is our trea - sure Ma - tris in gre - mi - o. _____

Al - pha es et O! _____ Al - pha es et O! _____

MORNING HAS BROKEN

Gaelic Melody
Words by Eleanor Farjeon

Slowly

Morn - ing has bro - ken Like the first morn - ing, Black - bird has

spo - ken Like the first bird. _____ Praise for the sing - ing

Praise for the morn - ing! Praise for them, spring - ing Fresh from the Word! _

PRACTICE ACTIVITIES

Identifying and Notating

1. You are given complete measures of rhythm patterns, notated without a meter signature, and a selection of possible meter signatures. Choose the correct signature for each measure and write its top and bottom numbers in the boxes.

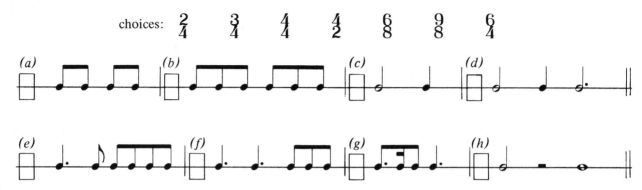

2. You are given incomplete measures of notated patterns, each with a correct meter signature. Select from the five choices one note that would complete each measure and actually notate it as the final note of the measure.

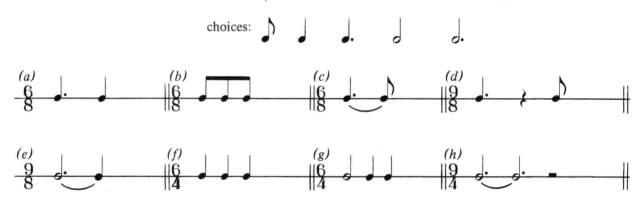

Identifying and Reading

3. Complete the following activities for each of the four (a, b, c, d) melodic rhythms: a) mark all beats with arrows as begun in the first melody; b) write in the blanks rhythm syllables for all patterns; c) think the melodic rhythm with syllables to a clapped beat, then read the rhythm with *lah*.

(b)
beats:

syllables: __ __ __ __ __ __ __ __

(c)
beats:

syllables:__ __ __ __

(d)
beats:

syllables: __ __ __ __ __ __ __ __ __ __

4. Continue to practice reading all rhythm exercises and song melodies presented in the *Study Activities*.

Creating

5. Complete part (a) so that you originate and notate eight measures of rhythm that might serve as a logical and musical rhythm for a melody in six-eight. Use some, but not necessarily all, notated patterns that are given. At your option, complete part (b) by creating and notating an original melody (any major key) based on the rhythm you wrote in part (a). Make adjustments, as needed, to the rhythm or pitch patterns until your melody is finalized.

(a) Create eight measures of melodic rhythm using any of the following patterns.

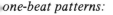 one-beat patterns: two-beat patterns:

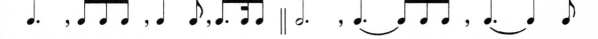

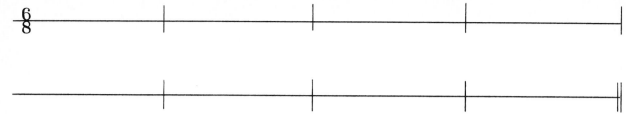

(b) Create an eight-measure melody using your rhythm from (a). Notate the melody in any key.

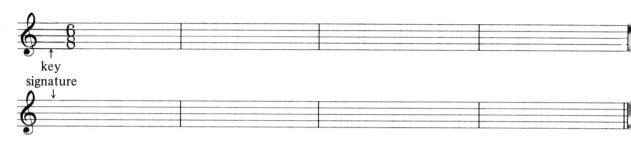

key
signature

Discriminating (Aural-Visual)

Activity 6 should be administered by an instructor or student assistant.

6. In each notated item (a through f) you see three different rhythm patterns; each pattern occupies a complete measure in the same meter. You will hear one pattern chanted on *lah*. Circle the number of the pattern that was chanted.

Performing

7. Sing with their texts, and play the melodies of, at least two of these songs:

    a. *When Johnny Comes Marching Home*
    b. *Blow the Man Down*
    c. *Down in the Valley*
    d. *In Dulci Jubilo*
    e. *Morning Has Broken*

8. Play the melody with chordal accompaniment (I–V^7) of *Blow the Man Down* and/or *Down in the Valley.*

AFTER YOU HAVE COMPLETED ALL **PRACTICE ACTIVITIES** AND RE-VIEWED THE **OBJECTIVES,** CONTINUE WITH THE **ASSESSMENT OF PROGRESS.**

ASSESSMENT OF PROGRESS

A. *Applied knowledge.* Part A can be completed as a self-administered test without reference to any other material. Write your responses in the blanks beside each item number and, when you have finished all of Part A, check your answers with those in *Keys to Chapter Assessments,* page 250. Correct all of your errors and restudy relevant material in the *Study Activities* and *Practice Activities* before continuing to Chapter Nine.

Answer questions 1 through 10 with reference to your selection of the correct note (choice 1, 2, 3, 4, or 5) to complete each of the incomplete notated measures (a through j). Observe the meter signature given for each measure.

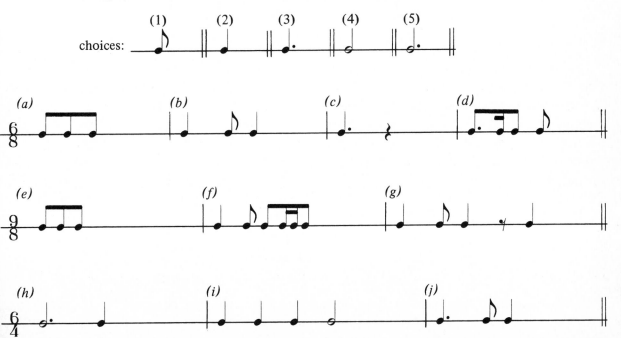

_____ **1.** Which note (choice 1, 2, 3, 4, or 5) would complete measure _a?_

_____ **2.** Which note would complete measure _b?_

_____ **3.** Which note would complete measure _c?_

_____ **4.** Which note would complete measure _d?_

_____ **5.** Which note would complete measure _e?_

_____ **6.** Which note would complete measure _f?_

_____ **7.** Which note would complete measure _g?_

_____ **8.** Which note would complete measure _h?_

_____ **9.** Which note would complete measure _i?_

_____ **10.** Which note would complete measure _j?_

Answer questions 11 through 19 with reference to your selection of the correct simple or compound meter signature (choice 1, 2, 3, 4, 5, or 6) for each of the notated complete measures (a through i).

choices:

(1)	(2)	(3)	(4)	(5)	(6)
$\frac{2}{4}$	$\frac{3}{4}$	$\frac{2}{2}$	$\frac{6}{8}$	$\frac{9}{8}$	$\frac{6}{4}$

Select correct signature for each complete measure:

_____ **11.** Which numbered meter signature is correct for measure _a?_

_____ **12.** Which numbered meter signature is correct for measure _b?_

_____ **13.** Which numbered meter signature is correct for measure _c?_

_____ **14.** Which numbered meter signature is correct for measure _d?_

_____ **15.** Which numbered meter signature is correct for measure _e?_

_____ **16.** Which numbered meter signature is correct for measure _f?_

_____ **17.** Which numbered meter signature is correct for measure _g?_

_____ **18.** Which numbered meter signature is correct for measure _h?_

_____ **19.** Which numbered meter signature is correct for measure _i?_

Answer questions 20 through 25 with reference to this notated melodic phrase:

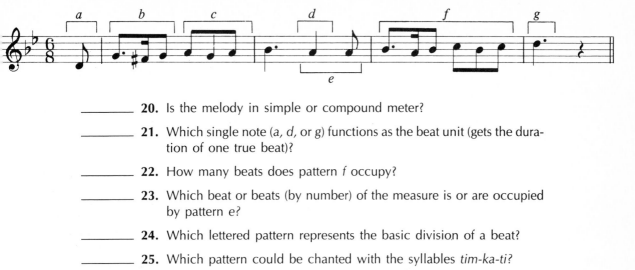

_____ **20.** Is the melody in simple or compound meter?

_____ **21.** Which single note (*a, d,* or *g*) functions as the beat unit (gets the duration of one true beat)?

_____ **22.** How many beats does pattern *f* occupy?

_____ **23.** Which beat or beats (by number) of the measure is or are occupied by pattern *e?*

_____ **24.** Which lettered pattern represents the basic division of a beat?

_____ **25.** Which pattern could be chanted with the syllables *tim-ka-ti?*

Answer questions 26 through 30 with reference to this notated melodic phrase:

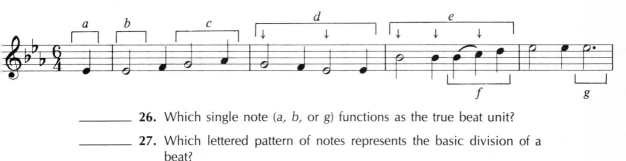

_____ **26.** Which single note (*a, b,* or *g*) functions as the true beat unit?

_____ **27.** Which lettered pattern of notes represents the basic division of a beat?

_____ **28.** How would you write with a number over a note the applied meaning of this signature?

_____ **29.** Are the true tempo beats marked correctly with arrows in measure *d* or in measure *e?*

_____ **30.** Does the anacrusis (note *a*) occur at an on-beat or after-beat point in the first incomplete measure?

B. *Skills.* Part B is an assessment of the level of skills you have developed in reading and performing rhythm patterns in compound meters. It should be administered to you by an instructor or a student assistant, and you should achieve the minimum acceptable level, or a higher level, before continuing to Chapter Nine.

1. Minimum acceptable level of performance:
 a. Chant, with either rhythm syllables or *lah* to a clapped tempo beat, the following:
   1) at least two exercises on each of these pages: 169–70, 172–73
   2) the melodic rhythm of at least one song of your choice from group a and one from group b:

        a) *When Johnny Comes Marching Home*
          Blow the Man Down
          Down in the Valley
        b) *In Dulci Jubilo*
          Morning Has Broken

b. Play, or sing with its text, at least one of the following songs:
   1) *Blow the Man Down*
   2) *Down in the Valley*
   3) *In Dulci Jubilo*

2. Higher level of performance:

a. Chant, with either rhythm syllables or *lah* to a clapped tempo beat, the following:
   1) any exercises selected by your instructor from all of those presented in the *Study Activities*
   2) all of the melodic rhythms in *Practice Activity* 3
   3) the melodic rhythm of all songs listed previously in section 1a

b. Play the melody, and a chordal accompaniment where indicated, of the following songs:
   1) *When Johnny Comes Marching Home*
   2) *Blow the Man Down* (chordal accompaniment)
   3) *Down in the Valley* (chordal accompaniment)
   4) *In Dulci Jubilo*

c. Sing with their texts at least three songs of your choice from among those listed in section 1a.

Chapter 9

Minor Scales, Melodies, and Chords

INSTRUCTIONS

1. Read the *Objectives* to obtain an initial acquaintance with competencies you should have acquired by the end of this chapter.

2. Complete all *Study Activities*. Your primary concern should be to understand minor scales and triads and to develop minimal skills in analyzing, reading, and performing melodies in minor keys.

3. Complete all *Practice Activities,* striving for accuracy in your responses, in order to gain experience in applying your knowledge and improving your skills.

4. As soon as you are ready, or when directed by your instructor, complete the *Assessment of Progress*. You should achieve the criterion levels indicated before continuing to Chapter Ten.

5. By the end of this chapter you will have acquired a great deal of knowledge and skill in dealing with music in major and minor tonalities that form the basis for organizing pitch in most pieces of traditional music. Optional Minichapter D presents pentatonic and modal scales and melodies. You might want to take a look at this material, for a few very good and familiar songs are based on these scale systems.

OBJECTIVES

1. Define the structure of, notate, and play minor scales in their three forms: natural, harmonic, and melodic.

2. Define *relative major and minor;* identify and name relative major and minor keynotes from given key signatures; identify and name the key (major or minor) in which a given melody is written.

3. Read and sing minor melodies with scale numbers and *so-fa* syllables, and, given a notated melody or scale, write appropriate scale numbers and *so-fa* syllables for all tones.

4. Define the structure of a minor triad, notate and name minor triads from given roots, and identify both minor and major triads from their notation.

5. Notate, name, and number the three primary chords (tonic, subdominant, and dominant-seventh) in selected minor keys, and play the i–iv–V^7 progression in at least two minor keys.

6. Play at least two song melodies presented in the *Study Activities*. (Chord accompaniments are possible with some of the songs.)

7. Given choices of notated major and minor triads or melodic patterns, identify the one you hear played (aural-visual discrimination).

STUDY ACTIVITIES

Ways of organizing pitch in music have formed a primary thrust throughout your study of music fundamentals. The concept of *tonality* was first presented in Chapter One. You will recall that tonality is the principle of "loyalty to a tonic" in which one tone takes on the role of a home tone, called the *tonic,* and all other tones in a scale or melody relate to it and, therefore, to each other. You also found that melody and harmony are based on some kind of scale.

Thus far all scales you have written or played, most melodies you have sung or played, and all chords you have used in accompaniments have been of major quality—melodies and chords in major keys based on major scales. Major mode is one of the two most prominent tonal systems used in traditional music since the seventeenth century; the other is minor. This chapter will acquaint you with minor tonality from the standpoints of minor scales, melodies in minor keys, minor chords, and chordal accompaniments in minor.

MINOR TONALITY

One of the quickest ways to establish an initial realization of minor tonality is to sing (or play) a familiar melody such as *We Three Kings of Orient Are* and draw some conclusions from the experience.

WE THREE KINGS OF ORIENT ARE   J. H. Hopkins

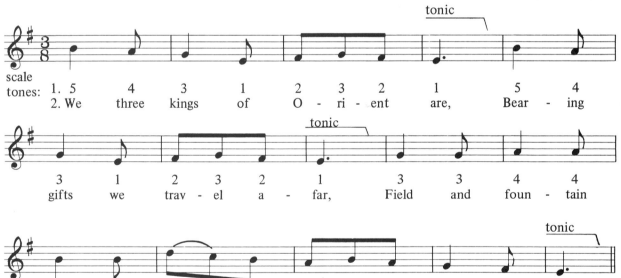

Can you confirm the following conclusions about *We Three Kings*?

1. Your mind (musical hearing) accepts and retains the pitch of E as the home tone, or *tonic.* This tone occurs at important points in the melody, including cadences of phrases one, two, and four. Other melodic pitches are strongly pulled downward by scale steps to it.

2. If E is the tonic (or *keynote*), the melody must be based on some kind of *E scale* and be in some kind of *E key*. When all scale tones found in the melody are placed in ascending scale order from their tonic E, we can analyze the scale structure and hear its sound (see illustration).

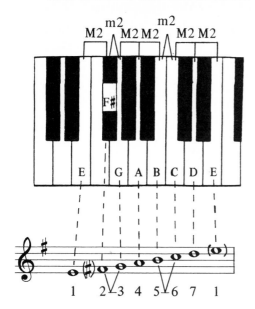

3. We find a different structure and sound in this scale compared with that of any major scale, due to the sequence of intervals that has minor seconds (half steps) between tones 2-3 and 5-6 instead of between 3-4 and 7-8 as found in major. All other step intervals in the scale are major seconds (whole steps). Such an organization of pitch in a scale, or a melody, produces an overall quality of sound called *minor*.

4. Therefore, *We Three Kings* has E as its tonic, uses notes of the E minor scale in its melody, is in the key of E minor, and sounds like minor tonality.

MINOR SCALES

Both major and minor scales evolved historically from older scale forms and became the two preferred tonalities for music in Western cultures from the seventeenth century into the early twentieth century. (Scales and melodies other than major and minor are presented in optional Minichapter D.) Minor tonality, un-

Comparative forms of a minor scale:

ascending- - - - - - - - - - - - - - - →   descending- - - - - - - - - - - - - - →

natural:	1	2 – 3	4	5 – 6	7	1	7	6 – 5	4	3 – 2	1
	la	ti–do	re	mi–fa	so	la	so	fa–mi	re	do–ti	la

1½ steps

harmonic	1	2 – 3	4	5 –⌐6	7⌐–1–⌐7	6⌐– 5	4	3 – 2	1
	la	ti–do	re	mi–fa	si–la–si	fa–mi	re	do–ti	la

↑   ↑
raise 7 one-half step ascending & descending

melodic:	1	2 – 3	4	5	6	7 –1	7	6 – 5	4	3 – 2	1
	la	ti–do	re	mi	fi	si–la	so	fa–mi	re	do–ti	la

↑   ↑   ↓   ↓
raise 6 & 7   lower to natural minor form
ascending   descending

like major, continued to evolve in response to preferences of persons who performed—and eventually those who composed—music until three forms of minor scales became functional. To understand minor tonality is to first understand its three scale forms, called *natural, harmonic,* and *melodic.* Study the structural chart showing comparative forms of a minor scale, and read the following summary statements about minor-scale structures.

1. *All minor scales* are diatonic scales: seven-tone scales comprised of step intervals. The seven tones can be numbered from the tonic—1 2 3 4 5 6 7 (1)—and assigned *so-fa* syllables starting with *la* and extending through an octave sequence from *la* to *la.* We could say that major scales are *do* scales and minor scales are *la* scales.

2. *Natural minor* can be thought of as the fundamental, original minor scale that corresponds directly to the older (Aeolian) mode, or scale, from which it descended. Its structure contains minor seconds between tones 2 and 3 (*ti-do*) and between 5 and 6 (*mi-fa*) and major seconds between all other tones. This sequence of major and minor seconds is retained in both the ascending and descending scale.

3. *Harmonic minor* is formed by making one modification to the natural minor scale: The seventh scale tone is raised one half step in both the ascending and descending scale. Such an alteration creates a true *leading tone* only a half step below the tonic (as in major) and also makes possible the use of a dominant-seventh chord for harmonic purposes (see the section on accompaniments in minor).

4. *Melodic minor* evolved from a desire to avoid the large scale interval (one and one-half steps, or an *augmented second*) left between tones 6 and 7 when the seventh tone was raised to create harmonic form. Its structure results from raising by one-half step both the sixth and seventh tones in the ascending scale, but lowering these tones back to their original pitches in natural minor in the descending melodic minor scale. Melodic minor is the only scale of Western cultures that differs in its ascending and descending structures. You also should note that the syllable name of raised 6 changes from *fa* to *fi* (*fee*) and that of raised 7 from *so* to *si* (*see*).

Now is the time to transfer generalizations about relative interval structure in minor scales to construction of specific scales. Study the three notated forms of the E minor and C minor scales and especially observe these features:

1. Natural form is constructed first to obtain exact scale tones to create its correct step intervals.

2. Sharped or flatted pitches in a natural minor scale become the *key signature for all forms of that scale.*

3. The raised seventh tone of harmonic minor, the raised sixth and seventh tones of ascending melodic minor, and the lowered sixth and seventh tones of descending melodic minor are notated with accidentals placed before the notes:
   ♯—raises a natural pitch
   ♮—raises a flatted pitch or lowers a sharped pitch
   ♭—cancels a natural sign and lowers the natural pitch

Use the reference keyboard to locate scale tones and visualize each scale interval. Play all notated forms of the E minor and C minor scales and sing them with scale numbers and *so-fa* syllables.

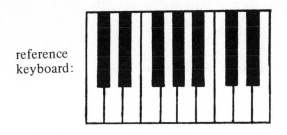

reference keyboard:

Three forms of the E minor scale:

E natural minor:

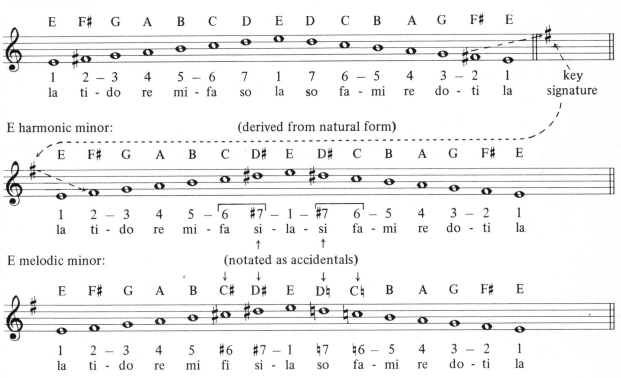

E harmonic minor: (derived from natural form)

E melodic minor: (notated as accidentals)

Three forms of the C minor scale:

C natural minor:

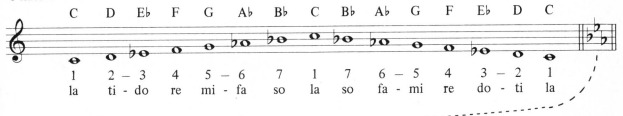

C harmonic minor:

C melodic minor:

C	D	E♭	F	G	A	B	C	B♭	A♭	G	F	E♭	D	C
1	2 – 3	4	5	♮6	♮7 – 1	♭7	♭6 – 5	4	3 – 2	1
la	ti - do	re	mi	fi	si - la	so	fa - mi	re	do - ti	la

RELATIVE MAJOR AND MINOR

You already may have questioned whether a relation exists between major and minor scales. The answer is yes. Every minor scale has a relative major scale with which it shares the same pitches and, therefore, the same key signature. But relative major and minor scales have a different tonic and, hence, a different sequence of scale tones to create the step intervals required to produce either major or minor sound. Study the relative scales, whose notations are superimposed on the same staff, and draw these generalizations:

1. The *relative major scale* is a *do* scale whose tonic is *do* and whose tones follow a *do re mi fa so la ti do* sequence that corresponds to the exact pitches that produce major scale intervals.

2. The *relative minor scale* is a *la* scale whose tonic is *la* and whose seven scale tones are the same pitches as those in relative major, but their sequence is *la ti do re me fa so la,* which forms natural minor scale intervals.

3. Each scale produces the same key signature, since each uses the same seven pitches.

4. The minor scale starts on a tonic that is three scale tones (or a *minor third*) below the tonic of its relative major. Stated conversely, the major scale starts on a tonic that is the third scale tone of its relative minor, or that is a *minor third above* the minor tonic.

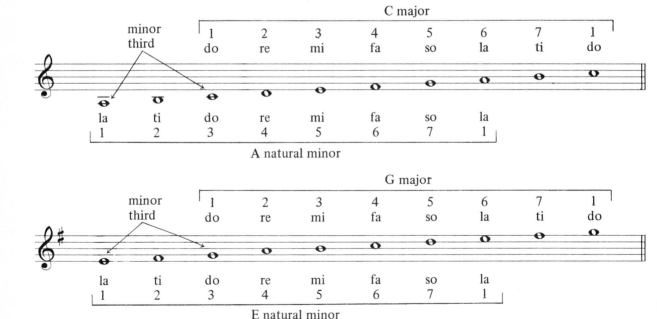

Minor Key Signatures and Keynotes

The point already has been made that relative major and minor share the same key signature. No separate system of signatures exists for minor; the signature for any minor key is that of its relative major. Locating and naming the minor keynote (tonic) from a given key signature is necessary for purposes of positively identifying the key in which a piece of music is written. These procedures will guarantee correct answers:

1. Look at the key signature and locate and name the major keynote in the same ways you learned in Chapter Three.
2. Locate the relative minor keynote a minor third (m3) below its relative major keynote and name that pitch, which is also the name of the minor key using that signature.

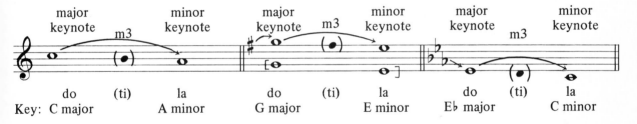

Here is a summary of relative major and minor key signatures and keynotes for all keys through four flats and four sharps:

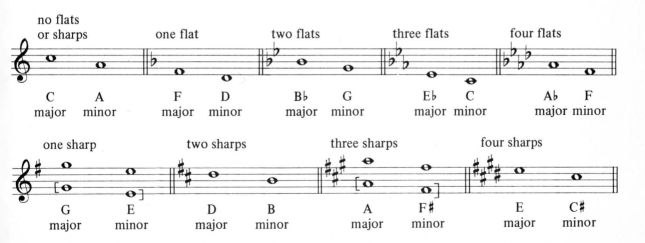

MELODIES IN MINOR KEYS

Positive Identification of Key

One should not attempt to read, anlayze, or perform a piece of music until its key has been determined. Positive identification requires naming both the keynote and quality: for example, B-flat major, G minor, F-sharp minor, A major. Given a notated melody that might be in either a major or minor key, you can name its key with a high degree of accuracy by following this procedure:

1. Observe the key signature and locate both the major and relative minor keynotes (see preceding section).
2. Determine which of the two keynotes functions as the true keynote by looking at the final cadence. If that note is the relative minor keynote, the melody is in the minor key of that name; if the final note is the major keynote, the melody is in a major key of that name. (You will recall from previous experiences that some melodies start on their keynote, or tonic, and others do not, therefore using the first note as an absolute clue to identifying the key is often inaccurate.)
3. Play and sing the melody to aurally confirm its true keynote and tonality (major or minor).

Study the final phrases of song melodies (1) and (2), each of which has a key signature of one flat. From what you see, confirm the reasons why (1) is in F major and (2) is in D minor, natural form.

(1) Key: F major — *keynote*

Go tell it on the moun-tain that Je-sus Christ— is born. *(do)*

(2) Key: D natural minor — *keynote*

Oh, sin-ner man, Where you gon-na run to? All on that day. *(la)*

Natural Minor Melodies

We now will work with several widely known traditional songs representing all three forms of minor. Your overall objective is to analyze, read, and perform them.

JOHNNY HAS GONE FOR A SOLDIER   American Revolution Song

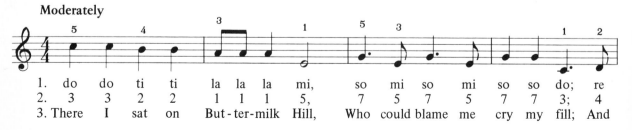

Moderately

	1. do	do	ti	ti	la	la	la	mi,	so	mi	so	mi	so	so	do;	re
	2. 3	3	2	2	1	1	1	5,	7	5	7	5	7	7	3;	4
	3. There	I	sat	on	But-ter-milk		Hill,		Who	could blame	me		cry	my	fill;	And

mi	mi	mi	re	do	mi	la	do;	do	do	do	ti	ti	so	la	la.
5	5	5	4	3	5	1	3;	3	3	3	2	2	7	1	1.
ev -	'ry	tear	would_	turn	a	mill;		John-ny	has	gone	for	a	sol -	dier.	

Johnny Has Gone for a Soldier appears to be in either C major or A minor (key signature of no flats or sharps). A quick look through the melody reveals a final cadence on A and no chromatic alterations (accidentals) raising either the sixth or seventh tone. Therefore, the key is A natural minor, and the melody begins on C, which is *do* (or 3) of the key. Read the melodic rhythm, play the melody, and sing the song with its text. Finally, sing the melody with *so-fa* syllables and/or scale numbers to enhance your sense of A functioning as the key-note, and begin to establish your ability to think some of the melodic intervals found in minor.

A La Nanita Nana is a two-phrase song in D natural minor. How do we know this? Observe that phrase one ends with an incomplete cadence (i.c.) and phrase two has a complete cadence (c.c.) on the minor tonic. Play this melody and sing it with *so-fa* syllables or numbers; doing so will help develop your musical hearing of scale-step and small-skip intervals in minor.

A LA NANITA NANA

Spanish Carol

Moderately

1.	la	la	ti	do	re	mi	mi	mi	fa	re	mi	mi	mi	fa	re	la	mi,
2.	1	1	2	3	4	5	5	5	6	4	5	5	5	6	4	1	5
3. A	la	na - ni - ta	na -	na,	na - ni - ta		e -	a,		na - ni - ta		e -	a,			

re	mi	fa	so	fa	mi	re	do	re	mi	do	re	do	ti	do	re	ti	do	ti	la.
4	5	6	7	6	5	4	3	4	5	3	4	3	2	3	4	2	3	2	1.
Mi	Je - sus	tie - ne		sue -	ño,	ben-di - to		se__		a,	ben - di - to			se__		a.			

Harmonic Minor Melodies

Joshua Fit the Battle of Jericho is also in D minor (one flat in the signature), but, in addition, we find an accidental C-sharp in the melody. C-sharp, of course, is the raised seventh tone and provides a good indication that the key is really D harmonic minor. First, read the melodic rhythm, which includes several patterns of syncopation, then play the melody and sing it with *so-fa* syllables in order to focus better on the sound of raised *so* (*si*) and to hear typical scale-step patterns in harmonic minor. (Observe the chord symbols; you will learn these progressions in the next section of this chapter.)

JOSHUA FIT THE BATTLE OF JERICHO

Spiritual

la si la ti do do re mi mi mi__ re re re___ mi mi mi_
1 #7 1 2 3 3 4 5 5 5___ 4 4 4___ 5 5 5___
3. Josh-ua fit the bat-tle of Jer-i-cho,_ Jer-i-cho,_ Jer-i-cho,_

la si la ti do do re mi mi mi__ do re mi re do ti la.
1 #7 1 2 3 3 4 5 5 5___ 3 4 5 4 3 2 1.
Josh-ua fit the bat-tle of Jer-i-cho,_ and the walls came tum-blin' down.

PAT-A-PAN

French Carol

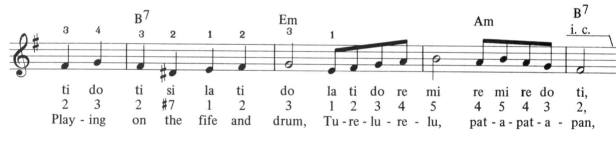

1. la la mi mi re mi do ti do re ti mi do ti;
2. 1 1 5 5 4 5 3 2 3 4 2 5 3 2;
3. Wil-lie, take your lit-tle drum; Rob-in, bring your fife, and come;

ti do ti si la ti do la ti do re mi re mi re do ti,
2 3 2 #7 1 2 3 1 2 3 4 5 4 5 4 3 2,
Play-ing on the fife and drum, Tu-re-lu-re-lu, pat-a-pat-a-pan,

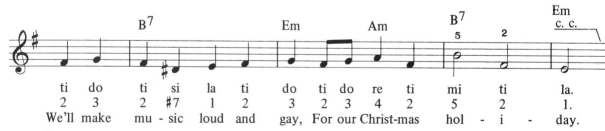

ti do ti si la ti do ti do re ti mi ti la.
2 3 2 #7 1 2 3 2 3 4 2 5 2 1.
We'll make mu-sic loud and gay, For our Christ-mas hol-i-day.

In what minor key (including its form) is *Pat-a-pan* written? What kinds of melodic cadences—complete or incomplete—occur at the ends of its three four-measure phrases? What is the meter signature, and what kind of note is the beat unit? Chant through the melodic rhythm with rhythm syllables or counts, then play the melody and sing it with *so-fa* syllables or scale numbers.

Melodic Minor Melodies

A melodic minor scale, you will recall, has both its sixth and seventh tones raised ascending but lowers these pitches descending. If in the process of determining that a melody is in a minor key we notice accidentals written before the sixth and seventh scale tones, we can reasonably conclude that the piece is in melodic minor. Such is the case in *Greensleeves*, where C-sharp (6) and D-sharp (7) appear as accidentals preceding the phrase cadences and are in addition to the F-sharp in the key signature. Sing and play *Greensleeves*; you should observe that it is in compound meter.

GREENSLEEVES

Old English Air

Moderately slow

CHORDS AND ACCOMPANIMENTS IN MINOR

The system of chord structures, names, and numbers in minor keys is parallel to that presented in Chapter Four for major keys. Our present concern is limited to the three primary chords—tonic, subdominant, and dominant-seventh—from which accompaniments can be provided to melodies in minor keys. You must understand minor triads before proceeding to chord progressions, for both the tonic and subdominant chords in minor tonality are minor triads.

Minor Triads

Triads—three-note chords built in thirds—produce different qualities of harmonic sound determined by the qualities and vertical orders of the thirds they contain. You can quickly grasp this idea by viewing a graphic illustration of generalized major and minor triad structures along with an application of these principles to a C major (C) and C minor (Cm) triad. Each chord contains one major and one minor third, but in reverse vertical orders: A major triad has a major third (M3) on the bottom, and a minor triad has a minor third (m3) on the bottom. We expect the two chords to have different qualities, or colors, of sound. You might want to remember a simple rule for converting triads from major to minor or from minor to major: A triad can be changed from major to minor by lowering its third (middle tone) a half step; a minor triad can be changed to major by raising its third a half step.

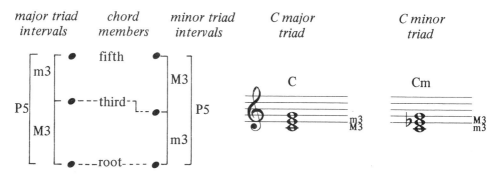

Study each notated minor triad shown constructed in thirds from a given root. Locate each interval, as well as each complete triad, on the reference keyboard. Observe that names of minor triads are written here with names of their roots (upper case letters) followed by a lower case *m*.

reference keyboard:

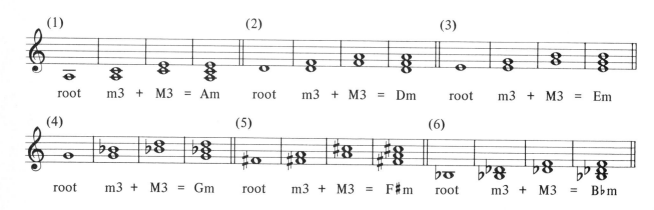

The Primary Chords in Minor

Knowledge you acquired in Chapters Four and Seven regarding construction and identification of primary chords in major will contribute to easier understanding of corresponding chords in minor. Chords in minor are usually based on harmonic form in which the raised seventh scale tone becomes the third of the dominant-seventh chord and results in exactly the same chord found in parallel major keys. Movement from this major dominant-seventh to the minor tonic provides a strong harmonic progression, especially at cadence points. Study the illustration that shows primary chords constructed on roots from the C harmonic minor scale, and give particular attention to relevant points in the three enumerated comments.

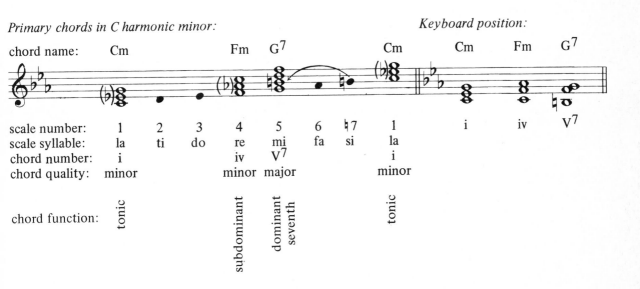

1. Tonic and subdominant chords are minor triads numbered with lower case numerals—i and iv.
2. The dominant-seventh chord always contains the raised seventh scale tone written with its appropriae accidental (natural or sharp sign). This chord is a major triad with an added seventh, and it is the same chord used in the parallel major key: V^7 is a G^7 chord in either C major or C minor.
3. Keyboard positions of the three chords follow the major-key model. Thus, the tonic chord is played in root position, and both the subdominant and dominant-seventh are inverted (see next section).

Chord Progression and Accompaniments

If you have had at least moderate success in playing left-hand chord progressions and accompaniments in major keys, you should have little trouble doing the same in minor keys. General patterns of pitch and finger movement are the same in both tonal systems, but the exact interval of pitch change for certain chord tones varies between whole and half steps. Study the chart that shows relatively in major and minor what happens to each chord in two basic progressions—tonic to subdominant and tonic to dominant-seventh.

Comparative rules for pitch movement in primary chord progressions in major and minor keys:

progression	chord tone	major keys	minor keys
tonic to	top	up one step	up a half step
subdominant	middle	up a half step	up one step
	bottom	same tone	same tone
tonic to	top	same tone	same tone
dominant-seventh	middle	up a half step	up one step
	bottom	down a half step	down a half step

Finger and pitch movement, which is relatively the same in all minor keys, is illustrated for the i–iv and i–V^7 progressions in C minor. Play these left-hand progressions on a piano.

Finger - pitch movement (left hand) in the i - iv progression:

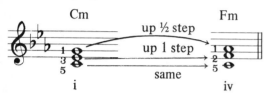

Finger - pitch movement in the i - V^7 progression:

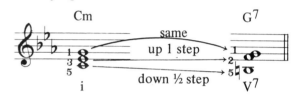

Now your are ready to try adding a chordal accompaniment to two song melodies you played and sang in the section devoted to harmonic minor melodies. Keyboard chords needed for this purpose are notated here in both treble (8*va*) and bass clefs; read from either clef. Be sure to practice separately the right-hand melody and left-hand progressions before attempting melody and accompaniment together.

Keyboard chords and optional guitar chords for Joshua Fit the Battle of Jericho:

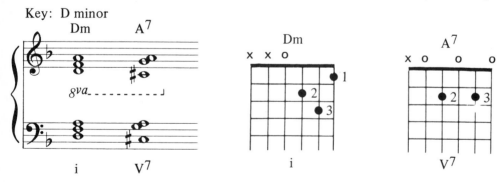

Keyboard chords and optional guitar chords for Pat-A-Pan:

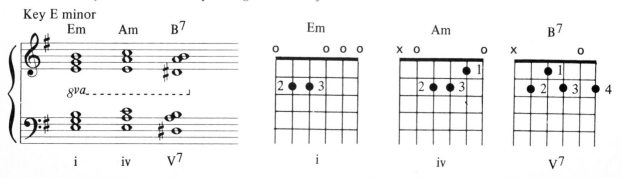

PRACTICE ACTIVITIES

Page references to relevant *Study Activities* are given in parentheses, and a keyboard is included for your optional reference.

reference keyboard:

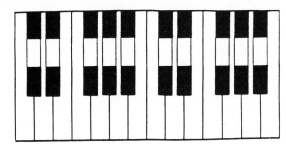

Notating

1. Follow the model (found on the reference page) for writing all three forms of a minor scale and construct and notate the G minor scale in all of its ascending and descending forms. Fill in all blanks with note names, numbers, and *so-fa* syllables, and write the correct key signature at points that are indicated. (185)

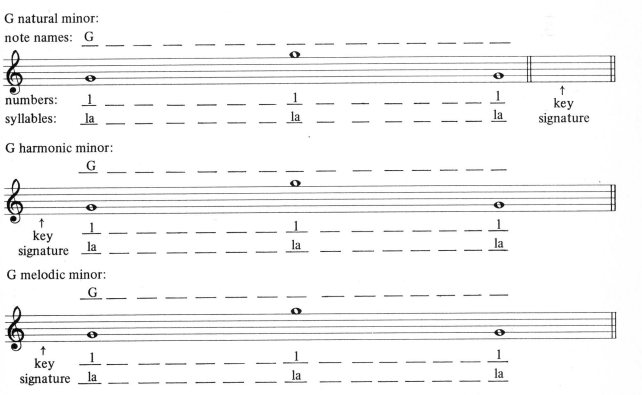

2. Follow the example. From each given root construct and notate a minor triad and write its name in the blank. (192)

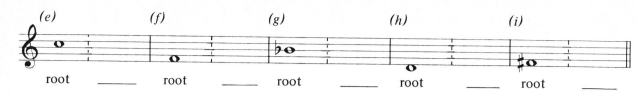

(e) *(f)* *(g)* *(h)* *(i)*

root _____ root _____ root _____ root _____ root _____

3. Follow the model worked out for a key signature of one flat and complete the following activities for (a) with a key signature of two flats and for (b) with a signature of no flats or sharps. (193)
   a. Notate in root position the three primary chords, spell each chord by writing names of its notes in the blanks, and write each chord name above the staff.
   b. Following the double bar line, notate each chord in its keyboard position and write its name above the staff.

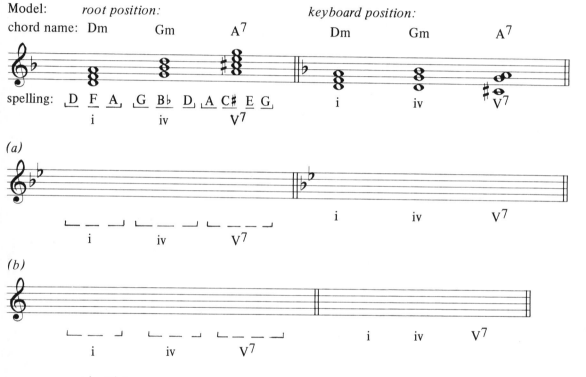

Model: *root position:* *keyboard position:*

chord name: Dm   Gm   A⁷   Dm   Gm   A⁷

spelling: D F A G B♭ D A C♯ E G
           i   iv   V⁷   i   iv   V⁷

(a)

i   iv   V⁷

i   iv   V⁷

(b)

i   iv   V⁷

i   iv   V⁷

Identifying

4. Follow the example and, for each given key signature, notate and name both the major keynote and its relative minor keynote. (187)

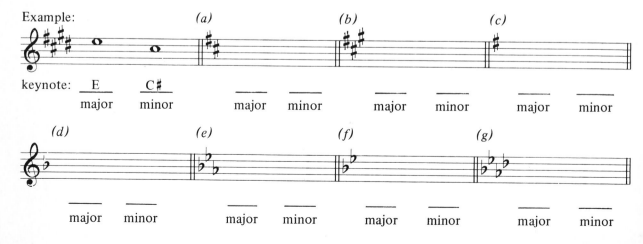

Example: *(a)* *(b)* *(c)*

keynote: E   C♯
        major   minor   _____ _____   _____ _____   _____ _____
                        major minor   major minor   major minor

(d) *(e)* *(f)* *(g)*

_____ _____   _____ _____   _____ _____   _____ _____
major minor   major minor   major minor   major minor

5. You are given isolated triads (*a* through *r*), of which some are major and others are minor. Follow the examples and write correct triad names in the blanks.

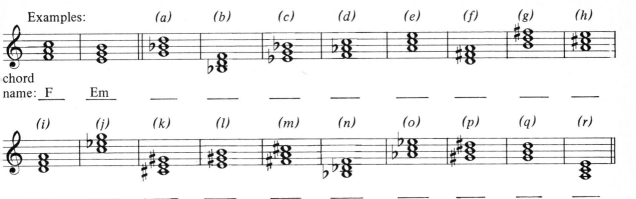

6. Three melodic excerpts (*a, b, c*) are given. You should be able to determine for each melody whether it is in a major or minor key by merely looking at its notation. Write key names, scale numbers, and *so-fa* syllables in the blanks provided for those purposes. (188)

Reading

7. Continue to read with *so-fa* syllables and/or numbers all song melodies presented in the *Study Activities*.

8. Sight read each of the following song melodies. First, chant the rhythm to a clapped beat; next, determine the key and play the melody; finally, sing the melody with scale numbers or syllables and with words of the text. You also might want to try the chordal accompaniment to *Charlie Is My Darling*.

AH, DEAR LOVE

English Round

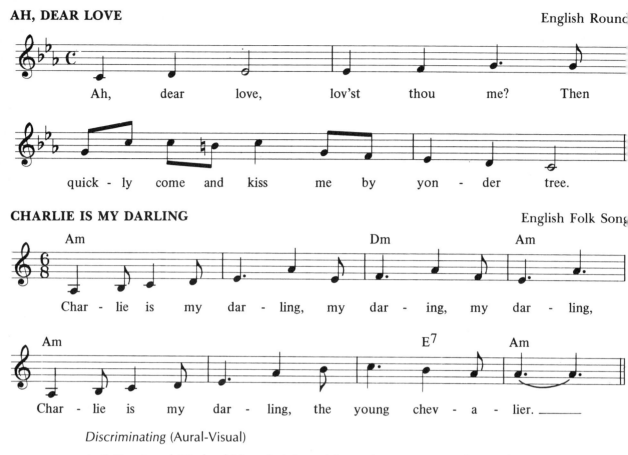

Ah, dear love, lov'st thou me? Then quick - ly come and kiss me by yon - der tree.

CHARLIE IS MY DARLING

English Folk Song

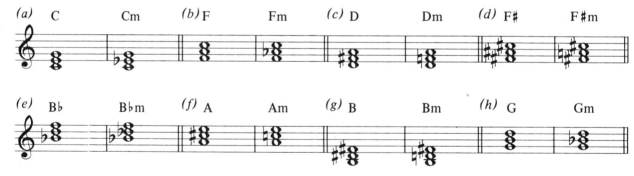

Char - lie is my dar - ling, my dar - ing, my dar - ling, Char - lie is my dar - ling, the young chev - a - lier. _____

Discriminating (Aural-Visual)

Activities 9 and 10 should be administered by an instructor or student assistant.

9. You are given pairs of notated triads of which one is major and one is minor. You will hear one of the triads played (it can be played first in *arpeggio*, then as a block chord). Circle the name of the triad you hear played.

(a) C   Cm   *(b)* F   Fm   *(c)* D   Dm   *(d)* F♯   F♯m

(e) B♭   B♭m   *(f)* A   Am   *(g)* B   Bm   *(h)* G   Gm

10. You are given five pairs (a, b, c, d, e) of parallel melodic pitch patterns in various combinations of major and minor keys. One pattern from each pair will be played; circle the number of the pattern played. (Reading all patterns with *so-fa* syllables would provide additional beneficial ear training.)

(a)

(1) D major   (2) D natural minor

do   la

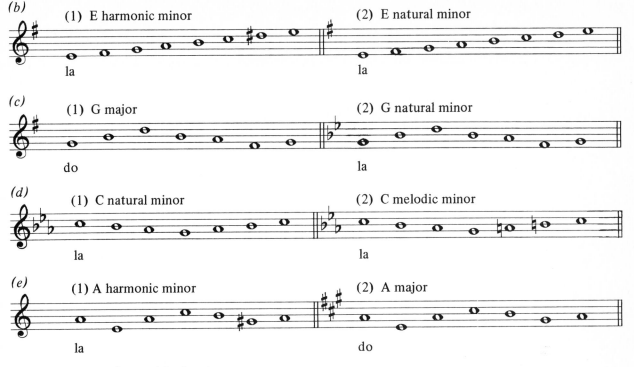

(b)

(1) E harmonic minor

la

(2) E natural minor

la

(c)

(1) G major

do

(2) G natural minor

la

(d)

(1) C natural minor

la

(2) C melodic minor

la

(e)

(1) A harmonic minor

la

(2) A major

do

Reading and Performing

11. Continue to practice the following material presented in the *Study Activities:*

    a. Sing with *so-fa* syllables and/or scale numbers:

        1) *We Three Kings of Orient Are*

        2) *Johnny Has Gone for a Soldier*

        3) *A La Nanita Nana*

        4) *Joshua Fit the Battle of Jericho*

        5) *Pat-a-pan*

        6) *Greensleeves*

    b. Play (and sing) the E minor and C minor scales ascending and descending in all three forms—natural, harmonic, and melodic.

    c. Play the melody of at least three songs listed in 11a.

    d. Play the melody with chordal accompaniment for *Joshua Fit the Battle of Jericho* and/or *Pat-a-pan.*

> AFTER YOU HAVE COMPLETED ALL **PRACTICE ACTIVITIES** AND RE-VIEWED THE **OBJECTIVES,** CONTINUE WITH THE **ASSESSMENT OF PROGRESS.**

ASSESSMENT OF PROGRESS

    A. *Applied knowledge.* Part A can be completed as a self-administered test without reference to any other material. Write your responses in blanks beside item numbers and, when you have finished all of Part A, check your answers with those in *Keys to Chapter Assessments,* page 250. Correct all of your errors and restudy relevant material in the *Study Activities* and *Practice Activities* before continuing to Chapter Ten.

Use this reference keyboard when it is needed as an aid in answering any of the questions.

reference keyboard:

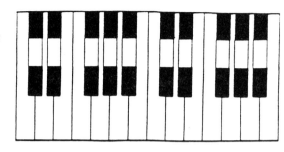

Answer questions 1 through 4 with reference to these four notated scales:

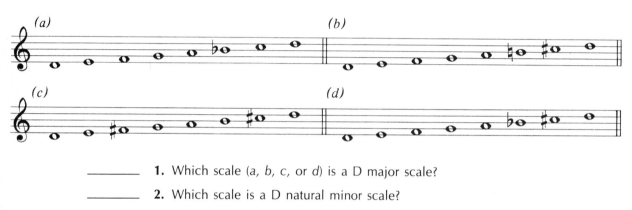

_____ **1.** Which scale (a, b, c, or d) is a D major scale?

_____ **2.** Which scale is a D natural minor scale?

_____ **3.** Which scale is a D harmonic minor scale?

_____ **4.** Which scale is a D melodic minor scale?

Answer questions 5 through 10 with reference to these key signatures (you might want to locate and name relative major and minor keynotes for each signature before continuing):

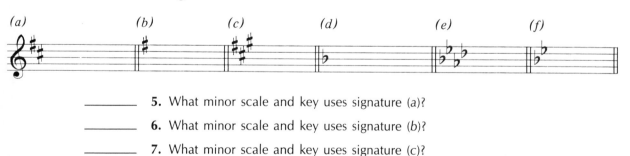

_____ **5.** What minor scale and key uses signature (a)?

_____ **6.** What minor scale and key uses signature (b)?

_____ **7.** What minor scale and key uses signature (c)?

_____ **8.** What minor scale and key uses signatrue (d)?

_____ **9.** What minor scale and key uses signature (e)?

_____ **10.** What minor scale and key uses signature (f)?

Answer questions 11 through 16 with reference to these notated triads:

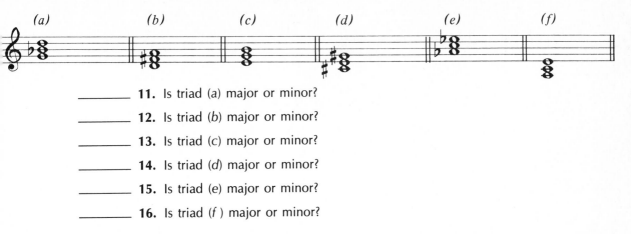

_____ **11.** Is triad (a) major or minor?

_____ **12.** Is triad (b) major or minor?

_____ **13.** Is triad (c) major or minor?

_____ **14.** Is triad (d) major or minor?

_____ **15.** Is triad (e) major or minor?

_____ **16.** Is triad (f) major or minor?

Answer questions 17 through 25 with reference to the final phrases of *Masters in This Hall* quoted here. (Your answer to question 17 will affect your answers to all remaining questions.)

MASTERS IN THIS HALL
French Carol

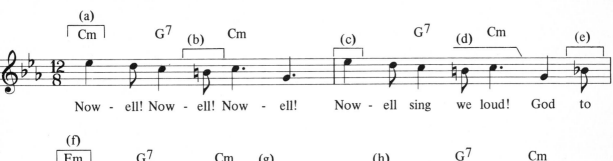

_____ **17.** In what key is the music written?

_____ **18.** Is note (c), (g), or (h) the keynote?

_____ **19.** What pitches (by name) comprise chord (a)?

_____ **20.** What *so-fa* syllable is correct for note (b)?

_____ **21.** What *so-fa* syllable is correct for note (e)?

_____ **22.** Is the phrase cadence on note (d) complete or incomplete?

_____ **23.** What is the number (numeral) for chord (f)?

_____ **24.** What is the scale number of note (h)?

_____ **25.** What is the scale number of note (c)?

B. *Skills.* Part B is an assessment of the level of skills in singing and playing music in minor tonality that you have developed during your study of this chapter. An instructor or a student assistant should administer this part, and you should achieve the minimum acceptable level, or a higher level, before continuing to Chapter Ten.

1. Minimum acceptable level of performance
   a. Sing with scale numbers and/or *so-fa* syllables two songs of your choice:
      1) *We Three Kings of Orient Are*
      2) *Johnny Has Gone for a Soldier*
      3) *A La Nanita Nana*
      4) *Joshua Fit the Battle of Jericho*
      5) *Pat-a pan*
      6) *Greensleeves*
   b. Play the melody of two songs of your choice from those listed in 1a.
   c. Play either the C minor or E minor scale ascending and descending in all three forms—natural, harmonic, and melodic.

2. Higher level of performance
   a. Sing with scale numbers and/or *so-fa* syllables any songs selected by your instructor from those listed in 1a.
   b. Play the melody of four songs of your choice from those listed in 1a.
   c. Play the C minor, E minor, and G minor scales ascending and descending in all three forms—natural, harmonic, and melodic.
   d. Play the melody with chordal accompaniment for either *Joshua Fit the Battle of Jericho* or *Pat-a-pan*.

Chapter 10

Form, Expression, Analysis and Synthesis

Chapter Ten is the final basic learning chapter contained in this book (optional minichapters A through E provide additional material for those who want to expand their knowledge), and its design differs in some respects from that of previous chapters. New subject matter in the areas of musical form and expression is presented in the *Study Activities* but is not extended into practice and assessment activities devoted solely to this new material. Instead, a final section on *Analysis and Synthesis* will give opportunities to demonstrate to yourself and others how well you can apply knowledge and skills learned throughout all the basic chapters to analyzing and performing selected pieces of music.

INSTRUCTIONS

1. Read the *Objectives* to obtain an initial acquaintance with competencies you should have acquired by the end of this chapter.

2. Complete all *Study Activities*. Your primary concerns should be: (a) learning how to identify and relate units of form within a melody and how to categorize and name its structure-at-large, and (b) interpreting various terms and signs that provide in the score indications of expressive musical qualities and incorporating these qualities into performance of the piece.

3. Analyze and perform each song included in the section on *Analysis and Synthesis*. Such experiences provide culminating practice and assessment activities for this and all preceding chapters. Check your responses with those given in the *Key to Score Analyses,* page 250.

OBJECTIVES

1. Recall and define the following terms associated with melodic form, and correctly use and interpret them in written or oral communication:

binary form	period
cadence	phrase
complete	repetition
incomplete	sequence
contrast	ternary form
motive	unitary form
part	

2. Define and interpret repeat signs and terms commonly used in music.

3. Pronounce, define, and interpret Italian words commonly used to indicate tempo; interpret metronome markings, such as ♩ = 90; relate tempo words and metronome markings.

4. Define and interpret Italian terms, abbreviations, and signs commonly used to indicate dynamics (levels of loudness).

5. Name and define basic kinds of articulation (legato, staccato, marcato), identify appropriate articulation for a given musical passage, and demonstrate proper articulation in the performance of a melody.

6. Recognize various kinds of phrase contours and accents (stresses) in a melody and perform the melody with a sense of these expressive features.

7. Given a notated song melody, (a) analyze important aspects of its pitch organization, rhythm organization, and form; (b) interpret all signs and terms that relate to tempo and dynamics; (c) play and/or sing the melody with accuracy and expression.

STUDY ACTIVITIES

FORM

A general idea introduced in Chapter One was that of form as the structural framework that results from ways patterns of sound are organized into *units* of a kind we can perceive on the basis of our psychological and cultural tendencies to group sound stimuli. Musical form can be said to have two dimensions—form *within* music and form *of* music. Form within the music has to do with how patterns of pitch and duration create units such as phrases, motives, and periods, as well as how these units are structured and related through designs such as repetition, sequence, and contrast. Form of music, on the other hand, refers to structure-at-large. The whole piece is a form (an art object), and this form usually can be analyzed, defined, and named.

Units of Form

We are primarily concerned with musical units of three relative sizes or scopes—motives, phrases, and periods. You already have dealt rather extensively with phrases, but we will redefine and illustrate phrases along with the other units.

Phrase. Phrases are natural divisions of a melody (similar to sentences of speech) and constitute its primary structural units. A *phrase* is perceived as a configuration of pitch movement (sound in motion) ending in a sense of finality or closure called a *cadence*, of which there are two kinds: 1) A melodic phrase ends in, and is punctuated with, a *complete cadence* (c.c.) when its final note is the keynote (tonic). 2) An *incomplete cadence* (i.c.) occurs when the final note is any scale tone other than the keynote—often the second, third, or fifth scale tone.

Motive. Many, but not all, melodic phrases divide naturally into smaller units, or subunits, called *motives*. Traditional song phrases often divide into two motives of similar length.

Period. Phrases sometimes divide into motives, and they sometimes combine into larger units called *periods*. A musical *period* is comprised of two phrases in a special *antecedent-consequent* relationship. The antecedent (questioning) phrase usually ends in an incomplete cadence and tends to be followed by a consequent (answering) phrase that ends in a complete cadence. Also, the two phrases usually are of the same length and often contain similar melodic patterns.

Michael, Row the Boat Ashore (key of D major), which you played with chordal accompaniment in Chapter Seven, illustrates all three kinds of structural units. The complete melody constitutes a musical *period* consisting of two four-measure *phrases* that contain two two-measure *motives*.

MICHAEL, ROW THE BOAT ASHORE

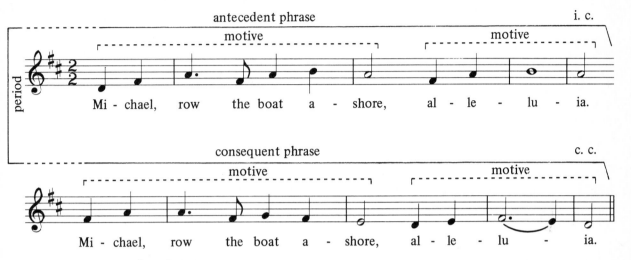

Structural Techniques

Motives and phrases are the main building blocks in a piece of music and are cohesively formed into a unified whole through the basic principle of all form—*unity in variety*. Unity sometimes is achieved through techniques of *repetition* and *sequence,* which produce a degree of likeness among motives and/or phrases. On the other hand, unity can also result from *contrast,* which introduces differences that add a distinct kind of variety.

Repetition.   Each motive and phrase can be thought of as a small musical idea within the whole. *Repetition* is an immediate restatement of an idea and can be of two kinds: 1) *Exact repetition* is a note-for-note restatement of the original. 2) *Modified* (altered) *repetition* is a recognizable restatement of an idea with changes having been made to one or more notes, often for purposes of approaching and ending in a different cadence. Repetition that is not immediate—that occurs following intervening ideas—is more properly called a *return.*

Sequence.   Restatement of a musical idea at a higher or lower pitch level is a *sequence.* Either a motive or an entire phrase can be sequential, therefore related, to a preceding motive or phrase. The sequential unit sounds and appears in notation to be similar to what preceded it, but note for note it is a certain interval—usually a second or third—above or below the original.

Structural design by repetition, sequence, and modified repetition can be seen and heard in *Skip to My Lou,* which is another musical period whose second phrase is a modified repetition of the first phrase. The first motive in each phrase is the same, providing sufficient likeness to qualify the entire second phrase as a repetition, but modification occurs in the second motive and leads to a complete cadence on the keynote. Why is the second motive in phrase one labeled a sequence?

SKIP TO MY LOU

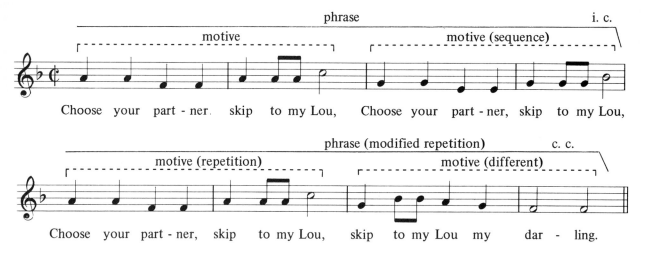

Choose your part-ner, skip to my Lou, Choose your part-ner, skip to my Lou,

Choose your part-ner, skip to my Lou, skip to my Lou my dar-ling.

Contrast. The first phrase of a melody is considered to be its first musical idea, or unit. Successive phrases can consist either of similar or different material. Each new (different) idea provides *contrast*. Phrases are traditionally labeled with small alphabet letters to symbolize structural relationships among phrases that constitute the entire melody. Letter *a* is assigned to phrase one and to any repetition of that phrase. Letter *b* represents the first contrasting phrase, letter *c* the second contrast, and so on. Modified repetitions and sequences of phrases can be indicated by adding a prime sign to their original letter (*a'*, *b'*). Most song melodies contain no more than two or three truly different phrase ideas.

MARINES' HYMN

U.S. Marine Corps Song

From the halls of Mon-te-zu-ma, to the shores of Tri-po-li,

We fight our coun-try's bat-tles in the air, on land and sea.

First to fight for right and free-dom, And to keep our hon-or clean;

We are proud to claim the ti-tle of U-nit-ed States Ma-rines.

Marines' Hymn has a phrase structure of *a a b a*. Phrase two is an exact repetition of phrase one, phrase three is contrasting from the standpoint of its pitch movement, and phrase four is a return of the first melodic idea. Variety within the melody is provided mainly by a change in pitch movement found in phrase three. A strong sense of unity results not only from the sameness of three phrases but also from a continuance of essentially the same rhythm patterns through all phrases.

Forms of Melodies

Identification of form *within* a melody—its motives, phrases, periods, repetitions, and contrasts—provides a basis for identifying the form of a whole melody. Determination of structure-at-large requires an additional level of analysis, namely, recognizing if and how individual phrases relate and combine into larger parts, or sections, of the whole. A *part* of a musical form can be defined as a unit comprised of two or more phrases that relate in such a way as to create a distinct entity. Parts usually contain two to four phrases, and a two-phrase period is probably the most common example of a part in simple melodies.

Most song melodies are formed of either one part, two parts, or three parts. Part forms can be most easily illustrated and understood by first considering two-part, then three-part, and, finally, one-part form.

Two-part form. Phrases, you will recall, are labeled with small alphabet letters; parts are labeled with capital letters. *Two-part form* (also called *binary form*) simply is made up of two contrasting parts that are identified as Part A and Part B. We can name the form in either of three ways: two-part form, AB form, or binary form. Typically, a short song melody in this form begins with two phrases that unite into a period (A) followed by two phrases that create another period (B) of different, contrasting, material. You will discover through the following analysis and summary statement that Brahms's *Lullaby* is a two-part (AB, binary) form. Carefully study the analysis and confirm it as you perform and listen to the melody.

LULLABY (two-part form)   Johannes Brahms

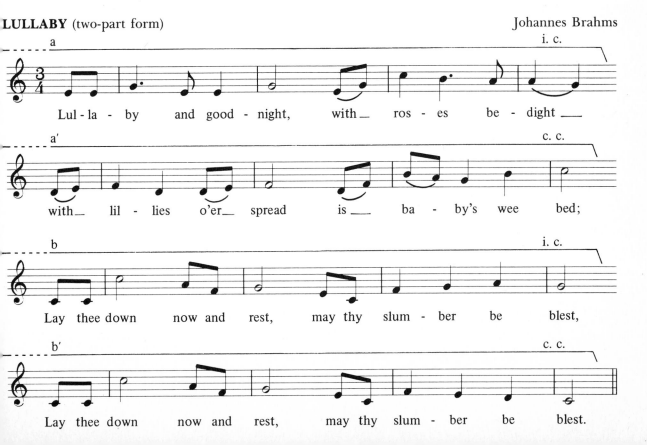

Summary of the form of Brahms's Lullaby:

AB form—a structure-at-large of two contrasting musical periods

Part A—a two-phrase period

phrase *a*—a four-measure phrase with incomplete cadence

*phrase *a'*—a four-measure phrase that is actually a *modified sequence* of phrase *a* and ends in a complete cadence

Part B—a two-phrase period of contrasting material

phrase *b*—a four-measure phrase of new melodic content

phrase *b'*—a four-measure phrase that is a *modified repetition* of phrase *b* and ends in a complete cadence

*Sequential relationship between phrases one and two of Lullaby:

Three-part form. Three-part (ABA, *ternary*) *form* is characterized by a return of Part A following the contrast of Part B. *The Ash Grove,* a well-known Welsh song, illustrates ABA form; study the analysis of its melody. You should observe that all of Part A is immediately repeated—via employment of a repeat sign—before continuation to Part B. Such a repetition does not alter the basic form.

THE ASH GROVE (three-part form)   Welsh Folk Song

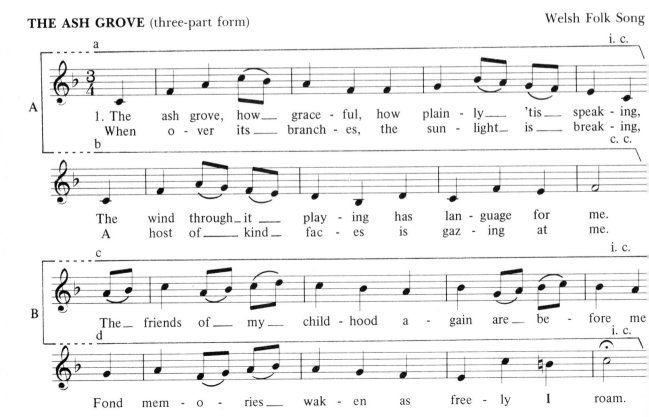

Summary of the form of The Ash Grove:

> A :‖ BA form—a structure-at-large of three musical periods of which the third is a repetition, following a contrast, of the first
>
>> Part A—a two-phrase period comprised of unlike phrases (*a, b*) and repeated in its entirety with different words
>>
>>> phrase *a*—a four-measure phrase consisting of two two-measure motives and ending in an incomplete cadence
>>>
>>> phrase *b*—a four-measure phrase of two two-measure motives ending in a complete cadence
>>
>> Part B—a two-phrase period of contrasting material ending on the dominant of F major
>>
>>> phrase *c*—a four-measure phrase of new melodic content comprised of a two-measure motive followed by a two-measure sequence ending in an incomplete cadence
>>>
>>> phrase *d*—a four-measure phrase that starts as a continuing sequence to phrase *c* and leads to a cadence on the dominant tone (5, *so*)
>>
>> Part A—an exact restatement of the original Part A, without a repeat (return)
>>
>>> phrase *a*
>>>
>>> phrase *b*

One-Part Form. Phrases in many two-, three-, and four-phrase melodies combine into an undivided whole instead of differentiated parts. This kind of structure-at-large can be called *one-part* (or *unitary*) *form*. In general, we encounter three types of one-part structures:

1. All phrases are based essentially on the same melodic material (see *Music Alone Shall Live,* notated here).

2. All phrases are different, but they possess similarities in their melodic rhythm and/or pitch movement (see *The Water Is Wide,* Chapter Seven).

3. Phrases relate through repetition and contrast, but they unite in an indivisible part structure of the whole (see *Marines' Hymn*).

MUSIC ALONE SHALL LIVE (one-part form)   German Round

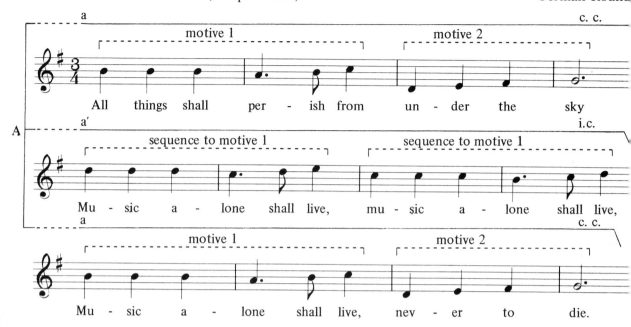

Repeat Signs and Terms

Notation of repeated passages in music can be accomplished in some cases by employing repeat signs and terms, thereby avoiding additional space and printing costs that would accrue if the same music was written again. You should be able to interpret any of the following situations:

Repeat sign.   The traditional repeat sign is a double bar with two dots on either the right side (facing ahead) or the left side (facing back). Repeat signs are found in two basic situations: (1) one sign facing back, and (2) two signs facing each other.

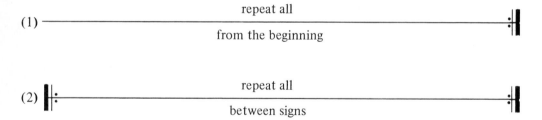

First and second endings.   In cases where all that is to be repeated is the same except for the final tone or tones, first and second ending brackets are used in conjunction with repeat signs. Tones under bracket 1 are performed the first time through, and those under bracket 2 are substituted on the repeat.

D.C. al Fine.   D.C. is an abbreviation for the Italian word *da capo*, meaning from the beginning, and *al Fine* means to the end. Hence, the performer is directed to go back to the beginning and continue to a point at which the word *Fine* (end of piece) is written.

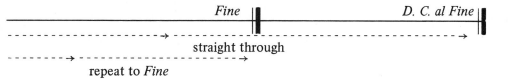

EXPRESSION

Acceptable musical performance assumes accuracy in pitch and duration—the right notes at the right time—and, in addition, requires that patterns of sound be delivered in an expressive, musically sensitive, manner. Musical expression is essentially a response to changes, or fluxes, that occur during movement of sound through a piece, thereby bringing about various degrees of musical tension and relaxation within and among the patterns.

Our concern with expression in music is threefold. First, we must acquire knowledge of, along with an ability to interpret, various words and signs that appear as part of a written music score and provide information about its potential expressiveness. Second, we must try to incorporate this intended expression into our performance of the piece. Third, we can develop a better idea of responses to subjective, feelingful affects of music, for these are stimulated in part by so-called expressive factors such as tempo, dynamics (loudness), articulation, and phrase shapes.

Tempo

You previously have read and performed a variety of rhythm patterns while clapping or internally sensing beats at a speed that was generally categorized as a fast, moderate, or slow tempo. *Tempo,* then, is the rate or speed of the beat, which in turn governs durations and the relative speed of patterns of sound and silence. The intended appropriate tempo for a piece of music can be indicated as part of a written score in two ways—with a metronome marking or with a tempo term.

Metronome marking.   The metronome was invented in 1816 by Johannes Mälzel, a friend of Beethoven's. Today's metronomes have either a spring-activated pendulum or an electronic mechanism. Both kinds are calibrated so they can be set to produce an indicated number of ticks (beats) per minute.

When a *metronome marking* is used, it appears—usually in parentheses—above the staff at the beginning of a piece of music. It consists of an equation containing a note and a number, and this marking is interpreted to mean a tempo at a rate of that many of that kind of note per minute, which actually translates into that many tempo beats per minute. The illustration showing three representative metronome markings and their meanings should clarify how such markings are interpreted and used to establish an appropriate tempo.

Metronomes and metronome markings:

(♩ = 120)

120 quarter notes, or
quarter-note beats,
per minute

(♩ = 72)

72 half notes, or
half-note beats,
per minute

(♩• = 96)

96 dotted-quarter notes,
or dotted-quarter beats,
per minute

Metronomes manufactured by Franz Mfg. Co., Inc.,
of New Haven, CT.

Tempo terms. Tempo can be indicated also by a word (or words) written above the staff. We have used English words, such as "Slowly" and "Moderately fast," in previous chapters. Although words of the language where the music originated can be used, Italian words are more traditional and universal. Some of the most common Italian tempo words are listed here in two classifications. Terms for *fixed tempo* appear at the beginning of a piece, or a major section thereof, and indicate a constant rate that should be maintained throughout the entire piece. *Variable tempo* refers to certain kinds of deliberate and temporary changes in tempo or beat that occur within some compositions.

Tempo terms are less rigid indicators of speed than metronome markings. How fast is *Allegro*, or how slow is *Adagio*? Variations occur between different pieces carrying the same term; some *Allegros,* for instance, are faster than others. Therefore, we have included a range of metronome markings, more or less applicable to each term, in order to provide a concrete frame of reference for establishing relative tempos.

Fixed tempo:

TERM	PRONUNCIATION	MEANING	METRONOME REFERENCE
Largo	LAHR-goh	broad, large	50– 60
Lento	LEHN-toh	slow	50– 60
Adagio	ah-DAH-zhoh	leisurely	56– 66
Andante	ahn-DAHN-teh	going or walking	72– 80
Moderato	maw-deh-RAH-toh	moderate	80– 92
Allegretto	ah-leh-GREH-toh	moderately fast	92–104
Allegro	ah-LEH-groh	lively	108–132
Vivace	vee-VAH-cheh	vivacious	136–160
Presto	PREH-stoh	quick	168–192

Variable tempo:

TERM	PRONUNCIATION	SIGN OR ABBREVIATION	MEANING
Accelerando	ah-chel-leh-RAHN-doh	*accel.*	gradually faster
Ritardando	rih-tahr-DAHN-doh	*rit.*	gradually slower

TERM	PRONUNCIATION	SIGN OR ABBREVIATION	MEANING
Rallentando	rah-lehn-TAHN-doh	*rall.*	gradually slower
Fermata	fehr-MAH-tah	𝄐	pause, hold beyond notated duration, and cease tempo beat

Dynamics

Intensity is the physical, or vibrational, property of sound that results from amplitudes of sound waves measured in terms of differences in physical energy, or pressure, and commonly expressed in units called *decibels* (an approximate range of 20–100 decibels represents softest to loudest unamplified musical sound). *Loudness* is the psychological correlate of intensity; it is a subjective sensation of the magnitude or strength of sound on a continuum from very soft to very loud. Degrees, or levels, of loudness in music are called *dynamics*.

Dynamics comprise one of the most effective and easily identified components of expression in music. Traditional Italian words, abbreviations, and signs written in the score are common indicators of intended dynamic levels and effects. Those frequently encountered are listed here in two categories: *stable dynamics* and *variable* (gradually changing) *dynamics*. Abbreviations are placed in column one because they, along with the signs for gradual change, are what usually appear in a score.

Stable dynamics:

ABBREVIATION	TERM	PRONUNCIATION	MEANING
pp	*Pianissimo*	pee-ah-NEE-see-moh	very softly
p	*Piano*	pee-AH-noh	softly
mp	*Mezzo Piano*	MEH-tsoh pee-AH-noh	moderately softly
mf	*Mezzo Forte*	MEH-tsoh FOR-teh	moderately loudly
f	*Forte*	FOR-teh	loudly
ff	*Fortissimo*	for-TEE-see-moh	very loudly

Variable dynamics:

ABBREVIATION	SIGN	TERM	PRONUNCIATION	MEANING
cresc.	⊏	*Crescendo*	creh-SHEN-doh	gradually louder
decresc.	⊐	*Decrescendo*	DEH-creh-shen-doh	gradually softer
dim.	⊐	*Diminuendo*	dih-min-you-EN-doh	gradually softer

Articulation

Articulation refers to the manner in which we perform consecutive tones within melodic patterns. It involves the degree to which we connect, separate, or emphasize these tones. Nothing does more to capture music's expressive life than appropriate articulation, which is traditionally classified into three kinds: *legato*, *staccato*, and *marcato*. Study and play or sing this four-note pattern in each style of articulation:

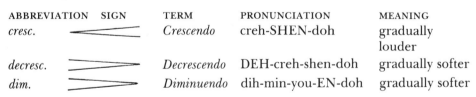

(1) legato:
connected, smooth

(2) staccato:
detached, separated

(3) marcato:
marked, with emphasis

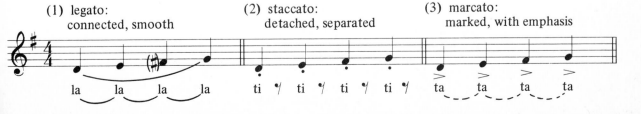

Notes encompassed by a curved line (slur) should be performed legato, those with dots above or below them should sound staccato, and those with an accent sign should be done marcato. But most song melodies are written without such markings. In these cases we must determine the appropriate articulation from our sense of how the music is supposed to sound—how we would expect to hear it done expressively—and perform it accordingly. Determine for yourself which articulation is most appropriate for each of the following melodic excerpts.

YANKEE DOODLE

MARINES' HYMN

THE WATER IS WIDE

Shaping Phrases

Phrases, along with motives, were cited earlier as the main building blocks of musical form. They also are the units through which musical expression is essentially achieved. Response to all aspects of artistic phrasing can be complex and sophisticated, but two basic and important ingredients can be fairly easily understood and applied, namely *contour* and *accent*. These two factors are among the fundamental forces that elicit musical expression.

Contour. Direction of pitch movement through a phrase creates its *contour*. You will recall from Chapter One that as melodic pitch moves forward in time, it either ascends (rises), descends (falls), or repeats (stays the same). If you were to trace a solid line through the principal note heads of a phrase, omitting repetitions and small detours, you would produce a graphic representation of phrase contour (see *The First Noel*).

Melodic contour for phrase one, The First Noel:

Ascending pitch usually creates a feeling of increasing musical tension and calls for a degree of *crescendo*, descending pitch is accompanied with a sense of relative relaxation and *diminuendo*, while either repeated pitches or small up and down fluctuations have an effect of calmness and stability. Try a subtle application of these ideas to singing (and playing) the first four measures of *All Night, All Day*.

ALL NIGHT, ALL DAY

Accent. *Accent* refers to an effect caused by placing greater stress on one tone than on those that precede and/or follow it. Most people tend to think of only one kind of accent called a *dynamic accent,* which is written with a traditional accent mark above (|) or below (>) a note head and requires a definite and sudden increase of loudness on the attack of that tone. But other kinds of accents are even more important and more frequent, for they are involved in expressive performance of any melody. These accents have no special markings in traditional music notation. However, we can insert poetic metric markings above notes to call attention, for our purposes, to the relative emphasis they should receive: a straight line (−) indicates a point of stress, and a concave line (∪) represents a point of relaxation of sound.

Here is a rather complete listing of kinds of accents that occur in melody. Study them and apply their effect as you play and sing the musical examples.

1. *Dynamic accent* makes one tone louder than others and is indicated by an accent mark (or abbreviations for terms not included here) above or below the note.
2. *Duration accent* (also called *agogic accent*) places stress on a longer note that is preceded and/or followed by shorter notes.
3. *Metric accent* stresses the tone that occurs on the first beat of a metric group or measure.
4. *Pitch accent* emphasizes the highest or lowest note of a group (see *All Night, All Day,* above).
5. *Text accent* stresses the most important word or word syllable and applies only to vocal music.

JINGLE BELLS

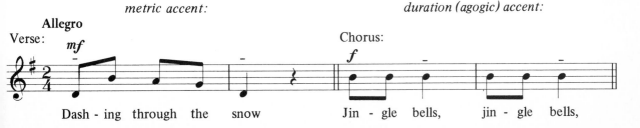

OH, SINNER MAN

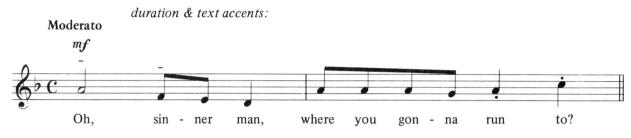

Oh, sin - ner man, where you gon - na run to?

A LA NANITA NANA

A la na - ni - ta na - na, na - ni - ta e - a, na - ni - ta e - a,

ANALYSIS AND SYNTHESIS

Perhaps the ultimate goal of studying music fundamentals is to be able to analyze, interpret, and perform music scores. *Score* refers to the written form of a piece of music and includes all facets of its notation plus all signs and terms. *Analysis* is a process of separating the whole piece into its components and examining how its patterns of sound are organized and related from the standpoints of pitch, rhythm, and form. *Synthesis* involves putting the components back together as an *expressive whole,* and this can be done best through performance—singing and/or playing the piece with accuracy, understanding, and expression.

You have built throughout this course a foundation of knowledge and skill that should enable you to analyze all, and perform at least some, of the next five pieces. We will do the analysis of each piece together. Your responsibility is to write, in the blanks provided, responses that will complete statements so they provide a significant commentary on how the sound is organized and interpreted. In some instances, you might need to restudy portions of this text where the subject matter was first introduced. Expressive performance of each song will require accurate reading of the score and practice in playing and/or singing it. You should check your write-in responses with those given at the end of *Keys to Chapter Assessments,* page 250.

AMAZING GRACE

Early American Melody
I Chronicles 17:16–17

A - maz - ing — grace! how sweet the sound That saved a —

wretch like me! ——— I once — was — lost, but

now — am — found, Was blind, but — now I see. ———

SCORE ANALYSIS AND PERFORMANCE:
Amazing Grace

Pitch Organization

1. The name of the keynote is _____, and the name of the key is

    _____.

2. The name of the first note is _____, its scale number is _____, and its *so-fa*

    syllable is _____.

3. Melodic intervals include a few scale steps, but most of them are _____.

4. The first five notes create skips among notes of the chord whose numeral is

    _____.

Rhythm Organization

5. The parenthetical marking above the meter signature is called a

    _____, and its meaning is _____. The Italian

    tempo term _____ would be an appropriate substitute.

6. A _____ note functions as the beat unit, each full measure receives _____

    beats (or counts), and the melodic rhythm starts on count _____ of an incom-
    plete measure.

Form

7. Phrase one is a, and its cadence is incomplete; phrase two is _____, and its

    cadence is _____; phrase three is _____, and its cadence is

    _____; phrase four is _____, and its cadence is

    _____. The four phrases form a structure-at-large that is

    _____-part.

Expression

8. *mp* is an abbreviation for the Italian word _____ and means

    _____; *mf* is an abbreviation for _____ and means

    _____; *cresc.* is an abbreviation for _____ and means

    _____; *rit.* is an abbreviation for _____ and means

    _____.

9. This song should be played and sung with _____ articulation.

Performance

10. Read the melodic rhythm to an appropriate tempo beat, making certain to give
    full value to half notes and tied notes.

11. Play and/or sing the song until you have achieved both accuracy and expres-
    sion.

WE WISH YOU A MERRY CHRISTMAS

English Traditional Song

SCORE ANALYSIS AND PERFORMANCE:
We Wish You a Merry Christmas

Pitch Organization

1. This melody ends at the point marked _____. The name of its keynote is _____, and the name of its key is _____.

2. Each of the first three phrases begins on the note (named) _____; its scale number is _____, and its *so-fa* syllable is _____.

3. The melodic interval on the first "we wish" is a <u>fourth</u>, on the second "we wish" it is a _____, and on the third "we wish" it is a _____. Furthermore, the melodic patterns in each of the three measures of "wish you a merry" are related by way of (repetition, modified repetition, or sequence) _____.

Rhythm Organization

4. The beat unit is a _____ note, and the meter is _____.

5. *Allegro* means a _____ tempo and could be equated to a metronome marking somewhere between _____ and _____ beats per minute.

Form

6. *D.C.* *al* *Fine* means repeat all from _____ to _____.Therefore, this melody has a total of _____ four-measure phrases.

7. Phrases one and two are similar, but one has an _____ cadence and two has a _____ cadence, causing these two phrases to combine into a larger unit called a _____ that can be labeled Part _____.

   Phrases three and four are of different material and provide a _____ to one and two. They, too, unite into a _____ and can be labeled Part _____.

   The *da capo* provides a return of Part _____, so the structure-at-large can be labeled with the letters _____, which is a _____-part form that is also called _____ form.

Expression

8. This melody has a strong feeling of triple meter that places stress, or metric _____, on beat _____ of each measure.

9. The spirit of both music and text requires _____ articulation through the first two phrases. But this spirit changes somewhat in phrase three, which probably should have a more _____ articulation. Phrase three also is one dynamic level (softer or louder) _____.

Performance

10. Play and/or sing this melody with musical expression, which depends mostly on clean articulation, an appropriate dynamic level, and a steady tempo at the proper speed.

SCORE ANALYSIS AND PERFORMANCE:
I May Not Pass This Way Again

Pitch Organization

1. The keynote is _____, the key is _____, and the melody both begins and ends on the _____.

2. The final melodic interval (B–D, *la–do*) is an ascending _____ third, which is a characteristic interval found in quite a few "lonely tunes."

Rhythm Organization

3. The meter signature in this piece means that each complete measure contains _____ half notes or the equivalent, the beat unit is a _____ note, and each measure receives _____ beats. Division of the beat, therefore, is represented by two _____ notes.

I MAY NOT PASS THIS WAY AGAIN

Words and Music by Rod McKuen

Moderato

4. The melodic rhythm begins at the (on-beat, off-beat) _____ point of

beat (number) _____, phrase two (word *And*) starts at the _____

point of beat _____, and phrase three (word *So*) is at the _____

point of beat _____.

5. The pattern on "Come along" could be read with the rhythm syllables _____

or counted _____.

Form

6. Each phrase is different from the others. Yet, there is a similarity in contour in
all but the next to final phrase, and a two-measure motive is repeated in phrase
three. These qualities of difference and likeness contribute to formal principles

of <u>unity</u> and _____ and result in a (unitary, binary, ternary)

_____ structure-at-large, due to the fact that phrases do not combine into differentiated parts within the whole.

Expression

7. The dynamic scheme through successive phrases goes from (Italian words) _____ to _____ to _____ and back.

8. The phrase intended to be articulated with more emphasis on each tone is marked _____; other phrases probably would be done with _____ articulation.

9. The tempo beat slows a little at the point marked _____ and actually stops momentarily while the note on *friend,* which has a sign called a _____ over it, is held slightly beyond its notated duration.

Performance

10. First, read the melodic rhythm to a tempo beat; second, play and/or sing the melody with accurate pitches and durations; third, play or sing the song with expression, which depends on responding to things written in the score along with a sense of phrase contour and accent (for example, combined pitch-text-duration accent on *build* and *pick*).

GO DOWN, MOSES

Spiritual

SCORE ANALYSIS AND PERFORMANCE:
Go Down, Moses

Pitch Organization

1. The keynote is _____, and the key is _____.

2. Accidental D♯ is scale tone number _____, and its syllable name is _____. The first melodic interval (B–G) is a _____ in size and occurs between scale tones numbered _____ and _____ whose syllable names are _____ and _____.

3. Chord numbers (numerals) for each of the chords indicated in the score are: Em _____, B^7 _____, and Am _____. Respective functional names of these three chords are _____, _____ and _____. The tonic chord is an E-minor chord whose root is _____, whose third is _____, and whose fifth is _____.

Rhythm Organization

4. The beat unit is a _____ note, and the meter is _____. Syncopation occurs on the word _____ and on the word _____.

5. *Andante* tempo is a going or walking rate that would fall within a metronome range of about _____ to _____ quarter-note beats per minute.

Form

6. The fourth four-measure phrase is actually a modified _____ of the first phrase, due to the fact that both phrases have the same second motive, and their first motives are characterized by a descending (name of interval) _____ from G to E. Therefore, the four phrases could be represented by the small letters _____ _____ _____ _____, which create a _____-part form.

Expression

7. Phrase one is at a dynamic level that is moderately _____, phrase two is one level (louder or softer) _____, and phrase three is marked with a _____ followed by a _____ corresponding to the phrase contour. Phrase four gets gradually _____ at its end, and its final note has a (term) _____ over it.

8. This song should be performed with _____ articulation.

Performance

9. Read the melodic rhythm to a tempo beat, making certain to perform correctly the syncopated patterns and to give all combined-beat notes (whole, half, dotted half) their full durations.

10. Play and/or sing the melody until both accuracy and expressiveness are achieved. As an option, add a chordal accompaniment comprised of chords whose symbols appear in the score.

GOOD-BY, MY LOVER, GOOD-BY

U.S. Folk Song

SCORE ANALYSIS AND PERFORMANCE:
Good-by, My Lover, Good-by

Pitch Organization

1. The keynote is _____, and the key is _____.

2. Melodic pitch movement is characterized mostly by intervals based on scale steps and descending thirds: B down to _____ is a (major, minor) _____ third, and A down to _____ is a _____ third.

3. This melody can be harmonized with only two chords: The tonic chord, whose name is _____, and the dominant-seventh chord, whose name is _____.

Rhythm Organization

4. The meter signature is _____, the beat unit is a _____ note, there are _____ beats in each complete measure, and division of the beat is represented by (number of) _____ eighth notes. This type of metric organization is classified as _____ meter. Melodic rhythm starts with a "pick-up" note for which the musical term is _____.

5. A fixed tempo is indicated at the beginning by a _____ marking of 90 _____ notes per minute, but this changes at the Refrain to 60 _____ notes per minute, which is a _____ percent reduction in rate of the tempo beat. *Accel.* at the beginning of phrase four stands for _____ which means gradually _____ to the point marked *a tempo* (original tempo).

Form

6. Phrase one (four measures) ends with an _____ cadence on the pitch of *re* (2), phrase two ends with a _____ cadence, and the two phrases combine to form a _____ that can be labeled Part _____. Each of these phrases contains two two-measure _____, and the first two measures of phrase two are a _____, a second lower, of the first two measures of phrase one. A _____ sign in conjunction with first and second _____ indicates that both phrases are repeated with different words, but this repetition does not alter the overall form.

7. Phrases three and four are different from the first part and can be labeled Part _____. The structure-at-large is a _____-part form that can be represented by the letters _____ and called _____ form.

Expression

8. The Verse is moderately loud and has rhythmic activity and bounce. By comparison, the Refrain has a dynamic level that is (louder, softer) _____, a tempo that is (faster, slower) _____, and an articulation that should be more _____. The *accelerando* in phrase four is accompanied by a _____.

Performance

9. Read the melodic rhythm to a tempo beat that responds to the changes in tempo.

10. Play and/or sing the song with correct tempos, dynamics, and articulations. As an option, add a chordal accompaniment with the I and V^7 chords.

Minichapter A

Bass Clef and Styles of Keyboard Accompaniment

Before continuing with bass-clef notation, review notation on the great staff (page 7) so that you are aware of relationships between treble and bass clefs.

PITCH NOTATION

Bass clef—also called F clef—is symbolized by the bass-clef sign which locates F below Middle C on the fourth line of a five-line staff. All other lines and spaces, including ledger lines and spaces above and below the staff, are named in ascending and descending alphabet order from fourth-line F.

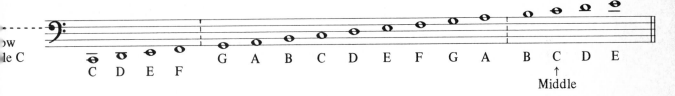

Practice naming the following bass-clef notes in forward, reverse, and random orders until you can do so at the rate of one note per second. Do not write in the names of notes; your objective is instantaneous recall.

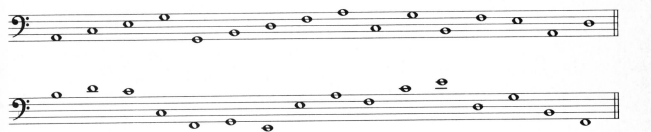

KEY SIGNATURES AND KEYNOTES

Key signatures written in bass clef involve the same sharped or flatted pitches in the same left-to-right order found in treble clef. Therefore, the location of keynotes of relative major and minor keys that share each signature follows the same principles and rules applied in treble clef. Here are signatures through five sharps and five flats written in bass clef:

Key signatures with relative major-minor keynotes:

BASS-CLEF SONG MELODIES

Melody can be written in either treble or bass clef. Treble clef is used mostly for song melodies intended to be sung primarily in unison or by women, children, and (strangely enough) tenors. Melodies for baritones and basses are usually written in bass clef. All adult male voices singing from treble-clef notation sound an octave lower than the music is written, and women's and children's voices sound an octave higher than music notated in bass clef.

Read the familiar *Ev'ry Night When The Sun Goes In* from its bass-clef notation and rewrite it in treble clef (one octave higher in pitch) on the blank staff.

EV'RY NIGHT WHEN THE SUN GOES IN

U.S. Folk Song

CHORD PROGRESSIONS

Keyboard positions of the three primary chords are shown written in both treble and bass clefs in several common major and minor keys. Practice reading and playing these (left-hand) progressions from their bass-clef notation.

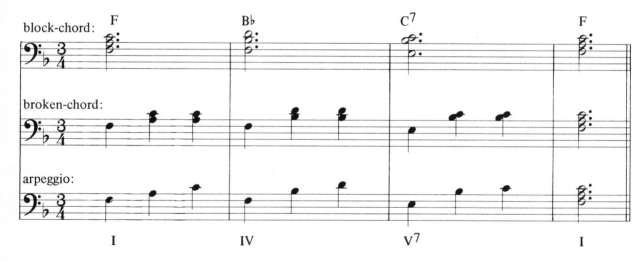

STYLES OF ACCOMPANIMENT

Chordal accompaniments that you played in other chapters were of a type called *block-chord style*. All three chord tones were played simultaneously and sustained for the same duration. Other styles are made possible by breaking up a chord and playing its notes separately at different points in time. The result can add both harmonic and rhythmic interest to an accompaniment. Practical styles for triple and quadruple meters (quadruple patterns also can be adapted to duple meter) are illustrated here. Practice playing each style in each meter.

Finally, improvise styles of accompaniment that are identified for two melodies you already have played with block chords: (1) *Down in The Valley*, key of F, in triple meter, and (2) *Merrily We Roll Along*, key of F, in quadruple meter.

Styles of accompaniment in triple meter:

Styles of accompaniment in quadruple (or duple) meter:

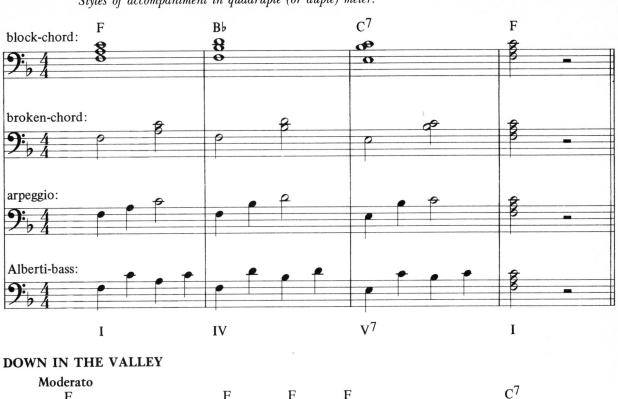

block-chord:

broken-chord:

arpeggio:

Alberti-bass:

DOWN IN THE VALLEY

Moderato

1. Block-chord style
2. Broken-chord style
3. Arpeggio style

MERRILY WE ROLL ALONG

Allegretto

1. Block-chord style
2. Broken-chord style
3. Alberti-bass style

Minichapter B

Guitar Accompaniments

TUNING AND STRUMMING

The classical *acoustic* (without electric amplification) guitar has six nylon strings numbered 1 through 6 from highest to lowest pitches produced. Strings are tuned to pitches shown on the keyboard and notated in bass clef.

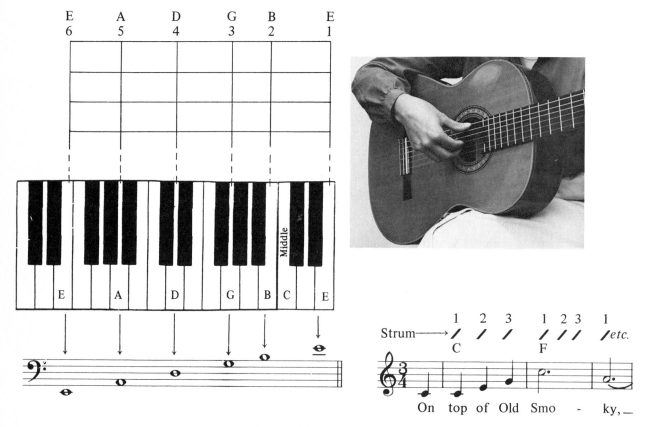

The correct playing position places the strings in a somewhat horizontal plane with the lowest-pitched string on top. Chords are played by strumming downward across all strings that produce pitches, low to high, contained in a given chord. A strum is executed with the right-hand thumb (cushion) and first three fingers, curved so that fingernails contact the strings, moving together in a brushing stroke across the strings (see illustration). A strum symbol above the staff is a bold diagonal line that indicates a strumming rhythm pattern.

READING CHORD FRAMES

Each string can vibrate as an open string over its full length from nut to bridge base and produce the pitch to which it is tuned. It also can produce other, higher pitches if its vibrating length is shortened by pressing it with a finger of the left hand against the fingerboard at a point just above one of the metal-strip inserts called *frets*. Thus, different combinations of open strings, strings not played, and left-hand finger positions on other strings produce various chords. Each individual chord (such as the D major chord that is illustrated) can be represented by a *chord frame* showing finger positions (1, 2, 3), open strings (o), and strings not to be played (x).

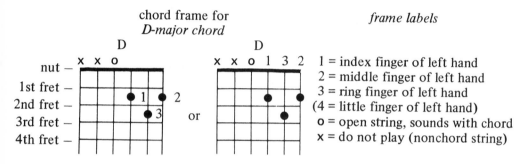

chord frame for
D-major chord

frame labels

1 = index finger of left hand
2 = middle finger of left hand
3 = ring finger of left hand
(4 = little finger of left hand)
o = open string, sounds with chord
x = do not play (nonchord string)

CHORDS AND ACCOMPANIMENTS IN A MAJOR AND D MAJOR

The acoustic guitar is an excellent instrument with which to provide harmonic accompaniment to song melodies and to singing. Such an accompaniment can be based on the same primary chords (tonic, subdominant, dominant-seventh) used for piano accompaniments in other chapters in this book.

A Major

A major is one of the easiest keys in which to chord on a guitar, due to relatively simple finger positions and chord changes. Independently practice the A (I) and E[7] (V[7]) chords as illustrated, then use them in an accompaniment to *Down in the Valley*. Next, practice the D (IV) chord and play an accompaniment, which includes all three chords, to *When the Saints Go Marching In*.

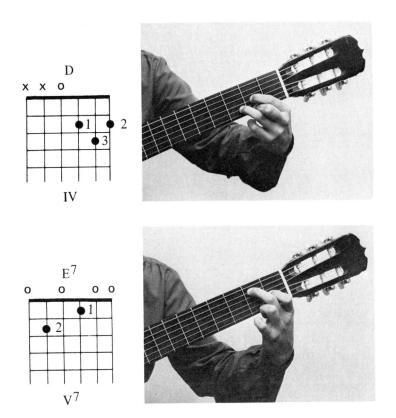

D
x x o
IV

E⁷
o o o o
V⁷

DOWN IN THE VALLEY

U.S. Folk Song

Allegretto
A   *mp*   E⁷

Down in the val - ley, val - ley so low, _____

E⁷   A

Hang your head o - ver, hear the wind blow. _____

WHEN THE SAINTS GO MARCHING IN

Street Band Processional

Allegro
mf   A   *etc.*

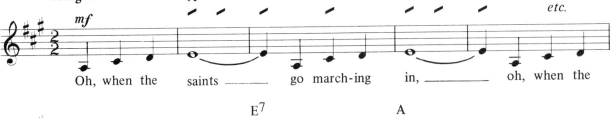

Oh, when the saints _____ go march-ing in, _____ oh, when the

E⁷   A

saints go march-ing in, _____ how I want to be in that

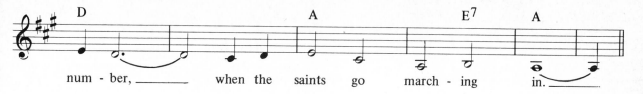

num - ber, _____ when the saints go march - ing in. _____

D Major

Practice this sequence of activities in the key of D major: 1) D and A⁷ chords; 2) accompaniment to *Skip to My Lou;* 3) G chord, D–G and D–G–A⁷ progressions; 3) accompaniment to *Michael, Row the Boat Ashore.*

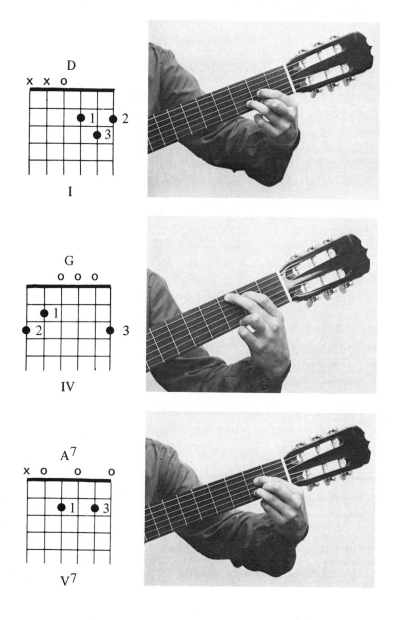

SKIP TO MY LOU

U.S. Folk Song

Moderato

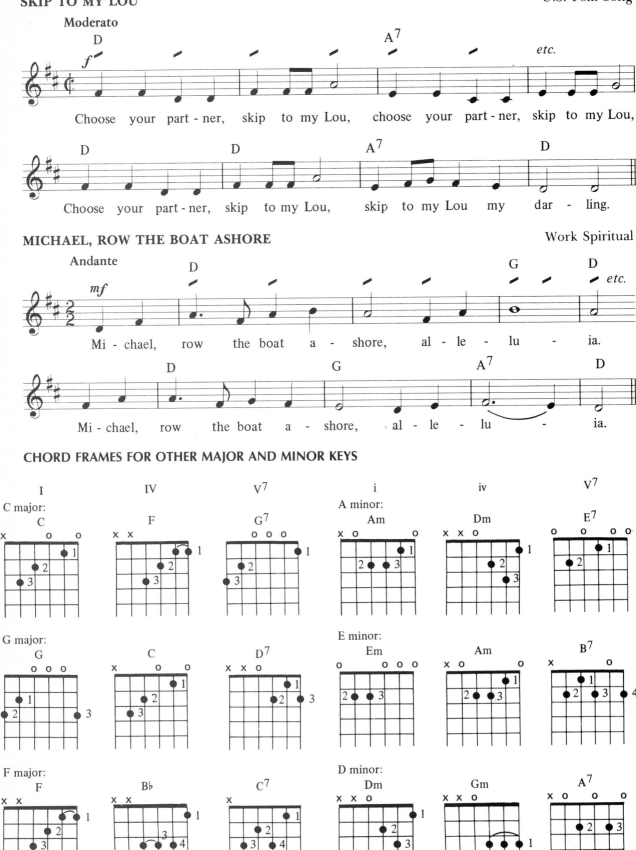

Choose your part-ner, skip to my Lou, choose your part-ner, skip to my Lou,

Choose your part-ner, skip to my Lou, skip to my Lou my dar-ling.

MICHAEL, ROW THE BOAT ASHORE

Work Spiritual

Andante

Mi-chael, row the boat a-shore, al-le-lu-ia.

Mi-chael, row the boat a-shore, al-le-lu-ia.

CHORD FRAMES FOR OTHER MAJOR AND MINOR KEYS

Minichapter C

Other Intervals and Chords

You learned in Chapters Three and Four to name and identify melodic and harmonic intervals used in constructing scales and primary chords. Specifically, you dealt with major and minor seconds and thirds, perfect fifths and octaves, and minor sevenths. A more complete presentation of intervals, including those previously studied, is given here.

DIATONIC AND MODIFIED INTERVALS

A particular interval, you will recall, is named with both its numerical size and its quality. Sizes within an octave range from one to eight, and qualities are of five kinds: *major, minor, perfect, augmented,* and *diminished.*

Perhaps the easiest way to understand fundamental constructs is to group intervals into diatonic and modified categories. *Diatonic intervals* are those created between the tonic of a major scale and each tone of that scale; they are either major or perfect intervals. The prime, octave, fourth, and fifth are perfect (P), and the second, third, sixth, and seventh are major (M). Here are all diatonic intervals notated from Middle C:

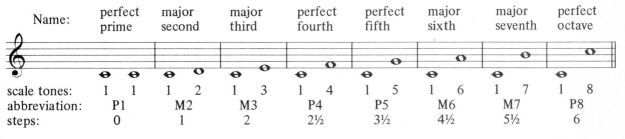

Name:	perfect prime	major second	major third	perfect fourth	perfect fifth	major sixth	major seventh	perfect octave
scale tones:	1　1	1　2	1　3	1　4	1　5	1　6	1　7	1　8
abbreviation:	P1	M2	M3	P4	P5	M6	M7	P8
steps:	0	1	2	2½	3½	4½	5½	6

Any diatonic interval can be modified in certain ways by chromatically raising or lowering the upper tone and notating it with an accidental (flat, sharp, or natural sign). These modifications result in intervals that are either minor, diminished, or augmented. Interval size remains unchanged, but the specific name changes to include the changed quality, for example: major sixth (M6) to minor sixth (m6) or perfect (P5) to augmented fifth (A5). Study the table of diatonic and modified intervals from C, giving special attention to how the upper tone is modified and to the abbreviated names of all intervals (we speak of a diminished fifth but label it d5).

Table of Diatonic and Modified Intervals from C:

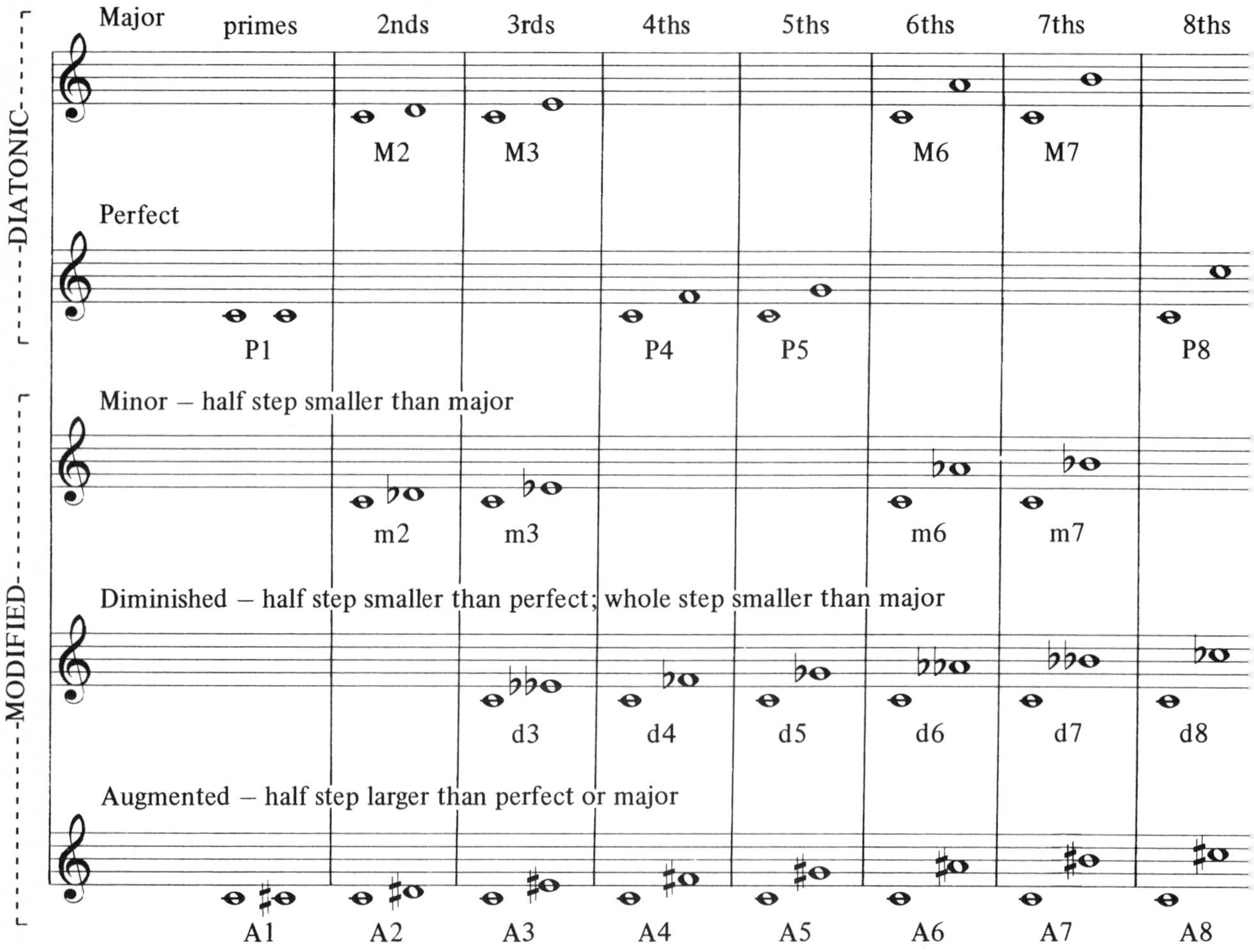
DIATONIC
MODIFIED
Major
primes
2nds
3rds
4ths
5ths
6ths
7ths
8ths
M2
M3
M6
M7
Perfect
P1
P4
P5
P8
Minor – half step smaller than major
m2
m3
m6
m7
Diminished – half step smaller than perfect; whole step smaller than major
d3
d4
d5
d6
d7
d8
Augmented – half step larger than perfect or major
A1
A2
A3
A4
A5
A6
A7
A8

Here is a generalized summary of interval modifications found in the preceding table:

INTERVAL	MODIFICATION	BECOMES
major	made *smaller* by one half step	minor
major	made *smaller* by one step	diminished
major	made *larger* by one half step	augmented
perfect	made *smaller* by one half step	diminished
perfect	made *larger* by one half step	augmented

The following practice exercises have intervals of seconds through sevenths written harmonically. Identify and name these intervals in one or both of two ways: 1) by considering the bottom note to be a tonic and determining whether the upper note is a normal diatonic tone of that scale or a chromatically modified tone, or 2) by treating the interval as an isolated one and determining the number of steps it contains. Use the reference keyboard as an aid to your determinations.

Reference Keyboard:

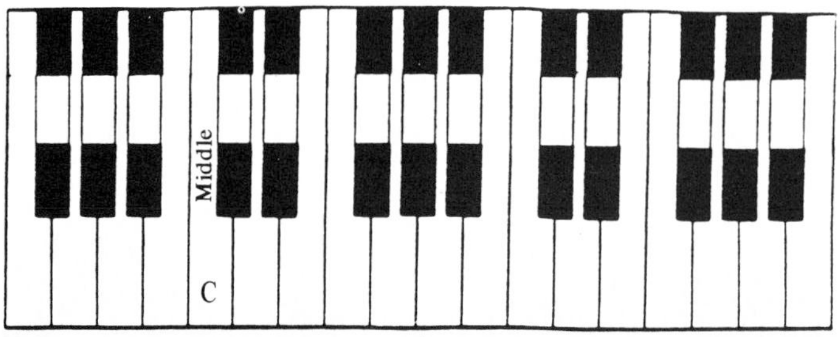
Middle
C

1. Complete naming these seconds:

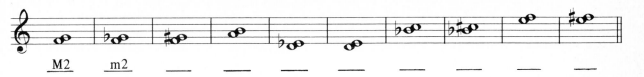

M2   m2   ___   ___   ___   ___   ___   ___

2. Complete naming these thirds:

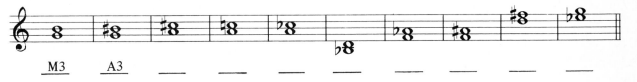

M3   A3   ___   ___   ___   ___   ___   ___   ___

3. Complete naming these fourths:

P4   A4   ___   ___   ___   ___   ___   ___   ___

4. Complete naming these fifths:

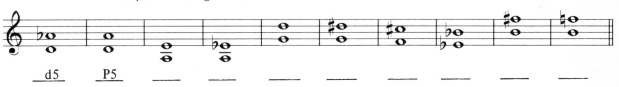

d5   P5   ___   ___   ___   ___   ___   ___   ___

5. Complete naming these sixths:

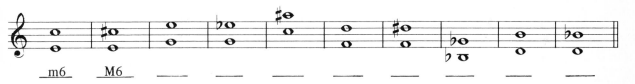

m6   M6   ___   ___   ___   ___   ___   ___   ___

6. Complete naming these sevenths:

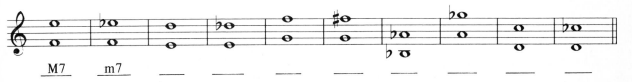

M7   m7   ___   ___   ___   ___   ___   ___   ___

INVERSIONS OF INTERVALS

An interval (melodic or harmonic) is inverted when the vertical positions of its two notes are rearranged so that the lower note becomes the upper note and the upper note becomes the lower note. Inversion always changes both size and quality of an interval according to specific principles, as follows:

Effects of Inversion on Interval Quality and Size:

Quality		Inverted Quality	Sizes	Examples
major	becomes ⟶ becomes ⟵	minor	sum of 9	M2 becomes m7 m3 becomes M6
perfect ⟵ remains ⟶		perfect	sum of 9	P4 becomes P5 P5 becomes P4
diminished	becomes ⟶ becomes ⟵	augmented	sum of 9	d5 becomes A4 A2 becomes d7

Inverted intervals:

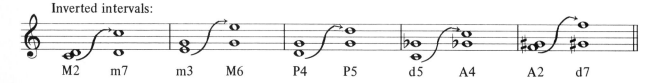

M2   m7   m3   M6   P4   P5   d5   A4   A2   d7

AUGMENTED AND DIMINISHED TRIADS

Construction of major and minor triads was learned in Chapters Four and Nine in terms of harmonic intervals contained within each kind of chord: Major triads, from their roots, have a major third and perfect fifth, or one major third plus one minor third; minor triads, from their roots, have a minor third and perfect fifth, or one minor third plus one major third. With this knowledge, structures of augmented and diminished triads can be easily understood. Study the following notated examples, and play each triad in order to hear its sound (quality, color) and compare it with the sounds of other traids.

Two views of an augmented triad:

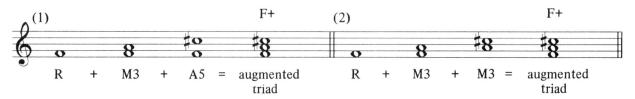

(1)   F+   (2)   F+

R   +   M3   +   A5   =   augmented triad   R   +   M3   +   M3   =   augmented triad

Two views of a diminished triad:

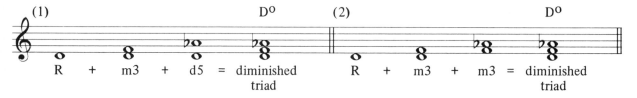

(1)   D°   (2)   D°

R   +   m3   +   d5   =   diminished triad   R   +   m3   +   m3   =   diminished triad

Any major triad can be augmented by raising its fifth a half step: *Any minor triad can be diminished by lowering its fifth a half step:*

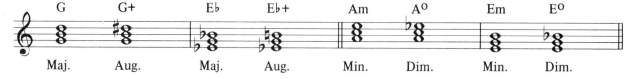

G   G+   E♭   E♭+   Am   A°   Em   E°

Maj.   Aug.   Maj.   Aug.   Min.   Dim.   Min.   Dim.

Minichapter D

Pentatonic and Modal Scales and Melodies

Major and minor scales studied in Chapters Three and Nine are the basis for a large majority of the music we encounter, but some well-known melodies are founded on two other kinds of scales, namely *pentatonic* scales and church *modes*.

PENTATONIC SCALE

Music based on the pentatonic scale can be found in nearly all early musical cultures, including those of ancient China, Africa, and native Americans; it might be considered the prototype of all scales. We also find pentatonic music among folk songs and art music of modern Western cultures.

A *pentatonic scale* is a five-tone scale that has no half steps. It contains one larger interval of one and one-half steps and three whole steps that together can be viewed most easily as relative tones represented by *do* ^{1} *re* ^{1} *mi* $^{11/2}$ *so* ^{1} *la*. Theoretically, any of these scale tones can be used as a tonic, making possible five forms of the scale. However, only the three common forms that have tonics on *do, so,* or *la* are illustrated here with *do* located on C.

Three forms of C Pentatonic:

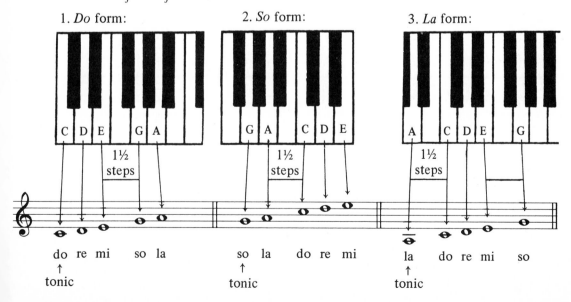

239

PENTATONIC MELODIES

Pentatonic melodies, like other traditional melodies, are usually written with a key signature. Here are some suggested procedures for determining whether a melody is pentatonic:

1. Locate *do* from the key signature (up one staff degree from the last sharp, or down four from the last flat).
2. Identify all different pitches used in the melody and arrange them in a one-octave sequence from *do*. If only five different tones are involved, and if they correspond to a *do-re-mi–so-la* order, the melody is based on a pentatonic scale.
3. Determine the form of pentatonic by identifying which of the tones sounds like a tonic in the melody. Most likely this tone will be the final note.

Pentatonic melodies are easy to play or sing, and when performed alone they have a distinctive tonal quality found only in pentatonic. But, when accompanied with chords they may sound either major or minor: *Do* form usually sounds major, *la* form usually sounds minor, and *so* form might sound either major or minor depending on the chords used. Sing and play each of the following folk songs and, as an option, add a chordal accompaniment. *Five Hundred Miles* is in F Pentatonic (*do* form) and *The Riddle Song* is in G Pentatonic (*so* form).

FIVE HUNDRED MILES   U.S. Folk Song

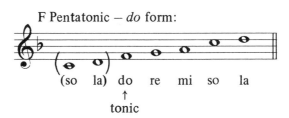

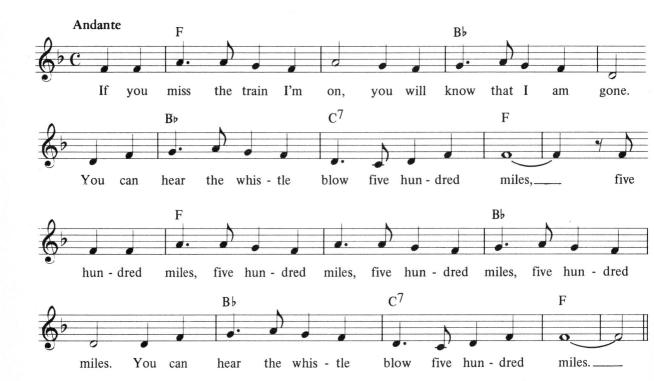

THE RIDDLE SONG

U.S. Folk Song

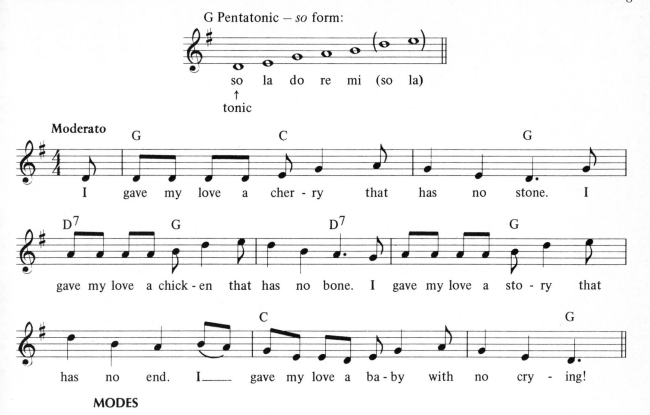

G Pentatonic — *so* form:

so   la   do   re   mi   (so   la)
↑
tonic

Moderato

I gave my love a cher-ry that has no stone. I
gave my love a chick-en that has no bone. I gave my love a sto-ry that
has no end. I___ gave my love a ba-by with no cry-ing!

MODES

Modes (also called *church modes* or *ecclesiastical modes*) are scale forms that provided the basis for most church music until the end of the Renaissance period (ca. 1600). We also find a modal tonality in some folk music of later eras as well as in certain twentieth-century classical and popular pieces. Our major and minor scales evolved from two of the six authentic church modes and dominated music between the late seventeenth and twentieth centuries. Of the other four modes, Lydian mode is rarely used and will be given no further consideration.

Modes are diatonic scales; that is to say, they have seven different tones in a step sequence that includes both whole and half steps. A clear idea of step intervals within each mode can be gained through identifying its tones with their relative *so-fa* syllables based on *do* as the major-scale tonic. Major—similar to the old *Ionian* mode—is a *do* scale encompassing an octave sequence from *do* to *do*, *Dorian* mode is a *re* scale whose tonic is *re* and whose tones consist of a *re–re* sequence, *Phrygian* mode is a *mi* scale, *Lydian* mode is a *fa* scale, *Mixolydian* mode is a *so* scale, and minor—similar to *Aeolian* mode—is a *la* scale. Five of these scales (excluding the uncommon Lydian mode) are notated here from Middle C as the major tonic. All scale orders can be transposed to other pitches that, in turn, would involve other key signatures.

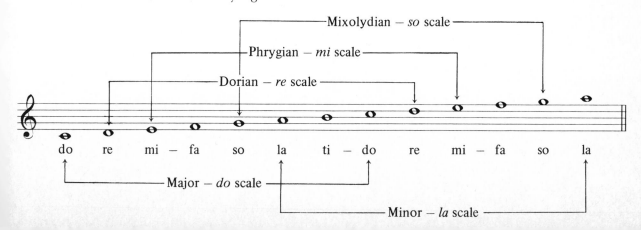

Mixolydian — *so* scale
Phrygian — *mi* scale
Dorian — *re* scale

do   re   mi — fa   so   la   ti — do   re   mi — fa   so   la

Major — *do* scale
Minor — *la* scale

MODAL MELODIES

Modal music is written today with the same key signatures used for major and minor, and identifying the mode or key follows similar procedures:

1. Locate *do* from the key signature.
2. Determine which tone in the piece is its tonic and name its tonality:

TONIC	TONALITY
do	Major
la	Minor
re	Dorian
mi	Phrygian
so	Mixolydian

Study, sing, and play the next two songs. *Scarborough Fair* is written with a signature of two flats that would locate *do* on B-flat. But C (*re*), not B-flat, appears to be the tonic. Play and sing the notated Dorian scale from C (*re*), then perform the song to confirm that its melody is based on that scale—that it is in Dorian mode. Follow a similar approach to the American folk song *Old Joe Clarke*, which, you will conclude, is Mixolydian mode. You also might want to take another look at *What Shall I Do With a Drunken Sailor?*—a song in Dorian mode that you sang and/or played in Chapter Five where focus was on its rhythm.

SCARBOROUGH FAIR

English Ballad

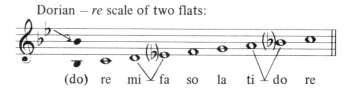

OLD JOE CLARKE

U.S. Folk Song

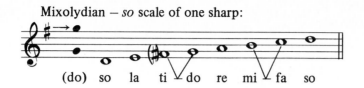

Mixolydian — *so* scale of one sharp:

(do) so la ti do re mi fa so

Allegro

Old Joe Clarke he had a house, Six - teen sto - ries high;

Ev - 'ry sto - ry in that house Was filled with chick - en pie.

Round and round, Old Joe Clarke, Round and round I say;

Round and round Old Joe Clarke, I have - n't long to stay.

Minichapter E
Other Metric Organizations

You have had fairly extensive experience with rhythm organized in both simple and compound meters and have read and performed a wide range of common patterns in music with meter signatures that encompass a very high percentage of traditional pieces. Yet, other metric organizations are used in music, and some of these are the focus of this minichapter.

QUINTUPLE AND SEPTUPLE METERS

Meter, you will recall, is the result of grouping strong and weak beats so that one strong beat followed by one or more weaker beats creates a *metric group* in which the first beat is a *metric accent*. In a fundamental sense, music has only two basic meters—duple and triple—and other meters are either a multiple of one of these or a combination of both. Study the table of comparative meters, all of which you have previously dealt with except for quintuple and septuple meters. Metric groupings of strong-weak beats are represented by metric counts that are marked to show both the primary accent (>) and secondary stresses (—) in each complete group or measure. Notice that quadruple (four) and sextuple (six) are really multiples of duple and triple, due to a psychological tendency to feel a secondary stress at the midpoint of each measure. *Quintuple* (five) *meter*, found in music with a five-four or five-eight signature, is a combination of one duple and one triple group within each measure, and the order in which this combination occurs in a specific piece can be either duple-triple or triple-duple. *Septuple meter* (seven-four or seven-eight) contains duple and triple metric groups that can take on three possible combinations within a measure: duple-duple-triple, triple-duple-duple, or duple-triple-duple.

Comparative Meters and Metric Groups:

METER	METRIC GROUPING WITHIN A MEASURE	METRIC COUNTS WITHIN A MEASURE
duple	two	$\overset{>}{1}\ 2$
triple	three	$\overset{>}{1}\ 2\ 3$
quadruple	two + two	$\overset{>}{1}\ 2\ \overset{-}{3}\ 4$

quintuple	two + three	> – 1 2 3 4 5
	or	
	three + two	> – 1 2 3 4 5
sextuple	three + three	> – 1 2 3 4 5 6
septuple	two + two + three	> – – 1 2 3 4 5 6 7
	or	
	three + two + two	> – – 1 2 3 4 5 6 7
	or	
	two + three + two	> – – 1 2 3 4 5 6 7

You should approach reading and performing melodic rhythm in quintuple or septuple meter in the same manner used for music with other meter signatures where the lower number corresponds to the beat unit. For example, sight read the melodic rhythm of *One May Morning* (English Folk Song). It has a quarter-note beat unit at a rate of 116 per minute throughout the entire piece. Each five-four measure contains a complete metric group of five tempo beats in a duple-triple (two plus three) combination that is sensed from the melodic pitch movement, words, and note durations. One triple group stands alone in the single three-four measure, but this fits easily into an ongoing flow of quarter-note beats and patterns of duration. Play and sing the song (key of G minor) in this same rhythm.

Melodic Rhythm of One May Morning:

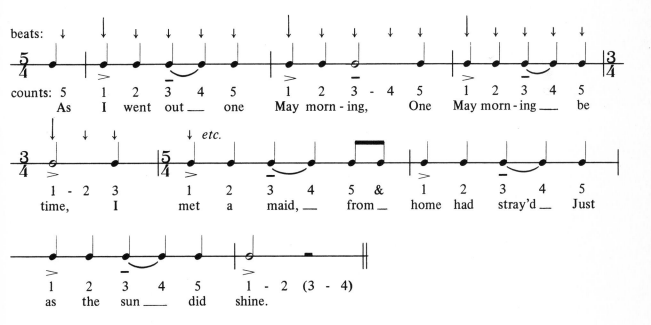

ONE MAY MORNING   English Folk Song

MIXED METERS WITH A CONSTANT BEAT UNIT

Most traditional melodies remain in the same meter and have one meter signature that holds true from beginning to end. However, some melodies (old and new) are based on *mixed meters*—an organization that involves changes from one meter to another within the piece. These kinds of meter changes are indicated by placing a different signature at the beginning of the measure in which a change occurs. One category of mixed meters is based on using the same beat unit through all changes in meter. Thus, a change from a signature of two-four to one of three-four signals a change from duple to triple metric groups, but a quarter note still represents a beat's duration and continues as a constant beat unit. Mixed meters with the same beat unit are easy to read and perform; merely keep a steady tempo beat and read the patterns of duration in a continuous movement through all measures. *Shenandoah* is a good illustration.

SHENANDOAH

U.S. Folk Song

MIXED METERS WITH VARIABLE BEAT UNITS

A considerable amount of music created in the twentieth century has a rhythmic organization in which duple and triple metric groups that occur either among or within measures are represented by tempo beats of different values. When this happens within a measure we have an organization called *asymmetric meter,* which means an unbalanced temporal division of the measure into beats of different value and duration—one beat is longer than others. Study the illustration of asymmetric meter notated in both five-four and five-eight. Unlike *One May Morning,* some music in metric groups of five moves at a pace fast enough to prohibit feeling or maintaining beats on every note represented by the signature's bottom number. Beats are sensed only at points of primary and secondary stress that divide the measure into duple and triple metric subgroups. A plain note (half note in five-four, quarter note in five-eight) represents the beat unit for a duple pattern, and a dotted note (dotted half note in five-four, dotted quarter note in five-eight) is the beat unit for a triple pattern.

Practice each of the notated two + three measures this way: (1) Chant (count) the pattern of five notes at a quick speed, giving all notes equal duration. (2) Repeat chanting the five-note pattern with a stress on counts 1 and 3. (3) Repeat step two and add a clapped beat on counts 1 and 3. Next, chant the three + two measures with a stress and clapped beat on counts 1 and 4. Asymmetric groups in seven (seven-four and seven-eight, not illustrated) are organized along the same principles.

Some twentieth-century music is based on mixed meters that include asymmetric measures as well as other measures in duple or triple meter. In these cases, one of the two asymmetric beat units will also apply to each of the other measures. The result is a melodic rhythm in mixed meters with variable (two) beat units. Shifts take place between plain-note beat units for duple patterns and longer, dotted-note beat units for triple patterns.

Illustration of Asymmetric Meter in Fast Five:

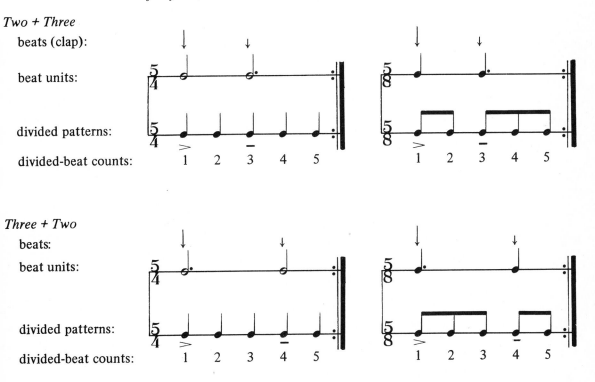

Observe the notated melodic rhythm of *It Is Good To Be Merry.* Based on a metronome marking of 92 dotted half notes per minute, we must decide to use a dotted-half-note beat unit for one-beat triple patterns that occur in three-four measures and on the second beat of five-four measures. Half-note beat units must be used for duple patterns found in the four-four measure and on the first beat of five-four measures. With the assistance of an instructor, practice reading the melodic rhythm and singing the melody of *It Is Good To be Merry*.

Melodic rhythm of It Is Good to Be Merry (♩. = 92)

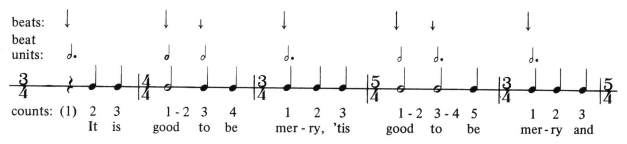

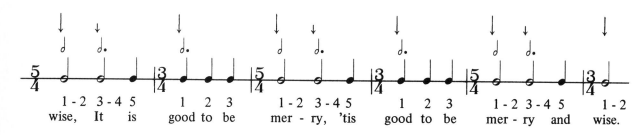

IT IS GOOD TO BE MERRY

Jean Berger

Vivace e ritmico (♩. = 92)

Beginning measures from *It Is Good to Be Merry* by Jean Berger. Copyright MCMLXI by Neil A Kjos Music Co., Publisher, Park Ridge, Ill. Used by permission.

Keys
to Chapter
Assessments

ONE: Part A

1. treble clef sign **2.** ledger lines **3.** staff line **4.** staff space **5.** beam **6.** stem **7.** flag **8.** note head **9.** *b, c, e, f* **10.** D-12 **11.** D-5 **12.** B-3 **13.** A-9 **14.** G-15 **15.** B-10 **16.** E-6 **17.** G-8 **18.** A-16 **19.** C **20.** C **21.** *so* **22.** 6 **23.** phrase **24.** incomplete **25.** D, G, E, C, C

TWO: Part A

1. *a, c, d, f, h* **2.** *b* **3.** *d* **4.** *c* **5.** *a* **6.** *a* **7.** *c* **8.** *b* **9.** *a* **10.** triple **11.** quarter **12.** c **13.** a **14.** d **15.** 3 **16.** b **17.** quadruple **18.** off-beat **19.** d **20.** b **21.** a **22.** slur **23.** c **24.** incomplete

THREE: Part A

1. a. *17* b. *12* c. *22* d. *7* e. *19* f. *12* g. *3* h. *24* i. *9* j. *14* **2.** (a) *D Ab F Eb C Bb* (b) *G# E D F# B C#* **3.** a. *m2* b. *M2* c. *M2* d. *m2* e. *M2* f. *m2* g. *m2* h. *M2* **4.** (a) F G A Bb C D E F (b) D E F# G A B C# D **5.** a. *E* b. *Bb* c. *Eb* d. *G* e. *A* f. *Db* **6.** F **7.** F **8.** 3, 1 **9.** seventh or 7 **10.** M2 **11.** m2 **12.** M2 **13.** m2 **14.** prime or unison or 1 **15.** complete (c.c.) **16.** mi mi mi re mi fa so la ti do **17.** 5 5 5 4 5 6 4 4 4 3 4 5 **18.** A A A G A Bb C D E F

FOUR: Part A

1. a. *m3* b. *M3* c. *P8* d. *P5* e. *m3* f. *m3* g. *m7* h. *M3* i. *P5* j. *m7* k. *M3* l. *P5* m. *m7* n. *P8* o. *M3* p. *M3* **2.** E **3.** G B D F **4.** D^7 **5.** Eb G Bb **6.** (c) **7.** G **8.** 4 8 11 **9.** (I) 9 13 16; (V^7) 8 14 16 **10.** m3 **11.** (I) 2 6 9; (V^7) 1 7 9 **12.** 5 9 12 **13.** F major **14.** F C^7 **15.** I(F) **16.** m3 **17.** $V^7(C^7)$ **18.** I(F) **19.** V^7 (C^7) **20.** (I) 7 11 14; (V^7) 6 12 14

FIVE: Part A

1. d **12.** 4 **3.** tim-ka **4.** 4 **5.** $\frac{2}{4}$ **6.** a, c, d **7.** 1 & **8.** 1 e & a **9.** ti-ti-ka **10.** off-beat **11.** yes **12.** c and d **13.** triplet **14.** 1 **15.** one **16.** 2

SIX: Part A

1. (4) **2.** (2) **3.** (2) **4.** (1) **5.** (3) **6.** (1) **7.** (4) **8.** (4) **9.** (4) **10.** b, d, f **11.** ti-ti-ka **12.** 1 & **13.** (5) **14.** one **15.** two **16.** $\frac{3}{2}$ **17.** three **18.** two **19.** 1-a2 **20.** tim-ka ta **21.** ta ta ta **22.** ta-i-ti **23.** five **24.** one **25.** 4 5 6

SEVEN: Part A

1. 5-11-13 **2.** B♭ **3.** 6-11-15 **4.** G, D7 **5.** 7-13-15 **6.** 8-13-17 **7.** E♭ **8.** IV **9.** 4-8-11 **10.** 3-9-11 **11.** D major **12.** 3, *mi* **13.** G **14.** G-B-D **15.** 3-7-10 **16.** 3-8-12 **17.** *b, c, g* **18.** *a, d, e, f* **19.** *a, f* **20.** I **21.** C **22.** IV **23.** C **24.** V^7

EIGHT: Part A

1. (3) **2.** (1) **3.** (1) **4.** (2) **5.** (5) **6.** (3) **7.** (1) **8.** (4) **9.** (2) **10.** (5) **11.** (5) **12.** (1) **13.** (4) **14.** (3) **15.** (4) **16.** (2) **17.** (6) **18.** (1) **19.** (5) **20.** compound **21.** *g* **22.** two **23.** 2 **24.** *c* **25.** *b* **26.** *g* **27.** *f* **28.** 2 **29.** *d* **30.** after-beat

NINE: Part A

1. (c) **2.** (a) **3.** (d) **4.** (b) **5.** B minor **6.** E minor **7.** F♯ minor **8.** D minor **9.** F minor **10.** G minor **11.** minor **12.** major **13.** minor **14.** minor **15.** major **16.** minor **17.** C harmonic minor **18.** (g) **19.** C-E♭-G **20.** *si* **21.** *so* **22.** complete **23.** iv **24.** 5 **25.** 3

TEN: Score Analyses

Amazing Grace: **1.** E♭ , E♭ major **2.** B♭, 5, *so* **3.** skips **4.** I **5.** metronome marking, 66 quarter notes per minute, *Adagio* **6.** quarter, three, 3 **7.** *a'*, incomplete; *b*, incomplete; *a'*, complete; one-part **8.** *mezzo piano*, moderately soft; *mezzo forte*, moderately loud; *crescendo*, gradually louder; *ritardando*, gradually slower **9.** legato

We Wish You a Merry Christmas: **1.** *Fine*, G, G major **2.** D, 5, *so* **3.** fifth, sixth; sequence **4.** quarter, triple **5.** lively, 108–132 **6.** beginning, *Fine;* six **7.** incomplete, complete, period, A; contrast, period, B; A, ABA, three-part, ternary **8.** accent, 1 **9.** marcato or staccato, legato, softer

I May Not Pass This Way Again: **1.** D, D major, keynote (tonic) **2.** minor **3.** two, half, two, quarter **4.** off-beat, 1; on-beat, 2; off-beat, 2 **5.** ti-ka-ti, 1 e & **6.** variety, unitary **7.** *mezzo piano, mezzo forte, forte* **8.** marcato, legato **9.** *rit.*, fermata

Go Down Moses: **1.** E, E harmonic minor **2.** 7, *si;* sixth, 5 & 3, *mi & do* **3.** i, V^7, iv; tonic, dominant-seventh, subdominant; E, G, B **4.** quarter, quadruple; people, land **5.** 72–80 **6.** repetition, minor third (m3), aaba', one-part **7.** soft, louder, *crescendo, diminuendo*, softer, fermata **8.** legato

Good-by, My Lover, Good-by: **1.** G, G major **2.** G, major; F♯, minor **3.** G major, D^7 **4.** $\frac{6}{8}$, dotted quarter, two, three; compound; anacrusis **5.** metronome, dotted quarter, dotted quarter, 50%; *accelerando*, faster **6.** incomplete, complete, period, A; motives, sequence; repeat, endings **7.** B; two-part, A–B, binary **8.** softer, slower, legato; *crescendo*

Index

AB form, 207
ABA form, 208
Accent:
  defined, 215
  kinds of:
    agogic, 215
    duration, 215
    dynamic, 215
    metric, 26, 215, 244
    textual, 215
  notation of, 215
Accidentals, 53
  flat, 53, 184
  natural, 53, 184
  notation of, 53
  sharp, 53, 184
Accompaniment:
  guitar, 149–51, 194, 231–34
  harmonization of, 153–54
  keyboard:
    I-V⁷, 92–94
    I-IV-V⁷, 148–52
    i-iv-V⁷, 193–94
  styles of:
    Alberti-bass, 229
    arpeggio, 228–29
    block-chord, 228–29
    broken-chord, 228–29
Alla breve, 126
Anacrusis, 38, 109, 170
Analysis:
  defined, 216
  of melodies, 217–24
Antecedent phrase, 204
Articulation, 213
Asymmetric meter, 246
Augmented intervals, 236
Augmented triads, 238

Bar line, 30
Bass clef, 7, 225
Beam, 29
Beat:
  defined, 25, 134
  duration, 26
  in asymmetric meters, 247

Beat (*cont.*)
  in very fast tempos, 134
  points within:
    off-beat, 35, 109
    on-beat, 35
  tempo of, 25
  unit, 31 (*see also* Beat units)
Beat units, 30–31
  dotted-half note, 134–35, 172
  dotted-quarter note, 134–35, 166
  eighth note, 131
  half note, 126
  in asymmetric meters, 247
  in fast tempos, 134
  in mixed meters, 246
  quarter note, 31
Binary form, 207

Cadence, melodic, 14, 204
Chord, 83 (*see also* Triads)
  accompaniment (*see*
    Accompaniments)
  dominant-seventh (V⁷), 88–89
  functions, 87
  names, 87
  numbers, 87
  progressions (*see* Chord
    progressions)
  qualities, 87
  skips in melody, 95, 152
  subdominant (IV), 144
  tonic (I), 88
Chord progressions:
  I-V⁷, major:
    guitar, 231–34
    keyboard, 90
    notated, 89–92
  I-IV-V⁷, major:
    guitar, 231–34
    keyboard, 145–48
    notated, 147–48, 227
  i-iv-V⁷, minor:
    guitar, 234
    keyboard, 194
    notated, 194, 227

Chromatic:
  pitch:
    names, 53–54
    keyboard locations, 53–54
  scale, 53–54
  signs:
    flat, 53
    natural, 53
    sharp, 53
  tones, 70
    neighboring, 70
    passing, 70
Clefs:
  bass, 225
  treble, 7
Compound meter, 164–65
  beat units, 165–66
  compared with simple meter, 164
  patterns, 167–68
  signatures, 165–66
Consequent phrase, 204
Contour, melodic, 214
Contrast, 206

Da capo (D.C.), 211
Decibel, 213
Diatonic:
  half step, 35
  intervals, 235–36
  scales, 11, 59, 184
Diminished intervals, 236
Diminished triads, 238
Dominant-seventh chord:
  in major, 88–89
  in minor, 193–94
  keyboard position, 89, 193
Dorian mode, 241–42
Dot, 33
Dotted notes, 33–34, 36, 108, 110
Duple meter, 27, 126, 131, 166
Duration:
  defined, 3
  patterns in asymmetric meters,
    247–48
  patterns in compound meters:
    beat, 167, 172